T0065499

CHRISTIAN - MUSLIM RELATIONS
IN SUDAN

A STUDY OF THE RELATIONSHIP
BETWEEN CHURCH AND STATE
(1898 - 2005)
3RD EDITION

GABRIEL GAI RIAM

WESTBOW
PRESS®
A DIVISION OF THOMAS NELSON
& ZONDERVAN

WestBow Press books may be ordered through booksellers or by contacting:

WestBow Press
A Division of Thomas Nelson & Zondervan
1663 Liberty Drive
Bloomington, IN 47403
www.westbowpress.com
844-714-3454

ISBN: 978-1-6642-6382-6 (sc)
ISBN: 978-1-6642-6383-3 (e)

Print information available on the last page.

WestBow Press rev. date: 05/12/2022

CONTENTS

Dedication xi

Acknowledgements xiii

Abbreviations xv

Glossary xix

Abstract xxi

1: Chapter One 1

  1.1: Introduction 1

  1.2: Scope and Structure of the Book 3

  1.3: Research Method and Sources 6

    1.3.1: The Historical Background 6

    1.3.2: Christianity in Ancient Nubia 7

    1.3.3: The Coming of Islam 9

    1.3.4: The Turco-Egyptian Period (1821-1881) 9

    1.3.5: The Mahdi State (1881-1898) 11

PART ONE

2: The Anglo-Egyptian Condominium: 1898-1946 17

  2.1: Introduction 17

  2.2: The Anglo-Egyptian Condominium 17

  2.3: The Role of the Christian Missionaries, evidence by
      the CMS (1900-1946) 19

  2.4: CMS Activities in Sudan and Expedition to the South 20

  2.5: Education Development in Southern Sudan 22

2.6: McMichael and Southern Policy: 1930-1946 23
2.7: Government and Missionary Spheres 26
2.8: Critique of Missionary Education in Southern Sudan 28
2.9: Political Economy 30
2.10:Islamic Revival (Mahdist Movement and Khatmiyya
      Orders 31
2.11: Religion and Law 32
2.12:Conclusion 34

3: Anglo-Egyptian Condominium: 1946-1956 35
3.1: Transitional Arrangements 1946 – 1955 35
3.2: Change of British Policy: 1946 35
3.3: Juba Conference 1947 37
3.4: Legislative Assembly: 1952 38
3.5: The Anglo-Egyptian Agreement of 1953 39
3.6: Torit Uprising – August 1955 41
3.7: Historical, cultural and economic factors of disparities 42
3.8: Conclusion 44

4: The First Period of the Development of Sudan as an
Independent Republic: 1956 -1972 47
4.1: Introduction 47
4.2: Education Policy in Southern Sudan (1956 – 1958) 48
4.3: Development of Religious and Cultural Conflicts
      (1958-1964) 49
4.4: Church and State Relations (1962-1969) 51
4.5: Missionary Societies Act 1962 51
4.6: Education and Religious Policies of the Government 53
4.7: Southern Reaction to Educational Policy 55
4.8: Civilian Government: 1964-1966 56
4.9: The Goodwill Visit of (AACC) to Sudan (1966) 57
4.10:The Sudan Communist Party's approach to Federalism 59
4.11: Numeiri's Policy Statement: 1969 60
4.12:The Anya Nya Movement 63
4.13:The First Ecumenical Initiative to Resolve the Civil War .. 64
4.14: Conclusion 66

5: The Ecumenical Inervention Leading to the Addis Ababa
Peace Conference 68
5.1: Introduction 68
5.2: The Dynamic of Sudanese Conflicts 69
5.3: Theresa Scherf's Mimeographed Paper "The Sudan
conflict" 69
5.4: The WCC Concern about Unity and Justice in Africa 70
5.5: AACC/WCC Approaches to the Conflict 73
5.6: The Negotiations 75
5.7: Ratification of Addis Ababa Peace Agreement 28
February 1972 79
5.8: Critique of the Addis Ababa Agreement 80
5.9: Conclusion 83

6: Second Period of Numeiri's Rule (1973-1985) 85
6.1: Introduction 85
6.2: Sudan's Permanent Constitution 86
6.3: Northern Political Parties Approaches to
Islamization (1973 -1977) 87
6.4: National Reconciliation (1977-78) 91
6.5: The Situation in South Sudan (1980 – 1983) 93
6.6: Southern fears about Arabisation 93
6.7: The Discovery of Oil in the South and Boundary Disputes 94
6.8: Numeiri's "Conversion" From Pan- Arab Socialism
to Islamization 95
6.9: The Process of Application of Shari`a Law (1980-1983) ... 96
6.10: Public and church Responses to Islamic Codes 97
6.11: Conclusion 100

7: Military and Parliamentary Periods (1985-1989) 101
7.1: Introduction 101
7.2: General Swar al-Dahab (1985-86) 101
7.3: Sadiq al-Mahdi Era (1986-1989) 103
7.4: Conclusion 107

8: Islamisation Under the National Salvation Revolution of
General Omar Al-Bashir 109
  8.1: Introduction 109
  8.2: Omar al-Bashir (1989 – 2020) 110
  8.3: NIF Federal Structures and Powers 111
  8.4: NIF Educational policy 113
  8.5: The 1998 Constitution 115
  8.6: Church-State Relations (1998 – 2005) 120
  8.7: Conclusion 124

9: Searching for a Viable Peace Process 126
  9.1: Introduction 126
  9.2: SPLM "Solution Modalities" to Sudan Conflicts
    (1994 – 2003) 127
  9.3: The Development of the Peace Process between the
    GoS and SPLM 129
  9.4: The analysis of Sudan Council of Churches/New
    Sudan Council of Churches toward the Peace Process 133
  9.5: Conclusion 136

10: Toward a Cuk (People's) Contextual Theology 138
  10.1: Introduction 138
  10.2: Toward a Sudanese contextual theology 139
  10.3: Covenant Theology of the Nuer 143
  10.4: Covenant in Islam (Mithâq; `Ahd) 148
  10.5: Covenant in Christianity (Berit and Daithike) 151
  10.6: Covenant and its Implications for Christian Mission
    and Islamic Da'wa 157
  10.7: Conclusion 163

11: Inter-Relgious Reconciliation and Peace-Building 165
  11.1: Introduction 165
  11.2: A Nigerian Example: Christian-Muslim
    Reconciliation and Peace-Building in Wusasa 166

11.3: Experience of Women's Action Group for Peace and
    Development in Sudan 168
11.4: A Pakistani Approach to Christian-Muslim Dialogue 170
11.5: Constitutional Implications of Post-Machakos Sudan 172
11.6: The Comprehensive Peace Agreement (CPA) 174
11.7: Conclusion 175
11.8: Conclusions of the Book 177

Bibliography 181
About the Author 193
Appendixes 195
Conclusion 233
Index 237

DEDICATION

This book is dedicated to all those Christian
Missionaries who came to
Sudan in 18th and 19th centuries to preach the Gospel.
This is for you in Christ's Name! "AMEN".

GGR

ACKNOWLEDGEMENTS

The research for this book was first written in fulfilment of requirements of the Degree of MPhil at the Graduate School of Divinity in the Centre for the Study of Christianity in non-Western World, New College – University of Edinburgh. Accomplished in the company of exceptional supervisors, friends, especially the staff of computer department of the faculty of Divinity at New College, Church Missionary Society's' Archives, Birmingham University; World Council of Churches in Geneva, and the National Library of Scotland for their support and guidance during my research periods.

Iam deeply indebted to late Professor David Kerr whose guidance gave me the focus to map out my research project adequately. His knowledge of Islamic World and Christian-Muslim relations especially in Sudan made valuable contribution to my understanding of the complex Sudanese situation and through his unparalleled leadership made me to produce this document successfully. I thank Dr. Elisabeth Keopping whose useful suggestions contributed to the quality of this work, Rev. Dr Terry McMullan for his useful comments on the proposal of the book. My gratitude goes to many friends: Dr. Peter Tibi Opi, Dr Wall Duany, Matthew Abur, Michael Mario Dhuor, Stephen Lul Nyak and James Sigin Banak, who provided some information and comments that, have greatly added to the quality of this work. Many thanks to late Revds. John Gatluok Chol, Michael Chot Lul, Stephen Kuony, Elder Gabriel Yoal Dok, Paul M Ayom, Amb. Philip Obong, and Mr, Dhil Chol, with whom I had useful conversations about the subject. Many thanks to the Presbyterian Church in Ireland, Church of Scotland whose financial support made my stay in Edinburgh a success, as well as the Presbyterian Church of Sudan for offering me this opportunity for writing this project – Christian Muslim relations in Sudan, an investment a person could cherish in life. I owe special thanks to Dr. Douglas H. Johnson for his useful material and financial support without which, it would have been difficult to complete the final phase of my research work. To my family their support and prayers; all endured my absence during the period of while writing this book.

Gabriel Gai Riam

ABBREVIATIONS

AACC: All Africa Conference of Churches
AAC: Armenian Apostolic Church
AIC: Africa Inland Church
ANC: African National Congress
AS: Armed Struggle
CCIA: Churches Commission on the International Affairs
CAS: Centre for African Studies
COC: Coptic Orthodox Church
CMS: Church Missionary Society
CPA: Comprehensive Peace Agreement
CMSA: Christian Missionary Society Act
CSCNWW: Centre of the Studies of Christian in the Non-Western World
CWS: Church World Service
DP: Dialogue and Proclamation
DUP: Democratic Unionist Party
DIP: Diplomatic or International Pressures
Dop: Declaration of Principles
ECS: Episcopal Church of the Sudan
EOC: Ethiopian Church of Sudan
GoS: Government of Sudan
GoNU: Government of National Unity

GOC: Greek Orthodox Church
HEC: High Executive Council
IGADD: Inter-Governmental Authority on Drought and
            Development
ICF: Islamic Charter Front
IARA: Islamic African Relief Agency
ICG: International Crisis Group
IDPs: Internal Displaced Persons
MSA: Missionary Society Act
MPs: Members of Parliament
NCP: National Congress Party
NF: Nasir Faction
NPG: Nile Provisional Government
NSCC: New Sudan Council of Churches
NT: New Testament
NUP: National Unionist Party
NIF: National Islamic Front
NGOs: Non-Governmental Organizations
NDA: National Democratic Alliance
NSR: National Salvation Revolution
OAU: Organization of African Unity
OAVWA: Organization of Alien Voluntary Act (1988)
OAVA: Organization of Alien Voluntary Act
OT: Old Testament
PCOS: Presbyterian Church f the Sudan
PS: Political Settlement
PUI: Popular Uprising or *Intifadha*
PN: Political Negotiations
PTD: Peace Through Development
RCCC: Roman Catholic Church Club
RCC: Roman Catholic Church

RSD:	The Right to Self- Determination
RTC:	Round Table Conference
SCC:	Sudan Council of Churches
SCC:	Sudan Council of Christ
SSLM:	South Sudan Liberation Movement
SAACDNU:	Sudan African Closed District National Union
SANU:	Sudan African National Union
SCP:	Sudan Communist Party
SF:	Southern Front
SSPG:	Southern Sudan Provisional Government
SSLF:	South Sudan Liberation Front
SRA:	Society Registration Act (1957)
SIC:	Sudan Interior Church
SCC:	Sudan Council of Churches
SPLA:	Sudan People's Liberation Army
SSU:	Sudanese Socialist Union
SSDF:	South Sudan Democratic Forum
SPLM:	Sudan People's Liberation Movement
SPC:	Sudan Pentecostal Church
SPEC:	Sudan Presbyterian Evangelical Church
SIC:	Sudan Interior Church
SPDF:	Sudan People's Democratic Front
SRA:	Societies Registration Act
UNHCR:	United National High Commission for Refugees
UN:	United Nations
UDI:	United Demand for Independence
UDSF:	United Democratic Salvation Front
UNC:	United National Charter
WAG:	Women Action Group
WWCC:	World Council of Churches
WCC:	World Council of Churches

GLOSSARY

Awqäf: Religious endowments

Da'wa: The call to faithful in obedience to God, used by some to identify Muslim missionary activity

Dhimmi: The protected status afforded to non-Muslim communities by Islamic Law, where such communities are guaranteed rights of religious, administrative and political freedom within the larger Muslim community, in return for their loyalty and payment of the *jizya* tax.

Hudûd: Offences in Islamic Law for which there are mandatory punishments laid down in the Qur'an.

Hadîth: The collected written reports of the sayings and actions of the Prophet Muhammad.

Imâm: The one who leads the community in prayer at the mosque.

Islâm: Submission and commitment to the will of God; the faithful, obedience and practice of Muslim people, the final perfected religion of God.

Ijtihâd: The exercise of independent judgment by Islamic legal experts whereby a consensus of the community is reached on a given matter.

Jizyah: Poll tax required of Dhimmi peoples under Islamic law.

Khalîfa: The successor or to the Prophet as the ruler of faithful.

Masjid: Mosque, the place or house of prayer for Muslims.

Muslim: One who practices or Islam; one who submits to the will of God

Mujahidîn: Muslims who participate in jihad in defence of Islam

Qiûâû: Crimes under Islamic law for which Qur'anic punishments may be waived in favour of compensation.

Qur'an: The holy book that Muslims believe contains the eternal Word of God revealed to Prophet Muhammad.

Shari'a: Islamic law, comprising the legal provisions of the Qur'an and Hadith, elaborated by Islamic legal scholars.

Sûfi: An Islamic mystic

Sufism: Islamic Mysticism.

Sunni: A Muslim who follows the Sunna; or custom of the Prophet Muhammad First four Caliphs of Islam.

Sûra: A Chapter in the Qur'an,

Shârâ: The process of consultation, or a consultative Council.

Ulamâ: The learned scholars of Islam; the custodians of Islamic teachings

Umma: The whole community of Islam, the community that God creates out of those who follow Islam

Zakât: Almsgiving; the third pillar of Islam

ABSTRACT

This book is about Christian-Muslim relations in Sudan, examined form the perspective of church-state relations in a country where Islam, the majority religion, has increasingly been identified as the religion of the state, and where the state has, since 2000, declared itself to be Islamic Republic. The book therefore, addresses Christina-Muslim relations within the constitutional arena of Sudan's national identity and integrity.

In order to understand the evolution of Christian-Muslim relations in Sudan, the book examines both the pre-independence period of the Anglo-Egyptian Condominium (1898-1956), and Sudan's history as an independent state from 1956 to 2005. Within this time-frame, the book examines the main factors that have influenced the course of church-state relations. In the period of the Anglo-Egyptian Condominium, this entails the role of mainly European missionaries and the colonial administration. The five decades of Sudanese independence (1956-2005) have witnessed an almost constant state of civil wars between the north and the south, the effect of which has been to polarize Christian-Muslim relations. This period will be examined in two phases: (a) from independence to the 1973 constitution, the later based on the Addis Ababa Agreement on 1972 that brought a temporary cessation of the civil war; (b) from 1973 to the present in which the state has been progressively Islamized by ideological movements and presidential degrees, and civil war resumed. I conclude with an examination of the 2002 Machakos Protocol, and the Comprehensive Peace Agreement (CPA) between the government of Sudan and the Sudan People's Liberation Movement.

The book advances four main arguments: (1) both Christianity and Islam in Sudan have allowed themselves to become polarized by political, ethnic and cultural factors: (2) the policy of successive governments and military regimes since independence has been to deploy Arabisatin and Islamization as means of national unity; (2) Both Christianity and Islam have ethical and theological resources that can contribute to national reconciliation (4) that the African traditionalist have theological resources that can contribute to consolidate peace building mechanisms among the Sudanese communities.

The book is divided into four parts comprising of eleven chapters. Part one deals with church-state relations during the Anglo-Egyptian Condominium. Parts two and three analyses church-state relations in the two periods into which the history of the Republic of Sudan can be divided: 1956-1972/3; and 1973-2005. Part Four discusses resources for a contextual theology of Christian-Muslim relations in Sudan with the aim of contributing to consolidate the peace agreement that has been concluded in January 2005 within the framework of the Machakos Protocol.

The research for this book was based on a combination of primary (archival and secondary sources, and included unpublished as well as published literature and interviews that I have conducted in Sudan and Britain

Gabriel Gai Riam

CHAPTER
ONE

1.1: INTRODUCTION

The aim of this book is to present an analysis of Christian-Muslim relations in Sudan through the perspective of church-state relations in the history from the pre-independence period of the Anglo-Egyptian Condominium (1898-1956), through the five decades of Sudanese independence (1956-2005).

The term "church-state relations" refer to constitutional dimensions of the history of Christian – Muslim relations in Sudan. The book will examine relationships between the Protestant churches, either as denominations (e.g. the Presbyterian Church or the Episcopal Church) or as ecumenical bodies (e.g. Sudan Council of Churches and the New Sudan council of churches), and the central government. In the pre-independence period this relationship involved churches under missionary leadership on the one hand, and the Anglo-Egyptian colonial administration, led by British colonial administrators, on the other. Since independence, and especially since the Missionary Act of 1962, church-state relations have engaged national Christian leaderships and national government, and have focused on the governments' policies of Arabization and Islamization as strategies for national unity that have been perceived and experienced by most Southerners as the imposition of Northern colonialism over the South. In this context, and for purpose of this book, church-state relations therefore focus on constitutional, political and social acts of Christian-Muslim relations.

The term "Christian-Muslim relations" can be applied to a wide range of religious concerns than those of church-state relations. In this book the term is used descriptively to refer to cultural and social that influence relations between the Christian and Muslim communities in Sudan. Based on the analysis of these factors, it will also be used theologically (in part four with reference to the challenges that faces Sudanese Christians and Muslims to find theological resources in their respective religious traditions that can contribute to strengthening and sustaining the current Machakos peace process that was formally concluded in January 9, 2005, bringing an end to the civil war that has raged through the greater part of Sudan's history as an independent state.

The book seeks, therefore, to analyses the institutional history of church-state relations in Sudan in a wider framework of the history of Christian-Muslim relations, and to identify the challenges that face Sudanese Christians and Muslims at the beginning of the 21st century.

Within this perspective, the book is concerned to identify the complex factors that have contributed to the religious character of the North-South conflict in Sudan as a struggle between: Arab" Muslims in the North and "African" Christians in the South. The term "Arab" is used as an internal reference Sudan to mean both the Arab immigrants who settled in the North Sudan in early 18th century and "Islamised African" whose self-identity is shaped through acceptance of, and adaptation to the Islamic region that spread through the regions of present-day Northern Sudan, especially from the 14th century. The term "African" Christian refers to the several Nilotic tribes -e.g. Dinka, Nuer, Shilluk - that traditionally lived in the riverain regions of Blue and White Niles, their allegiance to Christianity beginning with the arrival of European missionaries, Catholic and Protestant, in the 19th century. The population of Sudan was about 30 million people: Christian represents 16%, thus constituting the third largest religious group after Muslims (62%) and followers of traditional religions (22%). In the South however Christians are about 48.4%; these figure only refer to baptized Christians and do not take into account the number of displaced people estimated about 4 million refugees since the beginning of the hostilities in 1983[1]. In the course of Sudan's modern history; the regional demarcations between these two major groupings of the population have been blurred by the settlement of Arab Muslims in the Southern towns, and by the displaced African Christian to the North, i.e. internal refugees escaping the military conflict of the civil war that been fought entirely in the South between the forces of the Government of Sudan (GoS) and Sudan People's Liberation Army/ movement (SPLA/M) and other Southern armed resistance groups.

The objective of the book is to contribute to an understanding of the modern history of Sudan by elucidating the complexity of the factors that influence the course of church-state relations, within an analysis of history of Christian-Muslim relations in the pre- and post-independence periods. It is hoped that this will help Sudanese Christian and Muslims to deal dispassionately with their common history, in such ways as will enable them draw lesson that can contribute to the challenge of reconciliation and peace-building among Christians and Muslims within the Sudan as a nation that represent the most important meeting place between Arab and African, Muslim and Christian in African continent.

1.2: SCOPE AND STRUCTURE OF THE BOOK

Parts One to three of the book deal with the history and analysis of church-state relations in pre- and post-independence periods of Sudanese history. Part one focuses on the history of Anglo-Egyptian condominium, established in 1898 when General Kitchener led a combined Anglo-Egyptian army to suppress the short-lived *Mahdiyya* " caliphate" created in 1881 by Muhammad Ahmad Al-Mahdi (the Guided One) as a pre-modern Islamic state. Under Anglo Egyptian administration Sudan emerged effectively as British colony, in which the British administered the North and South as quite separate regions, and

---

[1] Nicholas lo Polito, Christian – Muslim Relations in Sudan: An Update, (unpublished paper, 1/10/2003), Solihull, West Midlands, UK., p.1

restricted Christian missionary activities mainly to the South where the missionaries were permitted to Christian the Africa population through education. Part one of the book will examine relations between the missionaries and the colonial administration, with particular attention to the missionaries; vision of the political future of Southern Sudan

Part Two deals with the first period of the history of Sudan as an independent state from 1956 to 11972/3. Following an initial attempt to establish democratic rule (1956-1958) under President Isma'il al-Azhari, this period of Sudan's was characterized by the military governments of President Ibrahim abboud (1958-1969), and President Ja'far al-Numeiri (1969-1985), both of whom came to power through military coups d'e'tat. In the context of the civil war that broke out in 1955-the final year of British colonial administration – the Khartoum governments struggled to formulate a national constitution that would hold Sudan together as a unitary state. I will show that General Abboud's attempt to Arabise the South – culturally through the Arabic language and religiously through the expansion of Islam – served to provoke Southern Christian resistance, and resulted in the 1962 Missionary Act that expelled most foreign missionaries from the South. This changed the shape and character of church-state relations; whereas the missionaries had previously represent the church, national Christian leadership now engaged directly with the governments of Sudan and was able to call on the diplomatic bodies. This resulted in an amelioration of church-state relations during the first period of President al- Numeiri rule (1969-1972/3) in which the government tried to end the civil war by entering into negotiations with the South Sudan Liberation Movement (SSLM). This section of Part two will here examine the role of the All Africa of Council of Churches (AACC) and the World Council of Churches (WCC) in mediating between Government of Sudan (GoS) and South Sudan Liberation Movement (SSLM), and the Addis Ababa Agreement of 1972 that was enshrined in the federal constitution of 1973.

Part Three of the book covers the period from 1973 to the present, comprising the second period of the al-Numeiri government through the then government of General Omar al-Bashir. This period was characterized by the Islamization policy of the GoS, under influence of the National Islamic Front (NIF) that has resulted in a state-by-state implementation of Islamic Shari'a law through the national constitution. The process began with al-Numeiri's introduction of the had punishment in the so-called "September 1983 laws" and was continued under the government of General Bashir that, in January 2000, declared Sudan to be an Islamic state. These policies annulled the Addis – Ababa Agreement, and resulted in the resumption of civil war that was intensified by the ideological struggle between the GoS's declaration of Sudan as an Islamic state and the SPLM's commitment to a secular state with a secular constitution and system of governance. This Part Three, will examine the course of church-state relations through this controversial period, and highlight ecumenical attempts to contribute to a peaceful resolution of the conflict.

Part four of the book, addresses the implication of the analysis in Part One and Three for the future of Christian-Muslim relations in Sudan, especially in light of the then agreed peace arrangements. It will be argued that a constructive approach to Christian-Muslim relations is essential for strengthening the 2002 Machakos Protocol on which that peace agreement was based. This is equally the case internally in the South, where Muslims and Christians live together in most towns and cities, as it is nationally in terms of reconciliation between the Christian South and the Muslim North. I will identify the possible roles of the Sudanese Churches as contextual agents of peace building in religiously and ethnically plural communities. I will seek to defend the hypothesis, based on both personal experience and empirical study, that reconciliation among Christian South and Muslims North Sudan can be effective in local initiatives that address the actual problems of the Sudanese people, and that such local initiatives form the basis on which to build regional and nation reconciliation from "the bottom up" rather than "the top down". Evidence drawn from Sudan Council of Churches (SCC) and New Sudan Council of Churches (NSCC) on local peace initiatives will illustrate this argument.

As part of the Introduction, I will offer a brief overview of aspects of the pre-19th century history of Christianity and Islam in Sudan in order to show how 20th/21st century Christian perception of Islam and Muslim perceptions of Christianity are influenced by respective interpretations of history.

1.3: RESEARCH METHOD AND SOURCES

The research on which this book is based includes both primary (unpublished) and secondary (published) materials. Historical data on church-state relations in the pre-independence period, examined in Part One, have been drawn from the archives of the Church Missionary Society deposited in the University of Edinburgh. The research for Part Two, especially in relation to the Addis-Ababa Agreement has made use of the archives of the Churches Commission on the international affairs, held in the library of the World Council of Churches, Geneva. The examination of post-1972 church relations, especially under the present Islamic government of General Omar Bashir, is based on documentary materials from the Sudan Council of churches and the New Sudan Council of Churches, and conversations I have conducted among Sudanese in London, Nairobi and Sudan. Secondary sources for the entire period of the research comprise published material held in the Edinburgh University library, including the two specialist collections of the Centre of African Studies (CAS), and the Centre for the study of Christianity in the non-Western world (CSCNWW)

1.3.1: THE HISTORICAL BACKGROUND

It is often assumed, both in scholarly writing and in popular interpretations of e history, that conflict has been over-riding dynamic of inter-religious relations, especially between Christians and Muslims.[2] This brief historical survey of pre-colonial history of Christianity and Islam in Sudan will subject such generalization to critical review, and I will argue that the medieval history of Christian-Muslim relations in Sudan offers a model of "truce" (Arabic *Sulh)* that merits critical consideration in modern times.

---

[2] Abdel Rahim Mohammed, Imperialism and Nationalism in the Sudan, p. 1

1.3.2: CHRISTIANITY IN ANCIENT NUBIA

Christianity first came to the regions that now comprise Northern Sudan in the 3rd century AD when Coptic monks form Egypt fled to Nubia – the region south of the first cataract of the river Nile, to the confluence of the Blue and White Niles to escape religious persecution imposed on Coptic Christianity by the Roman Emperors such as Decius (d.251) and Diocletian (d.313). Trade between Egypt a Nubia reaches back still further, and was another factor in the gradual southward migrations of Coptic Christianity. It was not until the 6th century, however, that the Christianisation of Nubia really began to take effect in the three kingdoms into which Nubia was divided: Nobatia (Arabic *Al-Nubah;*Coptic Maris), Makuria (Arabic: *al-Mugarra)* – these two being untied in the late 7th century - and Alodia (Arabic: *Alwa*). The first apostle to Nubia was a certain Julian who, according to the historian John of Ephesus, visited the region in the 6th century. Toward the end of that century a Coptic bishop, Longinus, was sent by the patriarch of Alexandria to further Julian's work, and to him attributed the earliest ecclesiastical organisation of the Nubian Church. By the early 8th century there is evidence of at least four episcopal sees, each with its own cathedral, and a growing number of monasteries. Nubian Christian civilization reached its zenith in the 89th century, and the archaeological and artistic remains on display in the National Museum of Sudan in Khartoum testify to the ways in which this earliest form of Christianity adapted to the cultural context of ancient Nubia[3].

It is important to emphasize that Christian Nubia not only survived the rise of Islam in the 7th century, but also achieved its greatest civilization at the same time as the Islamic Caliphate was undergoing its earliest historical developments in Medina (632-66), Damascus (661-750) and Bagdad (750-1258). Egypt fell to Arab Muslim conquest in the mid-7th century. In 651 King Qalidurut of Dongola, the capital of Makuria defended his kingdom against Arab Muslim invasion from

---

[3] S. Jakobielski, "Christian Nubia at the Height of its Civilization", in. Melfasi (ed.), General History of Africa: III – Africa from the 7th to the 11th century, pp.194-223

the north. A peace treaty was concluded, known as the, *Baqt* that recognized the frontier between Egypt as a province of the Islamic Caliphate and Christian Makuria, and committed both sides to a set of mutual agreements: that neither should attach the other that "citizens" of each state had right of passage through the other as travelers, but not as settlers that under such conditions, each state would be responsible for the safety of visitors from the other fugitives were returned the Nubians would allow a mosque to be built in Dongola for Muslim visitors, while the Egyptian Muslims extended right of " protection" (Arabic *dhimma*) to Nubian Christian travellers, including the right to worship in Coptic churches. The *Baqt* treaty also provided for settled trade relations between the two states; the Nubians were to supply an annual tribute of 360 slaves to Egypt, in return for which the Egyptians were to supply wheat, wine, linen and other commodities.

The treaty had the character of a "truce" (Arabic *Sulh*), a concept that has important ethical value in the Qur'an and Islamic law, as also in the Bible and Christian ethics, It served to established relations between two African states, one Christian the other Muslim, for several hundred years. As Jabobielski comments: "In principle the truce was upheld throughout the next five centuries of Christian civilization in Nubia, and in its initial phase was crucial for maintaining peace and possibilities for national development at a time when Arab armies occupied large areas of North Africa and Spain and were threatening Byzantium"[4].

The name Nubia nevertheless survived this change of religious, cultural and political rule. The Ottomans recognized Nubia as being divided into two regions: Upper Nubia was under the sovereignty of the Funj Sultanate, with its capital at Sennar[5]. Lower Nubia, "the land of Barbara", included territory both north and south of modern Egypt-Sudanese Frontier. The Beja tribes, who were recognised by medieval writers as ethnically Hamitic, distinct from both the Nubians and the Arabs, inhabited the Red Sea Hills in eastern Nubia[6]. It was

[4] Ibid., p 195
[5] ibid., p.1
[6] ibid., pp.7-8

under the Funj Sultanate that the region of ancient Nubia assumed the geographical, religious and political shape that has continued to define Northern Sudan through the 19th and 20th centuries.

1.3.3: THE COMING OF ISLAM

It was not until the 13th century that the Christian kingdoms went into decline, the *Baqt* treaty was broken by increasing pressures from Arab Muslim traders who settled in Nubia, and the conquest of Makuria by the Mamluk Egyptian army in 1276 marked the inaugurated of the Muslim rule. In the 16th century the Islamic Funj Sultanate replaced the last Christian kingdom of Alwa[7]. At that time many Nubians were killed, some enslaved and those who remained free fled to the Upper Nile regions where they mounted a determined resistance to the southward expansion of Islamic power.

1.3.4: THE TURCO-EGYPTIAN PERIOD (1821-1881)

In the early 19th century the territory of the Funj Sultanate fell under the political rule of the Ottoman Turkish rulers of Egypt, the dynasty founded by Muhammad Ali, the son of Ibrahim Agha, who came to Egypt in 1801 as a young officer with the Albanian detachment of Ottoman expeditionary force sent out to counter Napoleon's invasion of Egypt at the end of the 18th century[8]. Ali succeeded in removing the former Mamluk[9] dynasty of Egypt, and destroyed Mamluk power

---

[7] P. Holt & W. Daly, The History of the Sudan: from the Coming of Islam to the Present Day, 1979,p 1

[8] Mario A. Awet, The Ideology of An Islamic State and their Rights of Non-Muslims: With Reference to Sudan's Complex Social Structures, Cultural Diversities, and Political Rivalries, pp.42-43

[9] Mamluks were the Mongol and Cirassian slave soldiers who converted to Islam and advanced themselves to high military post in Egypt. From this high military class sprung tow ruling dynasties the Bhari (1250-1382) and the Burji (1382-1517), both named ager places where the troops seized power and were quartered. The Arabic word Mamlik means "one who is possessed, or owned" as a slave. It was first used in Baghdad by the Abbasid Calipha al-Mu'tasim

in 1811. The remnants of the Mamluks fled southward to Sudan and established themselves in Dongola. It was for this reason that Muhammad Ali fought to extend his military power into Sudan. His son Ismail led the conquest of Northern Sudan in 1820[10]. This inaugurated the first period of colonial rule in which the entire northern region was governed as a Turco-Egyptian colony, known as the *Turkiyya*.

Thousands of slaves from the Nilotic regions to the south of the *Turkiyya* were captured and moved to the military camps. Ismail attempted to advance southwards along the Blue Nile but was met with resistance. His death in 1823 resulted in brutal retribution across the Nile Valley and consolidation of Turco-Egyptian authority. This period saw a vast extension of the enslavement of Black Africans as a means of maintaining a huge slave army to police the expanding Turco-Egyptian territories. However, Hassan Makki Ahmed argued that the Europeans were the initial masters of slave trade and their merchants were eager to exploit the human and; material resources of Equatorial Africa and that the northern Sudanese were only their servants and employees[11]. Attracted by the large reservoir of ivory, they quickly established their cruel trade among the Nilotic African tribes. By 1856 they were already in Bahr al Ghazal, where they built relationships with the local chiefs to facilitate the movements of goods. During the first half of 19th century, the slave trade became an essential part of the Turco-Egyptian and Northern Sudanese economy, supplying Egypt's domestic and military needs[12]. At its height the slave market extended through the East African trade networks connected Darfur, Sennar and Barnu with Ethiopia and East Africa coast.

In the second half on 19th century the rise of the anti-slavery movement in Europe pressured Egypt to stop its slave traffic. Khedive

---

(833-842) to denote the slave soldiers, and continued to be used in this sense throughout later Islamic history

[10] PM Holt and MW Dally, 1979,op. cit., p. 47

[11] Hassan Makki Ahmed, Sudan: Christian Design, A Study of the Missionary Factor in Sudan's Cultural and Political Integration: 1843-1986, The Islamic Foundation, 1989 p 77

[12] PM Hot and MW Dally, op.cit., pp.,38-39

Ismail outlawed slavery in Egypt form 1863. To implement this policy, he relied on the British colonial servants, who were already present in Egypt, to administer and police the Southern provinces. Charles Gordon was appointed Governor General of Equatoria Province with the task of suppressing the slave trade. However, efforts to protect the Southern peoples were undermined by unreliable officials on the frontiers that were opposed to the restriction of slavery,[13] and slavery was never effectively suppressed by the Turco-Egyptian administration.

Turco-Egyptian administration did not have a coherent religious policy until the conquest of Dargur in 1874 opened the way for Islamic expansion[14]. Limited support was offered to some *Sufi* leaders in terms of money or tax exemptions. Meanwhile, some northern Sudanese cadres were being educated at the Azhar Mosque-University in Cairo. Sudanese Islam continued to be deeply influenced by Sufism, as it had been during the centuries of the Fundj Sultanate. While the *Qairiya* Order was traditionally the most powerful *Sufi* movement in Northern Sudan, as elsewhere in Sub-Saharan Africa, the 19th Century saw the rise of new Sufi orders that emphasized more indigenous forms of *Sufism*. In Sudan it was the *Khatmiyya* Order that dominated the religious scene, and made a point of maintaining good political terms with the Turco-Egyptian administration.[15] But growing resentment against the Turco-Egyptian colonial presence, and its policies especially of taxation, led many Muslims to yearn for a more dynamic religious leadership that would defend local interests more effectively than did the *Khatmiyya* Order.

1.3.5: THE MAHDI STATE (1881-1898)

In June 1881 Muhammad Ahmad ibn Abdullahi Al-Dungulawai, a member of the *Summaniyya* Order, declared himself the expected *Mahdi*, the messianic leader chosen by God to establish righteousness

---

[13] Richard Olaniya (ed), African History and Culture, pp. 46-47

[14] ibid., p.35

[15] Holger B. Hansen and Michael Twaddle, Religion and Politics in East Africa, pp. 34-35

upon the earth before the Last Day[16]. He called the Muslim community to a genuine Islamic piety and declared *Jihâd* against the corrupt Turco-Egyptian colonialists whom he condemned as unbelievers *(kâfir* pl. *kuffâr)[17]*. Modelling himself on the Prophet Muhammad, he raised an army of devout Muslims known as the *Ansar* or "Helper". Dissatisfied with foreign administration, many other Sudanese gave their support to the *Mahdî*. The rebellion of the *Ansâr* began in Kordofan, and by 1884 they established themselves militarily throughout the Bahr al-Ghazal Province. In 1885 they mounted their attack on Khartoum, first laying siege to the town, and finally conquering it and killing the Englishman who was serving as Turco-Egyptian Governor (1874-1885(, General Gordon[18].

The *Mahdî* is revered in Sudanese history as re-establishing an independent political state in Sudan for the first time since the Funj Sultanate. Sudanese historians continue to debate whether it should be interpreted as a first step toward constructing an Islamic theocracy in Sudan, or whether it was the first flourish of Sudanese nationalism directed against the Turco-Egyptians. It seems clear that the *Mahdî* himself was a leader of genuinely religious inspiration, but his early death in 1885 meant that the state that he created passed to the leadership of his successor, the Khalifa Abd Allahi (1885-1898)[19] whose rule was more akin to that of a military dictator. The *Shari'a* was the acknowledge laws of the Mahdist state, but the *Mahdî* assumed the authority to abrogate the existing law schools, and promulgate laws as *Mahdî[20]*. In the effect this meant that the legal administration of the *Mahidiyya* was combinations of *Shari'a* and customary.

It has already been noted that the *Mahdi* emerged from a *Sufi* order, the *Summaniyya*. In this sense he can be classed as a *Sufi*, but it has been argued that he was also influenced by the *anti-Sufi Wahhabi*

[16] ibid., pp.35-36
[17] Masour Khalid, The Government They Deserve : The Role of the Elite In Sudan's Political Evolution, 1995, pp. 34-36
[18] PM Holt &. MW Daly, op.cit., 2000,pp.75-83
[19] PM Holt &. MW Daly, op.cit, 1979, pp.86 - 97
[20] HolgernB. Hansen and Michael Twaddle, op.cit., p.36

movement of Arabia that sought to purify Islam of all innovations, including much of *Sufi* practice, by returning to the literal word of the *Qur'an* and *Hadith*. The Mahdist state was not, therefore, a typical expression of *Sufi* Islam, and was opposed by the *Khatiyya* Order. The successors of the Mahdist movement continue to style themselves as the *Ansâr* and take the form of an ideologically political party rather than of a *Sufi* order.

The *Mahdiyya* never succeeded in extending its power permanently into the equatorial regions of the upper Nile. Karam Allah, one of the *Ansâr*, managed to take Amadi town on Yei River in Equatoria, but only with considerable difficulty and for a short period. After the *Mahdî's* death in 1885, his successors withdrew from the region where they made little religious impact[21]. In 1893 Congolese soldiers belonging to King Leopold of Belgium appeared in the region. They captured Western Equatoria up to Mongalla and established the Lado Enclave. Similarly the French established themselves in Bahr al Ghazal, Western Upper Nile and Fashoda (Shilluk Kingdom), with the intention of annexing them to the French colonies already established in West Africa. But the failure of a French expedition from Djiboti to link up with Fashoda in 1896 resulted in a territorial clash between France and Britain. The British signed agreements first with the French and then with the Belgians, requiring them to withdraw, and Britain assumed colonial control of what now began to emerge as Southern Sudan, although technically the colonial authority was invested in the Anglo-Egyptian Condominium.[22]

The Condominium was formally established in 1898 following the defeat of the Mahdist state by an Anglo-Egyptian army under command of General Kitchener. In the battle of Omdurman on 2 September 1898, the Khalifa's forces were decisively defeated and a fresh chapter in the history of Sudan was opened as the entire territory that today comprises Sudan – Northern Sudan and Southern Sudan – fell under

---

[21] PM Holt, The Mahdist state in the Sudan, 19881-1898: A Study of its Origins Development and Overthrow, pp. 94-95
[22] Mansour Khalid, op.cit., op. cit., pp.32 -33

the colonial administration of the Anglo-Egyptian Condominium.[23] It is to this period that we shall turn in part one that will examine the colonial administration of Southern Sudan as the context in which the Southerners were progressively Christianised, and the issue of relations between the predominantly Christian South, and the predominantly Muslim North first became an issue.

---

[23] ibid., p. 16

PART ONE

CHAPTER
TWO

THE ANGLO-EGYPTIAN
CONDOMINIUM: 1898-1946

2.1: INTRODUCTION

This chapter deals with the first period of Anglo-Egyptian administration of Sudan from the establishment of the Condominium, following the defeat of the *Mahdist* state, to 1946 when the colonial administration decided that Sudan was ready for independence as a united country. During these four decades, Sudan was administered in two regions, the North and the South. The chapter is mainly interested in developments in the South that led to its Christianization, while the North consolidate its unity under Islam. It will be demonstrated that this division compounded historic distinctions between a predominantly Muslim North and an increasing Christian South compounded historic distinctions between Arabs and Africans, and added to the tensions between the South and the North that were to remain a divisive factor in Sudanese political and religious life thereafter.

2.2: THE ANGLO-EGYPTIAN CONDOMINIUM

"The necessary Laws and Regulations will be carefully considered and issued as required, but, it is not mainly to the framing and publishing of laws that we must look for the improvement and good government of the country. The task before us all is to acquire the confidence of the people, to develop their resources and raise them to higher level. (Lord Kitchener 1900[24]).

The constitution of the Sudan as a condominium was laid down in the Anglo-Egyptian Agreement of 1899, and was confirmed by the Anglo-Egyptian Treaty of 1936[25]; to govern the region that constitutes the present political boundaries of the Sudan. Although both Southern and Northern Sudan fell under the same administration, the two regions were treated separately. From 1910 the Governor General discharged his executive and legislative powers in the North through an Advisory Council consisting of representatives of provincial councils, the commercial sector, and nominees of the Governor General. This was consistent with the British colonial policy of "indirect rule", wherever possible exercising colonial power through indigenous political commercial institutions.

This pattern of administration was judged to be inappropriate in the South that presented quite different problems to the colonial administration. In contrast to the North that since the Funj Sultanate had evolved a sense of political unity under a central government, the Upper Nile regions were divided among distinct ethnic peoples who had only been drawn into geo-political association with Sudan following their conquest by the Egyptians in the 1860s and their consequent annexation to the *Turkiyya*. Under the British administration the three Southern provinces Bhar el Gazal, Equatoria and Upper Nile, consisting of 250,000 squares miles – became a separate administrative unit[26]. The British viewed the Black Africans, whose religion and culture were different from those of the Arab Muslims of the north, as requiring

---

[24] Lord Kitchener, in the Government of Sudan, The Sudan: A record of Progress 1898-1947,p. 3

[25] The Sudan Government, The Sudan: A record of Progress 1898-1947, p. 8

[26] Gabriel Warburg, Islam, Nationalism and Communism in a Traditional Society: The case of Sudan, pp. 153

a different administration that could best be conducted by British officials. Slavery had left its enduring mark in African hostility to Arabs and Islam. The British therefore forbade the use of Arabic in the South and introduced English instead as the region's official language. In the religious sphere the authorities encouraged Christian missionary activities, especially, in the field of education. Nevertheless, the peoples of the South, being unused to any form of central government were suspicious of the British administration, and the British found it difficult to extend their rule effectively over the whole area. According to a report of the time, it took a quarter of a century before British rule in the region was firmly established[27]. It was therefore impossible to set up an advisory council similar to that of the North, and the British determined on a different administrative policy altogether. This came to be known as "the Southern Policy" that sealed the South from the North, and developed it as a separate region from the late 1920s

2.3: THE ROLE OF THE CHRISTIAN MISSIONARIES, EVIDENCE BY THE CMS (1900-1946)

The first Protestant missionaries arrived in Khartoum in 1899; a year after General Kitchener defeated the Mahdi and the Anglo-Egyptian Condominium was established. The Church Missionary Society (CMS) led the way and established a CMS school in Khartoum, open to both Muslims and Christians. The policy of indirect rule, however, was resistant of Christian missionary intervention in regions of Muslim predominance, and the missionaries were warned not to speak to Muslims about religion[28]. With the appointment of Wingate[29] as the Governor General, in 1903, and invitation was given to CMS to concentrate its work in the South. CMS headquarters was initially

---

[27] ibid., p. 12

[28] Heather J Sharkey, "Christian Among Muslims: The church Missionary Society in the Northern Sudan" Journal of African History, No 43, 2003, trinity College, hartford

[29] PM Holt and MW Dally, 2000, op.cit.,p 195 (Sir Francis Reginald Wingate, the Second Governor General of Anglo-Egyptian Sydab: 1899-1916

reluctant to accede to this request, but Wingate – who was eager to resist the influence of Catholic Missions entering the South from Congo – made an offer that would have been embarrassing to refuse: the opportunity to assume educational responsibility for the entire Southern region. The CMS agreed, interpreting the government invitation as a direct call to extend the Kingdom of God in Sothern Sudan. In 1905 Llewellyn Henry Gwynne (1893 – 1957)[30] met with Wingate to discuss the new venture.[31]

The CMS were not the only mission to take up work in the South. From 1901 Catholic missionaries from the Belgian Congo had begun work among the Shilluk at Lull upstream from Fashoda, and five years later they achieved considerable results. In March 1902, the American Presbyterian Mission founded a base at Dolieg Hill, and their pragmatic approach was making progress in agriculture and education. At the same time the Sudan United Mission (SUM) opened its first station among the Dinka in the area to the east of the River Nile.

2.4: CMS ACTIVITIES IN SUDAN AND EXPEDITION TO THE SOUTH

The CMS expedition to the South reached the new provincial capital, Mongalla, in January 1906. However, it was decided that this was not a suitable place to establish the mission. There was already a large population of Northern Sudanese Muslims, both official and merchants, in the town, engaged in construction, developing and serving the new provincial capital. The Governor of Mongalla, Angus Cameron, took the view that the presence of the missionaries would create a possible source of friction within his territory, and refused to allow the CMS to settle. Instead he advised them to proceed to Bor, now belonging to the Upper Nile Region. It was in Bor, therefore, that the CMS inaugurated the first station of the Gordon Memorial

---

[30] Andrew C. Wheeler, "The Ministry of the Church Missionary Society in Northern Sudan in Samuel E. Kayanga and Andrew C. Wheeler,, (eds.), but God is not Defeated!", P. 53

[31] Lillian P. Sanderson and Neville Sanderson, Education and Politics in Southern Sudan,pp.440-444

Sudan Mission in January 1906, the pioneer missionaries being Rev. F. Hadow, Mr. R.C.J.S Wilmot, Rev. Archibald Shaw, Thom Lloyd, Rev A. Thon, Mr J. Comely and Dr. A. r. Cook

For the first eighteen months the work was hampered by ill health among the missionaries and confusion as to the priorities of evangelization, health and education, and security problems. It was not until 1908 that the situation clarified, and the Governor approved a plan for the mission at Malek, comprising 30 acres. His objective was to extend the boundaries of the South to include Gondokoro, lakuta and Soroti- thus including part of Uganda protectorate – and to this end he guaranteed the CMS exclusive rights throughout the whole region, enabling them to extend their activities within the Lado Enclave.[32]

By 1909 Archdeacon Archibald Shaw's (secretary of the CMS mission) reading – class at Malek was functioning. Between twenty to thirty boys and young men from among the mission workers were being taught. The mission also developed a range of vocational training programmes in gardening, brick making and carpentry. In spite of the absence of a qualified person to run the clinic, a small dispensary was started to cater for minor injuries and ailments. Llewellyn Gwynne[33] requested London for more recruits to expand the work among the Dinka and to move into Lado Enclave that now reverted to Anglo-Egyptian Condominium after death of King Leopold in December 1909[34]

---

[32] Archibald Shaw, Rev.A at Malek April 27,1910, CMS.Archives, Birmingham University

[33] Llewellyn Gwynne accompanied CMS expeditionary force and acted as Chaplain at Khartoum, appointed Archdeacon of the Sudan in the See of Anglican Bishop in Jerusalem, Became bishop of Egypt and Sudan, built Anglican cathedral in Sudan and was consecrated at Khartoum in 1911

[34] Lilian Passmore Anderson and Neville Sanderson, op.cit., pp. 53 and 445

2.5: EDUCATION DEVELOPMENT IN SOUTHERN SUDAN

In the Anglo-Egyptian Sudan, the problem of providing education in the South was a central question facing the Administration[35]. What form should the education of the traditional chiefs take? Should they be sent to the Gordon Memorial College in Khartoum where they would associate with Muslims, and thus be taught in Arabic, learn Qur'an and Islam, with the probability that they would eventually become Muslims? Alternatively, should the Government set up a non-religious system for them, or should their education be entrusted, under government regulation, to the missionary societies? The Anglo-Egyptian Administration chose the last alternative.[36]

The main difficulties according to Sir Harold MacMichael were the diversity of languages, the absence of any system of orthography, and lack of funds and staff at the disposal of the missions. It was not until 1926 that a systematic scheme of Educational organization in collaboration with the missionaries was adopted. Missionaries were granted subsidies for education and medical work. Two levels of education were introduced in 1927: a four year elementary course, followed by a four-year intermediate course in separate schools. English was the language of instructions, and the aim was to produce a supply of clerical staff for the government administration of the South. In 1928 a language conference was held in Rajaf (Provincial capital of Equatoria in 1928) attended by representatives of Sudan, Uganda, and Belgian Congo Governments and the missionary societies. Resolutions were reached to develop languages according to the trial regions. Six major languages were selected for use in vernacular education. These "Roll A" languages were Bari, Dinka, Latuka, Nuer, Shilluk, and Zande. The provision of textbooks and grammar was explored, and linguistics experts were hired to carry the work further.[37]

---

[35] Harold MacMichael, The Anglo-Egyptian Sudan,p.265

[36] CMS, " The CMS Gleaner", 1 March 1918, p. 1-2 Achieve, University of Birmingham

[37] Roland Werner, William Anderson and Andrew Wheeler, (eds), op.cit, pp.271-272

The Director of Education in a letter to the secretary of Sudan Mission wrote: "if CMS is prepared to provide the staff and building required for schools in the South (Mongalla Province), the government will issue instructions to the local authorities of the provinces. People should be encouraged to send their children to schools. The local authorities would also facilitate alternatives in the out-lying districts, and will not establish other schools that would serve as rivals unless the CMS fails in its objective". The CMS agreed to the government policy. Rev Shaw who was the Secretary of the Mission submitted a proposal to the Headquarters in the United Kingdom that was subsequently approved, and the schools were established in the South for the son of chiefs[38].

According to a CMS report of March 1929, the government of Sudan gave a subvention of #150 per annum toward the Society's expenditure on the Omdurman Hospital, which was gratefully accepted by the Committee in return for their education work, The Committee then confirmed that the CMS would maintain their elementary schools in southern Sudan; on the understanding that the government would increase the subvention for this sphere of Society's educational work from #1950 to #3600 per annum. It was noted with satisfaction that the recruits (Rev. R.S Macdonald and Rev. W.L.M.Giff) were already available to fill the posts created by the Government in the South[39]

2.6: MCMICHAEL AND SOUTHERN POLICY: 1930-1946

While it was clearly the British intention to administer the South as a separate region from the beginning of the Anglo-Egyptian Condominium, the so called "Southern Policy" was not clearly articulated until 1930 by the Civil Secretary, Mr. Harold McMichael, in advice given to the Governors of Southern Provinces of Bahr el Ghazal, Equatorial and Upper Nile:

"The political object of "Southern Policy" was to create a solid barrier to protect the South against the insidious political intrigue

---

[38] Harol MacMichael, op,cit.,pp.266-267
[39] CMS Report,CMS Archive, Birmingham University, G# A 100,pp.85-86

which must in the ordinary course of events increasingly beset our path in the North[40]....The policy of the government in the Southern Sudan is to build up a series of self-contained racial or tribal units with structure and organization based to whatever extend the requirements of equity and good government permit, upon indigenous customs, tribal usage and beliefs"[41].

The administrative and commercial directives enacted under closed Districts policy reflect deeper concerns of the British administration. There were four reasons for the British administration's development of the Southern Policy: Firstly, the fear of the British that Africa might became an Islamic continent along the lives of the Mahdist movement of the late 19th century. Having suppressed Mahdist attempts to extend Islam into the South, the British were on the alert against any form of Islamization of the southern peoples. This is one of the reasons of setting up the Equatoria Corps to guard the South against Islamic incursions. Secondly, the British recognized that Southerners continued to be hostile towards the North on the account of slavery. Memories of the slave trade were still fresh within the Southern circles where it was feared that the presence of Northern traders would itself lead to further exploitation of human resources, and the expansion of Arab and Islamic influence. Thirdly, the creation of indirect rule was intended to strengthen indigenous African traditions in the South, which had been weakened during the previous century of chaos, and would probably not survive if they were brought under the Islamic political culture of the North[42]. Fourthly, the Anglo-Egyptian Administration used missionaries to its advantage by directing them to remote southern regions where they could consolidate the British presence by proxy; and at the same time, to minimize cost to the government of southern educational development. Missionaries thereby complied with, and

---

[40] ibid.,p.173
[41] T.S.Cotran, Khalifa Mahgoub and Lolik Lado, Report of the Commission of Inquiry into the Disturbances in the Southern Sudan,p.16
[42] The Government of Sudan, op.cit., pp.12-14

benefited from the colonial policies that help to reify the north and south and divide the Sudanese peoples[43]

The policy was pursued vigorously. For example, the border village Kafia Kinji in Bahr el Ghazal was abandoned, and a sort of a no-man's land was created between Bahr el Ghazal and Darfur to prevent intermixture of Arabs and Africans. Arabic was not to be used in the Southern educational system, and Southern Muslims were restricted in the practice of their religion. Administrators were instructed to speak the language of their local districts and to acquaint themselves with local customs as closely as possible.[44] English language was adopted as the official language of Government and the medium of instruction in schools in the South[45]

The goal of Southern policy was to build up a series of self-contained tribal units with structure and organization based upon indigenous customs and traditional beliefs. As a means of implementing this policy, MacMichael's Memorandum on Southern Policy stated that English should be used where "communication" in the local language was impossible, in order to discourage Arabic. This must be also applied to heterogeneous groupings such as the Sudan Defence Force and the Police. He continued to elaborate: "Indeed, every effort should be made to make English the means of communication among the men themselves to the complete exclusion of Arabic.[46]Southern Governors were instructed to implement these policies and to include educational progress in their reports.

The CMS agreed to work under the terms of the Southern Policy, and pay due regard to government's political and administrative desiderata.[47] Yet they never abandoned the wish to be agree to evangelize the whole of Sudan, including the Muslim North beyond the capital of Khartoum where they were permitted to build an Anglican Cathedral.

---

[43] Heather J Sharkey, ibid., p.57

[44] Oliver Albino =, A Southern Viewpoint, p. 21

[45] Hassan Makki Ahmed, op.cit., p. 75

[46] ibid.,p.174

[47] ibid.,p.266
    Muddathir Abdel-Rahim,op.cit.,p.4

The Governor General, Lord Cromer, strongly resisted this hope, and declared "I have no objection to giving the Missionaries a fair field amongst the black African population in the Equatorial regions, but to let them lose at present amongst the .... Muslims of the Sudan would, in my opinion be little short of insane".[48]

2.7: GOVERNMENT AND MISSIONARY SPHERES

The Anglo-Egyptian policy toward missionary societies in the South was to give each religion where it was permitted to operate without competition or interference from other societies. For teaching of religion they were free from government control as we have seen, education was the primary responsibility laid upon them by the government, and from 1927 the government supported this with substantial subsidies that were paid to the missionary societies to cover the cost of education.[49] The CMS was, however, unhappy with the fact that its work was limited to a sphere of influence defined by the government. In 1933 Archdeacon Shaw argued for the abolition of the missionary spheres. While the CMS sympathized with his view, it felt that the Sudan government would be placed in an intolerable position if they were to accept the opinion of the Archdeacon. So the CMS reluctantly accepted that the spheres of influence policy should be accepted and only pressed for a realignment of the sphere boundaries as suggested by the government. It has to be recalled that one of the features 1910 Edinburgh agreement on "comity of mission areas" was to give one mission agency the responsibility to evangelize a certain group of people in a country to avoid double occupancy of a region so that competition along denominational line would not confuse the local populace. The agreement recognized new mission efforts to go to unoccupied areas.

The result of this policy was that educational development in the South was divided among different missionary societies working in different areas, and lacked an effectively unified approach. This, in the my view, is one of the reasons for the weakness of the educational

---

[48] Ibid.,p.5
[49] T.S.Cotran, Khalifa Mahgoub and Lolik Lado,op.cit.,p.5

system in the South by comparison with the North, which was in turn one of the factors that created more fear I the minds of South Sudanese against their fellow countrymen in the North.

A brief review of statistical evidence makes clear that the educational system in the South failed to fulfil its initial promise. Prior to 1932 the total of pupils in bush schools rose sharply, from 2,600 to 4,100, and the number of pupils in post-elementary education increased from 280 to 500. In 1932, however, this rapid growth was abruptly halted, and a decline set in with 12% shrinkage intermediate schools by 1936. By 1938 the number of pupils was still falling.

This stagnation was of concern to the Southern administration since it was so evidently at odds with Harol MacMichael's 1930 policy that had entrusted so much of the implementation of education development to the missionary societies. LS Sanderson attributed the problem to lack of sufficient financial investment: "The total contradiction between the educational stagnation after 1932... is usually explained by the collapse of the Sudan revenue in the early 1930" In my opinion, however, the cause of the stagnation is more accurately revealed in the admission of the Civil Secretary in 1984: "The policy of advancing Southerners has suffered much through ignorance or inattention, resulting from its having been cloistered on the political side of this office"[50]. This suggests that the educational development of the South suffered on account of political considerations, among which the decision of the region into the missionary spheres of influence was imposed by the government, against which Archdeacon Shaw had protested.

This had the effect of perpetuating the disadvantage of the South as compared with the North. In the North, for example, all the traditional *Qur'an* schools which were run on the narrowest curricula and in deplorable conditions were upgraded to village schools, and were provided with qualified teachers and approved courses of instructions. In this manner the North had 239 schools by 1932. The Institute of Education was founded at Bakh er Ruda on the White Nile South of Khartoum, with a modernized system of education that concentrated on the training of new teachers and the in-service refreshment of

---

[50] T.S.Cotran,Khalifa Mahgoub and Lolik Lado,op.cit.,p.17

those already qualified. This, in addition to Gordon College that was founded in Khartoum in 1902, provided the North with an integrated system of primary, secondary and technical education, and significant progress was made toward developing education among girls.[51]

The result of this disparity was that relatively few southerners were educated to fill clerical posts in the region. For the most part those who were educated were the sons of the soldiers who came from outside the region. Indigenous people among the Nuer and Dinka, mainly from Pastoralist backgrounds, tended to be ignored. Those who completed primary education, that emphasized the learning of vernacular languages,, were expected to discontinue their studies after level four and to work for the local chiefs, usually as secretaries who would keep a record of court cases. While the missionary societies did their best to develop local schools, they were hampered by lack of sufficient funds, a disunited provision of education, and government neglect.[52]

2.8: CRITIQUE OF MISSIONARY EDUCATION IN SOUTHERN SUDAN

In this situation it is not surprising that criticisms were leveled against missionary education by some administrators in the South. These were investigated in the Commission of Inquiry into the disturbances of 1955 that marked the beginning of the civil war on the eve of the British withdrawal from Sudan.

The first accusation was that the missionaries were more interested in promoting Christianity at the expense of Islam than in providing education for the sake of national development. They were criticized for presenting Islam only in the negative terms of the slave trade, and of labeling all Northerners as slave traders. An expressed by a Catholic missionary from Nairobi to a Southern Sudan Student:

---

[51] The Government of Sudan,op.cit

[52] Douglas H. Johnson, The Root Causes of the Sudan's Civil Wars, 2003, p. 15

"The African population around is almost wholly Moslem, of Arabs, extraction and whenever I see them my thoughts run to the grim story of Arab slave raiders in Southern Sudan. The raiders were all Moslems – what a story of the utter abomination of that evil religion which makes no appeal to conduct, even including slave raiders in its scope, and directs its special hostility to the Christian religion of one who was both God and man, and laid down his human life to save humanity from the sin which Islam treats of lightly and then took that life again and is ALIVE TODAY, to give daily power over sin[53].

While the Commission of Inquiry noted the negativity of missionaries in the South toward Islam, it took the view that this was not the direct cause of the 1955 disturbances that were of political rather than religious nature. Neither the slave trade nor the differences in religion played a direct part in the problems, though they represented a legacy of tensions that alienated Southerners and Northerners.

The related criticism raised against the missionaries was that they used education as a means of evangelization rather than the training of teachers. The Commission noted that there was substance in this criticism, and that, with very few exceptions, the mission schools failed to produce a cadre of professionally-trained Southern able to assume senior positions in either the educational or administrative systems that were essential for the "Sudanisation" of the South. An official from the Ministry of Education whose evidence before the Commission of Inquiry showed that there had been a lack of regular inspection or control of the missionary schools by the colonial administration supported this criticism. The low standard of education of Southerners, it was argued, was one of the reasons why the government had to take over the direct control of southern education in 1946, with the aim of making up the lost ground by replacing the missionary educators. In the light of this background, Duncan argues that Southern education

---

[53] T.S.Cotran, Khalifa ahgoub and Lolik Lado,op.cit.,pp 5-6

in mission schools had not been satisfactory. He likened the role of missionaries to that of chaplains, rather than professional educators who could prepare Southerners in the skills that were essential for the development of South.[54]

Lastly, the Commission noted that there was too a great deal of mistrust and suspicion between colonial administrator and the missionaries that produced a cleavage between church and state, and between the North and South in all aspects of development.

2.9: POLITICAL ECONOMY

The Southern Policy was premised on the principle of the separate development of the South and the North. Under the Closed Districts Ordinance of 1930, free movement between the North and the South was restricted. Passport and permits Ordinances were promulgated and subsequently used to transform the Sothern provinces into "Closed Districts"[55]. As we have already noticed, Southern policy was meant to separate the populations of the two regions. This resulted in the transfer to the North of Northern official serving in the South, and the denial of trading licenses to northern traders who traditionally traded in the South. Under the Southern Policy these Northerners were replace by Greek, Armenian, ad Syrian and Egyptian Christian traders who took the reins of the economy into their hands rather than Southerners themselves.

As a result economic development in the South lay in the hands of a few, while Northern merchants were encouraged to expand their trade throughout the North. The colonial administration concentrated investments in the northern Sudan, especially in the cotton development of 90,000 acres of Gezira plain that enabled the North to become a major trader in the international market[56]. Tribal notables and religious leaders in the North benefited from an administrative system that issued contract that allowed them to accumulate rights to labor ad

---

[54] J.R.S. Duncan, The Sudan: A Record of Achievements, pp, 266 -217
[55] Mansour Khalid, 1990,op.cit.pp.58 -64
[56] The Government of Sudan, op.cit.p.30

land, and strengthen relations between the Muslim commercial elite and the colonial authorities. For examples, the son of Mahdi Sayyid (Sayyid: religious leader, notable) Abd al –Rahman gained considerable wealth through Government contracts for variety of items such as wood and fuel, and became a staunch supporter of the British as result. This pattern had no equivalent in the South where commerce continued to be in the hands of Greek, Syrian, Armenian traders.

It is clear, therefore, that the colonial policy of separate development resulted in the unequal development of the North and South under Anglo-Egyptian Condominium. The contrast became apparent from 1946 when the colonial administration changed the policy of separate development into one of national unification that was intended to bring Sudan to independence under a unity system of governance that was demanded by northern political parties, mainly based on the political visions of the *Ansar and Khatimiyya* Orders.

2.10: ISLAMIC REVIVAL (MAHDIST MOVEMENT AND KHATMIYYA ORDERS

The political development of the North also took a course that was very different from the South during the Anglo-Egyptian Condominium. The use of Islam as a means of political change had already occurred, as we saw in the introduction to the book, in the rebellion of the *Mahdî* against the corrupt Turco-Egyptian colonial regime and the establishment of the short-lived Mahdist state in Omdurman. After the fall of this state in 1898, the *Ansar* continued as a distinct religio-political group under the leadership of Abd Al-Rahman al-Mahdi, forming itself in the *Umma* Party that reconciled itself with the British and supported the colonial authority. During the same period, the *Khatmiyya* Order led by the Mirghani family, continued to be influential in the countryside; it formed the national Unionist Party that allied itself with Egypt, and acted as a moor opponent of Mahdism. Both the *Khatmiyya* and *Ansâr* groups were organized at the local levels through their local religious leaders, known *faki-s*[57].

---

[57] Nazib Ayubi, Political Islam: Region and Politics in the Arab World, p. 105

"Sectarian" (*tâ'ifi*) politics thus entered the political scene of the North, and dominated the Northern political culture during the 20th century. Differences in religious tradition were reflected in the character of these two parties. Thus, the reluctance of *Sufi* leaders to assume political roles gave primacy to secular and "modernizing" nationalist within the National Union Party (NUP) as compared to the Mahdist movement that ensured the primacy of the traditional *Ansâr* leadership within Umma party.[58] In contrast to these two traditionalist parties there emerged in 1949 an ideological Islamic movement, the Muslim Brothers, under the leadership of Hassan al-Turabi, who was influenced by the Egyptian Muslims Brothers, and entered a formal association with them in 1954. In 1964 the Sudanese wing of Muslim Brotherhood re-styled itself as the Islamic Charter Front (ICF). Its aim was to create Sudan as an Islamic state, and while it challenged the traditional influence of the Umma and National Unionist Parties, it was also opposed to the policies of a reformist ideological party known as the "Republican Brothers", established by Mahmud Taha in the 1940s.

Political life in the North was therefore very active during the Anglo –Egyptian Condominium as Muslims created political parties with clear views about the identity of state in an independence was declared in 1956, they were well placed to shape the governments of Sudan, both democratic and military. There was no comparable political development in the South and the change of colonial policy in 1946 therefore left the Southerners vulnerable to political domination by the North.

2.11: RELIGION AND LAW

During the Anglo-Egyptian Administration, law and religion were placed in separate compartments.[59] The main laws governing the Sudan were established on the secular principles of the Penal code of 1899 and the Criminal Code of 1890. These were remodeled in 1925, and

---

[58] ibid., p. 105
[59] Dougls.as H Johnson, 2003, op.cit. p. 13

later in 1929, by the introduction of a new Civil Justice Ordinance.[60] These enactments were amended from time to time to meet the need of changing conditions and developments of the societies as perceived by the colonial administration.

In the North *Sharî_`a* law was preserved, but with limited competence in the domain of family law for Muslims regulating marriages, inheritance and some property rights. In the Urban areas of the North, different forms of customary laws were also recognized for non-Muslim peoples from the South. A network of the religious courts was recognized under authority of a Grand *Qadi*. Aware of the traditionally orthodox *`ulama* to service the legal system, many of whom came from Egypt. The Grand *Qadi* remained an Egyptian until 1947.[61]

Islamic law was not extended to the South. Here the colonial administrators build legal systems on the basis of local religions and customs, approved ad embodied in tribal hierarchies. Islam was neither pursued nor expelled from the South during the colonial era, but it was confined, both geographically and legislatively. During the early 1920s the army and much of the police force comprised Northern Muslims, and after the dissolution of these Sudanese battalions *malakiyya-s,* or within civilian quarters designated to government officials. Here they were allowed to have their own schools and to apply law, but the colonial administrator maintained a clear division between the rural areas and town. Islamic influence of rural communities remained limited.[62]

In the rural areas customary laws prevailed, supported by traditional religion.

It was among the rural and village communities that conversion to Christianity and Christian students then pursues higher qualification in the towns where the main educational system was established. Here they came under the secular legal administration of the civil justice Ordinance. Southerners were discouraged from converting to Islam and adapting its culture.

---

[60] The Sudan, A record of Progress 1898 – 1947, Printed by Sudan Government, (C.A.S) Archives University of Edinburgh

[61] ibid.,p. 13

[62] ibid.,p. 13

This resulted in a clear legal differentiation between the South and the North, both between customary and religious law, and between the customary legislation itself, and provided a legislative undergirding of the Closed District Act to which reference has already been made. Christianity was increasingly identified as the religion of the South, while in the North Muslims encouraged greater uniformity of practice through Islam.

2.12: CONCLUSION

The examination that this chapter has undertaken of political, educational, economic and legal aspects of the Anglo –Egyptian Condominium demonstrates the tension that underlay the entire colonial administration. The aim of the Condominium was to develop Sudan as a single nation, including for the first time in its history both the North and the South. The colonial policy, however, was to develop the North and South as separate regions, each with its own ethnic and cultural characteristics. This was justified in colonial theory on the argument that the predominantly Muslim North had achieved a higher level of political and administrative development than had the South, and that Southerners needed time and space to catch up. It was not the intention of the colonial administration that the South should be Christianized, but by entrusting so much of the educational process of development in the South to Christian missionaries whose primary intention was evangelism through education, the colonial administration effectively confirmed the historic distinctions between Arabs and Africans along religious as well as cultural and ethnic lines. It was through Southern policy and the administration of the Anglo-Egyptian Condominium that the south came to be identified with Christianity, while the North continued to express its identity through Islam. The tension between these two identities was exacerbated from 1946 as the colonial policy changed to administering Sudan as a single state in preparation for national independence. It is to this development that we turn in the next Chapter.

THREE

ANGLO-EGYPTIAN
CONDOMINIUM: 1946-1956

3.1: TRANSITIONAL ARRANGEMENTS 1946 – 1955

The discussion of institutional arrangements prior to independence
effectively started during the Juba Conference 1947, and progressed in
haphazard steps through the Legislative Assembly of 1953, the Anglo-
Egyptian Agreement of 1953, and up to Torit Uprising in August 1955.

3.2: CHANGE OF BRITISH POLICY: 1946

With the end of the Second World War, Europe's pre-war colonial
arrangements came under review, with pressure especially from the
United States for colonized countries to be granted full independence.
The Anglo-Egyptian Condominium government had, therefore, to
make a decision about the future of Sudan. The tide of Sudanese
nationalism was rising in the North, and the cause of self-determination
for Sudan was being taken up by Egypt that, as early as 1936, indicated
its desire to end the Condominium. Shortly before the end of the war,
in 1944, initial steps were taken to establish an Advisory Council for
Northern Sudan with power to advise the Governor General on matters
relating to the creation of legislative body that would represent the whole
Sudan. It is hardly necessary to point out, given the Condominium's

policy of separate administration of the North and the South, that this Advisory Committee did not include representatives of the three provinces of Southern Sudan.

For almost two decades the Condominium government had been undecided what to do with the South, There were two options: the first was to link the South with the North in an independent Sudan; the second was to extract the South from an independent Sudan and link it politically with East Africa.

> "It is by economic and educational development that these people can be equipped to stand up for themselves in the future, whether their lot be eventually cast with the Northern Sudan or with East Africa (or partly with each)"[63].

By 1946, however, the government decided to reverse its Southern policy of Closed Districts and to "Cast the lot" of Southern Sudan wholly with the North. The new policy was expressed as follows:

> "It is necessary act upon the facts that the people of Southern Sudan are distinctively African and Negroid, but that geography and economic combine (so far as can be foreseen at the present time: to render them inextricably mixed to the Middle Eastern and Arabicized Northern Sudan: and therefore to ensure that they shall by educational and economic development they be equipped to stand up for themselves in the future as socially and economically the equals of their partners of the Northern Sudan in the Sudan of the future".[64]

The decision to link the South with the North in an independent Sudan has to be understood in the context of the influence of Arab

---

[63] T.S.Cotran, Khalifa mahgoub and Lolik Lado, op.,cit., p.18
[64] ibid., p. 18

nationalism in the Middle East., and in Egypt in particular where Egyptian nationalist struggle against Britain included the problem of the Suez Canal. The Canal was an important trade artery for Britain, and was protected by a British military contingent in Egypt; the Egypt nationalist demanded a complete British evacuation, including the military cautiously in respect of Sudanese independence, not wishing to cause further trouble with the Egyptians at the risk of the Canal. The United States that was just emerging as a power in the idle East also pressured Britain to placate Egypt and secure the Canal for western interests.

The Governor General of Sudan therefore appointed a special Sudan Administrative Conference, which began its proceedings in April 1946. In contrast to the Advisory Committee of Northern Sudan, this conference included the governors and representatives of the South as well as the North. It recommended that a subcommittee be sent to the South to negotiate the relationship between the Southern provinces and the North in a united Sudan. The Civil Secretary, J. W. Robertson, issued a directive to the Provincial Governors on 16th December 1946 informing them that the Southern policy was at an end, and that the South would be untied with the North.[65]

The Southern Governors responded by pointing out that the Civil Secretary had not obtained the opinion of Southerners on their future, and that the government should therefore convene a separate administrative conference for Southern Sudan[66].

3.3: JUBA CONFERENCE 1947

In order to meet the concerns of the Southern governors, an administrative conference was convened in Juba in 1947. Its participants comprised fifteen Southerners chosen by the Governors of Southern Provinces, six British officials, and six Northerners. Their remit was to explore the views of Sothern Sudanese and to determine whether it was advisable for the South to send representatives to the proposed

---

[65] Oliver Albino, op.cit., pp. 23-25
[66] ibid., pp. 24-25

Legislative Assembly, or whether they should have their own Advisory council similar to one established in the North in 1944.[67]

The conference was, from the point of view of the Southerners, unsatisfactory. The Northern representatives, led by Judge Mohammed Saleh Shinghti, were highly educated and had a define view in favour of Sudan's political future as a single state. The Southerners had differing opinions both from the Northerners and among themselves. It was clear from the minutes of Juba conference that few people from the South could visualize at this time what the political developments would be in the future.

The Civil Secretary who chaired the conference made remarks that were in favour of the unity of Sudan, rather than of the South joining an East African federation. This created fear in the minds of the Southern representatives that the aim of the conference was simply to inform them of a decision that had already been reached between the British and the Northerners, that the South would be handed over to the North. For Southerners this meant a new form of colonialism, this time from the North, and it is for this reason that the resolutions of the Juba conference are still seen by Southerners as having been biased against their interests, and therefore of questionable legitimacy, even though it was agreed that thirteen Southerners representatives would participate in the Legislative Assembly.

3.4: LEGISLATIVE ASSEMBLY: 1952

In April 1952 the Legislative Assembly enacted, with the agreement of both the British and the Egyptians, a draft Self-Government Statute that established a Council of Ministers, all of the Northern Sudanese that would exercise authority in a transitional period leading to full independence of Sudan. The Statute included safeguards for the South, vesting these in the authority of the Governor General. The Stature was, however, opposed by the *Khatmiyya* leader, Ali Mirghani, and his party boycotted the assembly in protest. The Northern political parties staged a series of meetings in Cairo without Southern representatives.

---

[67] Sir James Robertons, The Minutes of Juba Conference 1947, pp. 2-6

They then merged into National Unionist Party (NUP) that nominated Ismai'l al-Azhari as their candidate for the Presidency of an independent united Sudan.

The situation was complicated by the Egyptian revolution of July 1952 that deposed the Khedivate and replace it with the military government of the Free Officers, nominally led by General Neguib, himself half Sudanese. On 5th December 1952 an agreement was concluded between NUP and the new Egyptian government that rejected the draft Self-Government Statute as a satisfactory basis for Sudanese independence, and issued a statement declaring Sudan an indivisible entity.[68] The Northern parties presented a unified front and obliged Egypt to omit specific powers that were reserved to the Governor General for the protection of the interest of the South.

3.5: THE ANGLO-EGYPTIAN AGREEMENT OF 1953

The British therefore had no alternative but to revise the draft the Self-Government Statute for the Sudan. One of the major questions was the degree to which a national constitution based upon the unification policy of 1947 could include safeguards for the South. The Committee was sharply divided on the issue of Southern interests, as one of the British representatives commented.

"Without protection, the Southerners will not be able to develop along indigenous lines; will be overwhelmed and swamped by the North and deteriorate into a servile community hewing wood and drawing water. To pretend that there are no fundamental differences between them is like covering up a crack in a tree trunk with moss. Such a process, like any observing of truth, is unsound".[69]

However, by investing the power to safeguard the South in the office of the Governor General, the Self-Government Statute invited criticism from both the Northern and Egyptian politicians who saw the safeguard of Southern interests as a way of continuing British power over an independent Sudan. This critical issue was not definitively resolved in

---

[68] T.S.Cotran, Khalifa Mahgoub and Lolik Lado, op. cit., p.18

[69] ibid., pp.18 - 21

the Anglo-Egyptian Agreement that was signed on 12th February 1953. The agreement reiterated the unity of Sudan as a fundamental of the South were only acknowledged in a general commitment "to ensure fair and equitable treatment of all the inhabitants of the various provinces of the Sudan". Moreover, in the transitional period the authority of the Governor General would be exercised through an international commission consisting of two Sudanese Egyptian, a Pakistani and one British representative.

The process leading to this Agreement suggests that there was a diplomatic trade-off between the British sand the Egyptians: that the Egyptians would withdraw their demand for British evacuation of the Canal Zone in return for British support of the principle of Sudanese unity that would tie the South to the politically dominant North. The British Ambassador to Egypt emphasized that the accord would inaugurate an era between Egypt and Great Britain.[70]

The period from 1948 to the signing of the Anglo-Egyptian Agreement was marked by intensive "Sudanisation" of the South. Various economic, educational and administrative reforms were introduced that, while advancing the development of the South, were intended to affirm the principle of national unity. For example, the Nzara Cotton Industry of the Zande Scheme became a viable project, with its branches operational in the South. Communications were improved. A united system of education was introduced that included the teaching of Arabic, and local government was established in all districts. Trade was opened up to all Sudanese, and restrictions on free movement between the North and the South were relaxed.

In February 1954, a "Sudanisation Committee" was set up with the remit of replacing British officials with Sudanese cadres' in government posts. The Committee was made of three Northern and two British members, the South was not represented. When the names of the new Sudanese administrators were announced in October: out of 800 posts only six were assigned to Southerners. The highest of those posts was that of Assistant District commissioner (D.C). In their conference at Malakal Town Southerners, asked the Parliament to give them more

---

[70] Oliver Albino, op.cit.,pp.31-36

post. The Parliament responded by assigning four posts of Vice – D.C., and two of Mamurs.[71] Tensions degenerated into revolt in 1955 that ravaged the south until 1972, when Addis Ababa accord was concluded giving the south form of local autonomy.

One of the important consequences of these changes was that Southern people became more politically conscious than they were before. Accelerated Sudanisation was met by growing political consciousness among educated Southerners who gave voice to their opposition to the political arrangements that were being put in place for Sudanese independence.

3.6: TORIT UPRISING – AUGUST 1955

The Condominium administrators were clearly aware of the distrust ad hostility that was building up in the South. Southern opposition against the excessive migration of Northerners to South was becoming public. The possibility of a military uprising was foreseen in instructions issued by the government for the evacuation of Northern Sudanese and foreigners to Zaire and Uganda in the event of hostilities. As the situation became tenser, Isma'il al-Azhari, the leader of the transitional legislative Assembly, announced in January 1954 that armed forces would be increased.[72]

On 18th August 1955, with Sudanese Independence promised for the following year, the so-called mutiny started in Torit when the (Southern) Equatorial Corps refused to accept orders to relocate to Khartoum without ammunition. Just before these orders were issued, British officers were evacuated from the South, and platoons composed only of Southerners were ordered to move to Khartoum, allegedly to take part in a parade to mark the evacuation of foreign troops from Sudan. As the Torit garrison paraded in preparation for departure, the requested assurances from the officer in charge that their re-location would only be temporary. The requests were not granted, and fearing retribution the garrison broke into the armory, taking

---

[71] Nicholas lo Polito, op.cit., pp. 1-2
[72] Oliver Albino, op., pp. 19-21

guns and ammunition[73]. This marked the beginning of a general revolt throughout the Southern Sudan. Complete disorder and chaos prevailed for two weeks. On the 20th August a State of Emergency was proclaimed in the three Southern Provinces of Bahr al-Ghazal, Equatoria and Upper Nile, and the insurrection was suppressed with the help of the Royal Air Force[74]. The Torit uprising was put down, but the anger it had unleashed could not be suppressed, and the incident is taken as marking the beginning of the civil war in which the South fought against the North for the political rights of self-determination that had been denied them during the negotiations toward Sudanese independence.

On 19th December 1955 the elected parliament promised that: "the request of the Southern members of parliament for a federal system of governance for the South will be given due consideration by the constituent Assembly". But immediately after independence it became clear that the new government of Khartoum intended to follow a policy that was expressed in the slogan "One Language (Arabic), One Religion (Islam) and One Nation[75]". But to outline the mains causes of the incident and other external influences that might have contributed to North – South conflicts.

3.7: HISTORICAL, CULTURAL AND ECONOMIC FACTORS OF DISPARITIES

The bitterness of Southerners that resulted to the 1955 up rise highlighted the historical differences that existed between North and the South. They then expressed their opinion through violence to undermine the principle of national unity for the impending independence of the country. Racial, cultural and linguistic factors underlay the Sothern's political resistance to the North. There is very little in common between Northern and Southern Sudanese: racially, the Northerners

---

[73] Roland Werner., William Anderson. And Andrew Wheeler, op.cit., 367 - 368

[74] Oliver Albino, op. cit., pp 36 - 38

[75] Mom Kou Nhial Arou, In Post-Independence Sudan, p. 17

are Arab and Muslim, while the Southerners are Africans who, by the end of the Anglo-Egyptian Condominium, were significantly Christianized. Linguistically the Egyptian Northerners are Arabic-speaking while a variety of different Africa languages prevail in the South and by independence English was established as their *lingua franca*. For historical reasons the Southerners regarded the Northern Sudanese as their traditional enemies, and the memory of slavery and economic exploitation was still fresh in mind. These differences had, as we have seen, been consolidated rather than diffused under a quarter of a century of British administration of the South Sudanese from knowing and learning from each other. The missionaries who had most of the education in their hands threw in their influence in favour of Southern Policy, and encouraged the Southerners to view the Northerners as religious enemies.

In addition to these cultural antipathies, the South had not achieved equal educational or economic parity with the North. While Northern Sudan progressed quickly in every field under the Condominium, the South lagged far behind. Because there were more educated Northerners at the time of Sudanisation, they took up most of the key positions in the South with the advent of independence, often to the disadvantage of Southerners. For example, when the Northerners took over the management of Nzara Cotton Industry of the Zande Scheme in South Sudan in July 1955, three hundred Southern workers were immediately dismissed.[76] The dismissal induced the Nzara Workers Union to protest and demonstrate. The new administration called in army and the police who were ordered to fire at the demonstrators. The commission of inquiry estimated six people killed and many wounded in the incident. Southerners argued that this was a deliberate attempt by the Northern management to deprive local people of their livelihood.

The religious difference between North and South also affects the political culture. In Sudan as a whole, about 62% of the people are Muslims, 38% follow indigenous beliefs and Christians, expressing their religious beliefs through Sufi orders (*turuq*), and the Christians belonging to 'Roman Catholic, Protestant and Orthodox churches,

---

[76] ibid., p.17

the *Turuq* and the churches cutting across ethnic lines – the fact that Arabic is the language of the *Qur'an* links it's in the Southerners mind with Arabic culture and Islamic religion. It is for this reason, more than differences of belief and doctrine, that the South contested the role of Islam in terms of the constitutional framework of Sudan. Similarly Arabic was perceived as the language of Northern colonialism, and was therefore resisted[77] (See appendix I).

Furthermore, the lack of equity in political power sharing made it impossible for Southerners to seek redress of their grievances through parliamentary political process. Since the Juba conference of 1947, Southerners demanded federal status to safeguard their cultural, social and economic development[78]. None of the Northern political parties accepted this demand. They reasoned that federation would only be a step towards the complete secession of the South, and would encourage similar developments in the other regions such as Darfur and Nuba Mountains both of which had expressed their preference for a decentralization policy for the encouraging sectarianism among different Islamic and ethnic groups. Finally, the Southern problem was viewed as a legacy of British imperialism and therefore, had to suppress as part of the struggle to rid Sudan of British influence.[79]

3.8: CONCLUSION

The aim of this chapter has been to expose the political problems that were inherent in the period of transition from the colonial administration of Sudan to its emergence as the independent Republic of Sudan in the 1st January 1956. It has been demonstrated that these problems were essentially of a political and developmental nature. Religion was not the issue of dispute *per se*, but was an important factor in the culture in which the political conflict took shape.

The missionaries were not part of the process of political negotiation that took place from 1946. Their influence was confined to the educational

---

[77] Ann Mosely Lesch, The Sudan Contested National Identities
[78] ibid., p. 116
[79] ibid., p.155

responsibilities that were delegated to them under the Southern Policy that was decreed by the colonial administration. Education was, in my view, the most successful part of the development of the South during the Condominium period. While the missionaries always saw education as the means to development and Christianization – goals that were inseparable in their minds – they laid the foundations of education in the South, and educated most of the Southerners who were to emerge as the political leaders in the transition to independence and thereafter. Furthermore, the missionaries were successful in bringing the first generation of Southern Christians into leadership of the Catholic and Protestant Churches. It is not justifiable, therefore, to hold the missionaries responsible for the Southern resistance to the policy of Sudanisation and the independence of Sudan as a unitary state. Many of them may have harboured doubts about the viability of the principle of unity on which the independence movement was founded, but it was Southern Sudanese themselves who opposed the policy and took to the barricades in the 1955.

The efforts of the CMS and other missionaries in Sothern Sudan can be viewed as the most positive aspect of developing the indigenous people in the South. This helped the people of the south to become Christians and subsequently to resist internal colonization by the North in the form of Islamisation and Arabisation. The problems subsequent to independence derive not from mission but rather the self-interest and outright failure of the Northern political parties and the colonial powers.

Persistent interference of Northern administrators in the affairs of the South was a cause friction that erupted in 1955. This was substantiated in the Report of the Commission of Inquiry that gave many instances of arbitrary dismissal of Southern political representatives simply on grounds of their having voiced the preferences of the South for federation. The attitude of the North is suggested, at least, in a telegram that is attributed to Prime Minister Ismail al-Azhari about the beginning of July 1955, it originated from an unknown southern clerk in Juba and reads:

"To all my administrators in the three Southern Provinces, I have just signed a document of self-determination; do not listen to the childish complaints of the Southerners. Persecute then; ill-treat them according to my orders. Any administrator who fails to comply with my orders will be liable to persecution. In three months' time all of you will come round and enjoy the work you have done.[80]"

This telegram was widely circulated throughout the Southern provinces. It was sent to various politically minded clerks in government offices and to southern police officers and men in most parts of Southern region. It also reached Oboyo Saturlino, one of the leaders of the Equatorial corps. On receiving telegram he called a meeting of army officers and presented intelligence that the Prime Minister intended to disband the Corps and replace it with Northern soldiers, this fuelled the angers that erupted in the Torit uprising.

Therefore, it can be argued that ultimate responsibility for the 1955 crisis, however, lies with the colonial administration itself. As we have seen, the British policy of administering the South separately failed to achieve its goals as the South remained seriously under developed by comparison with the north after quarter of a century of colonial administration. We have also noted, in the first ten –year period of the Southern Policy during the 1930s, few Southerners qualified for executive work. It was not until 1942 that the first Southerner was allowed to compete for a public service position. In this respect the South lagged behind their Northern counterparts. The shift in colonial policy in 1946 from the implemented because the British caved into pressures form the Northern political parties and Egypt to hand the South over to the North in return for what eventuated as limited concessions in respect of British protection of the Suez Canal and other interests. Had the British handled the 1947 conference and the events that followed the 1955 uprising fairly, putting the interests of the South before their own, it was likely that the civil war could have been avoided, and Sudan could have emerged as a viable nation based on the peaceful – existence of all its peoples.

[80] ibid., p. 85

FOUR

THE FIRST PERIOD OF THE DEVELOPMENT OF SUDAN AS AN INDEPENDENT REPUBLIC: 1956 -1972

4.1: INTRODUCTION

In this chapter, I will offer a review of the first period of Sudanese independence from 1956 to 1972, analyzing the problems of constitutional and political structure of the new state – problems that were to a large degree the unfinished business of the former colonial administration. The focus will be on the ways in which church-state relations were influenced by the policy of both parliamentary and military governments to affirm the unity of Sudan by Arabizing and Islamizing the South. This led to the crisis of the Missionary Society Act (MSA) of 1962, and its repercussion on government policy toward religion and education in the South. Following the expulsion of foreign missionaries between 1962 and 1964, the All Africa conference of churches (AACC) embarked on a policy form 1966 of building new relations with the Khartoum government. This laid foundations for an international ecumenical peace initiative in 1970/1971 involving both the AACC and the world Council of Churches, and, for the first time, drew the Sudan Council of Churches into direct relations with the government.

4.2: EDUCATION POLICY IN SOUTHERN SUDAN (1956 – 1958)

It has to be recalled that during the Juba conference of 1947 referred to earlier, the Southern Sudanese initially demanded federal status as a solution to the North-South problem. They argued that peoples of such different racial, religious and cultural characteristics and the African and Arabs could only co-exist in the same state if constitutional recognition was given to their respective identities and political needs. This required a federal rather than unitary state. As already mentioned in this chapter that on 19th December 1955 the parliament promised that: "The request of the Southern members of parliament for a federal system of governance for the South will be given due consideration by the Constituent Assembly" but this did not happen. The common language of English and the Christian religion, both of which had taken root in the South during the Condominium, were viewed as obstacles to national unity. Tensions between the North and South were thus aggravated form the birth of independence, each region viewing the existence of the other in terms of imperialism: the Southerners feared the internal imperialism of the Arab Muslim North, while Northerners feared that the Southern demand for regional federation was an open door to renewed Western imperialist attempts to destroy Sudan by proxy.[81]

During the first two years of independence, 1956-1958, parliamentary politics was dominated by the question of the political status of the South. On the basis of promises given earlier at the 1947 Juba conference, Southerners continued to press for a federal status, but the Northerners objected to their demand, and instead they took over the administration of the South, supported by a police force and an army that were then manned by them.

The first Minister of Education, Sayed Ali Abdel Rahman, was the architect of the "Northern Education Policy". In a statement to the House of Representatives earlier in April 1955, He said: "It would be the policy of the Ministry of Education to have a unified system of

---

[81] ibid., p. 155

Education for the whole country.[82] According to the government, it was essential to reform the Southern system of education that had previously been administered by Christian missionaries, and to assimilate it into a national system based on what already existed in the North. Thus, the Minister projected that, by 1964, all entrance examinations to secondary schools in the South would be conducted in Arabic, just as in the North. Southerners viewed this educational policy as the beginning of Arabization of their educational system, and destruction of cultural traditions. The Government was unmoved by the protests from the South, and the policy was speedily implemented by the military government of General Abboud when it seized power in a bloodless coup on 17th November 1958, and suspended the constitution.

4.3: DEVELOPMENT OF RELIGIOUS AND CULTURAL CONFLICTS (1958-1964)

President General Ibrahim Abboud immediately dissolved the Parliament. But it quickly became clear that the military government had no better idea of how to administer the South than the civilian government that it replaced. The situation rapidly deteriorated, among romours that the government intended to embark on a policy of resettling Northerners in the South. Linking these romours with the military take-over, Southerners argued that the Northerners had in fact handed over the elected government to the military to implement the Arabisation of the South.

All forms of Southern protest were ignored. Masour Khalid has observed: "The crippling failure of the government was entirely to under-estimate the importance of the Southern factor"[83]. Indeed, the regime denied that there were any legitimate political demands in the South that required a political solution. Instead they argued that the problem in the South was due to the lack of law and order, and to Christina missionaries who refused to accept that Southern Sudan was legitimately part of the united Sudan. The missionaries were portrayed

---

[82] ibid., p. 120
[83] Mansour Khallid, 1990, op.cit. 187

as the source of all-evil. If they were removed, all would be well and national unity and integration would be achieved by assimilating the South into the Arab Muslim culture on the North. According to this argument, there would be no room for cultural diversity, and any dissent would be suppressed by military force. This policy was justified by the Governor of Equatoria, Ali Baldo, who in 1961, said:

> "We thank God that by virtue of the marvelous efforts of the revolutionary, the country will remain forever united. You should turn a deaf ear to any evil talk, which comes from the politicians, as you well know what has come of them in the past few years, and you certainly don't want bloodshed again in the South".[84]

Drastic measures followed. Sunday replaced by Friday as the religious holiday in the South, conforming to the Muslim practice of the North. This had immense symbolic meaning for the Southerners who perceived it as an attempt to coerce them to accept Islamic, not simply Arab culture. Christians were not allowed to pray anywhere except on Sundays, and only in Churches. Muslims on the other hand enjoyed freedom of worship which they practiced anywhere. Southerners were enticed to embrace Islam. An exceptional example was Chief Jambo of the Moru tribe who changed his name to Ibrahim when he was persuaded to accept Islam.

This was the impassioned situation in which the Abboud government determined to take drastic action against the Christian missionaries in the south by introducing the missionary Societies Act of 1962 that drastically curtailed the activity of foreign missionary societies[85].

---

[84] ibid., p. 188
[85] ibid., pp. 188 -190

4.4: CHURCH AND STATE RELATIONS (1962-1969)

The Missionary act (1962) provoked the first major crisis in church-state relations in independent Sudan. In this section, we shall examine the act itself, and its repercussions on church-state relations in the South over the next seven years.

To begin with, it is important to put the situation of the churches in the South into historical context. It was the policy of the British administration, during the Anglo-Egyptian Condominium, to maintain the variety and diversity of the several territories that fell loosely under British policy was to separate the religious spheres of Islam and Christianity. Islam was dominant in the North, and Christian missionaries were not allowed to work among Northern Muslims, Similarly, Islamic influence was not permitted to spread in the Southern provinces where the activities of Christian mission were mainly concentrated. This policy obviously created difficulties for the governments of independent Sudan that were faced with the challenge of developing the unity of the country. It was due to the gravity of this problem, and the inability of civilian politicians to solve it that the military government of General Abboud took over in 1958 and suspended the constitution. The military government viewed the presence of Christian Missionary groups in the South with extreme suspicion, and held them responsible for fermenting the movement for southern independence. Consequently, the government decided to take measure against the missionaries as foreigners who were diverting the loyalty of the Southern citizens.

4.5: MISSIONARY SOCIETIES ACT 1962

The Missionary Society Act (MSA) required all missionary societies to apply to the government for a licence to work in Sudan, and to comply with the terms of a licence. The normal activities of the missionary societies were effectively restricted with the sphere of existing churches, and written parental consent was required before any young person under the age of eighteen could identify him or herself Christian.

All foreign missionaries had to apply for permission to continue to work in the South, and for the most part this was withheld or denied. Within the next twelve months nearly two hundred and fifty foreign missionaries were required to leave the country. By February 1964 the GoS had expelled all remaining missionaries, on grounds that they were engaged in programs that diverted energy and resources from the services supplied by the government.

Faced by this crisis, the Church Missionary Society (CMS) moved to a policy of developing an indigenous Sudanese Church as quickly as possible, so that the South would be less reliant on missionary personnel and resources. The then President of the CMS, Sir Kenneth Grubb, wrote to the President of the Supreme Council of the Republic of the Sudan in February 1963, acknowledging the problems that were facing the government, and gave assurance that the Society wished to cooperate in the promotion of unity and good order. At the same time he expressed the Society's concession to allow a UK missionary to be appointed to the staff of the Minister of Interior who undertook to have the necessary permission granted.

At the same time the CMS made representations to the British Foreign Office on 23rd September 1964. They resisted the temptation to accuse the Sudan government of anti-Christian motives. However, they drew attention to the steadily government policy on education and the role of missionaries in the South would result in the stifling of the life of the Church. They pointed out that the Government was by-passing the authority of Bishop Allison who had episcopal charge of the Anglican Diocese of Sudan, who had been refused permission to enter the South; and that the government was ignoring the Sudanese Bishops by applying directly to the government of Nigeria for theological tutors for Mundiri. In light of these problems and the expressed protests of the Sudanese Bishops about the treatment of the Church questions were raised against the proposed visit of the British Queen to Sudan at the time[86].

---

[86] Brian de Saram, CMS Africa Secretary to Sir Kenneth Crubb, President, CMS; "Record of a meeting at eh Foreign Office 23-09-64

4.6: EDUCATION AND RELIGIOUS POLICIES OF THE GOVERNMENT

Mentioned has already been made of the Northern Education Policy that was introduced in 1955 and implemented by the Abound government. Here we must consider its impact on religion and on the relationship between church and state in the South. Education can be utilized as a powerful medium for the promotion, propagation and spread of religion[87]. Many African constitutions address this question ad adopt various positions. Traditional understandings of both Islam and Christianity, the later especially in its Calvinist form, hold that since all truth is revealed by God, there is; no such thing as objective knowledge or neutral education that is independent of religion. The concept of secular education is alien to such thinking, both in Christianity and Islam. For example, in several South African states where influence of Calvinism is strong, there is resistance to the spread of secular education, and Zambia opted to proclaim itself a Christian state[88].

In a comparable way successive Sudanese Government have been committed to a high standard of Islamic education where all subjects are taught in a way that corresponds to the principles of Islamic culture. While this may be perfectly suitable for the North with its majority Muslim population, it creates difficulties in the South. With the advent of Sudanese independence, the missionaries continued to run most of the education in the South as they had under the Anglo-Egyptian Condominium. The missionary schools continued to supplement the government system of education until 1957 when the GoS announced Northern Education Policy under which the Government took complete control of the education system and assimilated it to its Northern counterpart under a national system that looked to Islam for its guiding principles.[89]

---

[87] J. D. Van der Vyver, "Religious Freedom in African Constitutions", Abdullahi An-Na'im (ed) Proselytization and Communal Self-determination in Africa, p.132

[88] ibid., p. 132

[89] Joseph Oduho and William Deng, Problem of Southern Sudan, p. 45

One of the immediate changes was the replacement of village schools by the *såq* (market), school that taught in Arabic. To enter Arabic school a pupil had first to go through the Islamic *Khalwa* (kindergarten) where they were taught to memorize verses from the *Qur'an*. After passing through these primary levels of Islamic education, the student would proceed to the *Ma'had*, the Islamic institute for religious education. The government established these secondary level schools in the Southern cities of Juba, Kodok, Wau, Maridi, Yei and Raja[90] earlier in 1959.[91]

Arabic Language thus, became compulsory as the medium of instruction in government schools. The aim was to wipe out the linguistic foundations of the education developed under the former British administration and the missionaries, where English has been taught as the common language[92]. It followed that Southerners educated in missionary schools were considered illiterate by the standard of the Sudanese government because they could not write and speak Arabic, and therefore, were unlikely to find jobs in government institutions.

In the first two years of independence the missionary schools ran parallel to government schools in the South. With the implementation of the Northern Education Policy, and the expulsion of the missionaries under the 1962 Missionary Act, most children in the urban area had to attend government schools where they were taught in Arabic. The study of Islam was compulsory, regardless of the religion that a child professed. Given the government's lack of Sympathy with any form of Christian education, Christian churches found themselves under government pressure to stop their teaching programs. For example, in 1960 a Christian center was closed and the instructor prisoned because the District Commissioner of Yei found a blackboard with Roman characters (numbers) in the chapel[93].

---

[90] Roland Werner., William Anderson and Andrew Wheeler, op.cit., 375-376

[91] Sudanese Minister of Education, "The Educational Policy of the Republic of Sudan", Full text of speech delivered, 31st October 1959,pp.2-23

[92] ibid., pp. 46-48

[93] ibid., pp. 48

4.7: SOUTHERN REACTION TO EDUCATIONAL POLICY

The South rejected outright the government's educational policy[94]. The latent negativity toward Islam among Southerners now became focused on what was perceived as the GoS confusion of religion and education that threatened to erode the valued traditions of cultural and religious diversity among the Southern political organisation in exile, opposed to the Abound regime. It drew its popular support from the growing Southern resentment over the loss of civil liberties, coupled with increasing economic hardship. Several Southern members of Parliament (MPs) left the country to join the resistance. Others, like William Deng and Aggrey Jaden who were in the Sudan civil service, soon followed them. In 1962 the politicians and civil servants founded a political organization that was initially called the Sudan African National Closed District national Union (SACDNU), but renamed the Sudan African National Union (SANU) in 1963[95]. They petitioned the United Nations for self-determination for the South, arguing that their patience had come to an end, and that they were convinced that they were left with no option but to resort to force to bring a solution to the North-South conflict.

Already in November 1962, a group of Southerners had launched a military raid on government forces at Kajo-Kaji in Southern Sudan. The main participants in this operation were ex-servicemen in the Equatoria Corps who had taken part in the 1955 uprising, after which they had fled to the hills and to neighbouring countries. The success of the Kajo-kaji operation led to series of attacks on government forces in 1963, and the emergence of the first organized group of freedom fighters call *Anya-Nya*[96].

---

[94] ibid., pp. 190-191

[95] ibid., pp. 121-123

[96] *Anya-Nya*, the term was used in the 1960s by the Southern Regel Movement and it means, "Snake Venon" or "incurable poison". For detailed study of its origins, see Elias Nyamlell Wakoson, "The Origin and Development of the Anya-nya Movement", in Mohammed Omer Bashir, Southern Sudan:

4.8: CIVILIAN GOVERNMENT: 1964-1966

The failure of Abboud regime to redress the North-South relations, and the spread of guerrilla war in the South, led to a popular uprising in 1964 that resulted to his removal and his replacement by Sirr Al-Khatim Al-khalifa as head of transitional government.

On 10th December 1964 the new Prime Minister Mr. Al-khalifa, responded positively to a SANU memorandum by declaring amnesty to all Sudanese who had fled the country since 1955, and appealing to them to return home. However, SANU refused to return to Sudan without negotiations, which, they argued, should take place outside Sudan, under the international supervision. Their declared political objective was self-determination as distinct from full independence. This was in accordance with the policy of the Organization of African Union (OAU) that pledged to maintain the old colonial borders of the newly independent African states. Yet SANU help open the option for full independence for the people of Southern Sudan in the future, in a free and fair referendum.

The Prime Minister agreed to SANU's request for a conference, though it was decided that it should be held in Khartoum. Various groups that included representatives of the government, the main Northern political parties, and two main Southern political parties – SANU and the Southern Front (SF) - and foreign observers, attended the Round Table Conference of 1965. It was convened to address a range of constitutional options for the South: separation, federalism, and local government. The South presented two options: SANU pressed for federalism, while SF campaigned for full independence[97]. The North, on the other hand, preferred minimalist concessions for local government, and were not willing to discuss either separation or federation. The Southern demand for a referendum was refused, and the conference ended without agreement.

The optimism that the Southern representatives and the GoS had

---

Regionalism and Religion, Graduate University Publications, no. 10, University of Khartoum: Khartoum, 1984 pp. 127-204
[97] Douglas H. Johnson, 2003 op. cit., p. 41

brought to the conference was finally dissipated by the national election a few weeks later[98]. These resulted in the formation of a coalition government of the Democratic Unionist Party (DUP) and the Umma Party firstly under the leadership of Mohammad Ahmad Majob, then from 1966, of al-Mahdi as Prime Minister. This represented a re-establishment of the old Northern parties that had already failed to resolve the problems of South Sudan. The status of the South remained as ambiguous as ever, and the failure of the Round Table Conference (RTC) created a sense of pessimism in terms of finding a solution through political negotiation.

When al-Mahdi succeeded Mohammad Ahmad Majoub as Prime Minister he outline a two-Pronged approach to solving the problem between North and South: he aimed at "crushing the rebellion" in the South, while at the same time he would seek dialogue to find a political solution within a united Sudan under an Islamic constitution[99]. It was at this point that the All Africa Conference of Churches (AACC) made its first intervention into Sudan.

4.9: THE GOODWILL VISIT OF (AACC) TO SUDAN (1966)

The AACC decision to undertake a "Goodwill Visit" to Sudan in December 1966 was taken in light of the expulsion of the missionaries between 1962 and 1964 and the massacres of South Sudanese civilians by GoS forces in 1965[100]. The objective of the visit was to test the government's claim that the Missionary Act was intended to encourage the Africanization of the Sudanese churches, not the persecution of Christians. The AACC, delegation consisted of Sir Francis Akau Ibiam, the first President of AACC. Rev John Gatu, General Secretary of the Presbyterian Church in East Africa, Rev Swailem Sidhom, an Egyptian Pastor who had worked in Sudan, and Mr. S. H. Amissah, the General Secretary of AACC.

---

[98] M. W. Daly and Ahmad Sikainga (eds), Civil War in the Sudan, p. 15

[99] ibid., p. 231

[100] Roland Werner, William Anderson and Andrew Wheeler, op. cit, pp.434 - 435

The anti-colonial stance of the AACC at this time, and its own reservations about the role of the Christians missionaries,[101] made it very difficult for the delegation to appreciate the way in which South Sudanese perceived and experienced the policies of the Khartoum government in terms of colonial oppression. Because it lacked the black white dimension of the racial struggles that dominated AACC concern in Southern Africa, the South Sudanese perception of their problems with North in terms of Internal anti-colonialism was hard for the AACC to accept. In addition, the Organization of African Union (OAU) policy of confirming colonial boundaries meant that the AACC delegation would have no sympathy with those elements of the South that called for separate independence. The delegation assumed that a united Sudan was the only acceptable outcome of political negotiations, and that peace must be restored under essentially the same political and social conditions as already existed.

For this reason, the South Sudan Liberation Movement (SSLM) regarded the Visit as a betrayal and thereafter treated the AACC with mistrust. It took some years for the AACC to overcome the suspicions that it created during this first visit, and to play a constructive role in search for peace in Sudan. The delegation left Khartoum with a positive impression of the Sudan government, and the government also, for the first time, realized that there was another Christian voice in Africa to be listened besides that of the missionaries, and that the AACC spoke the language of nationalism and anti-colonialism.

Al-Mahdi now set about forming a National Constitution Commission to draft a permanent constitution. The Commission was charged with a number of functions including the geographical definition of the South, and provision of its claim for a federal status. The Commission reported its recommendations to the Constituent Assembly in January 1968. It recommended that a regionally based form of federal administration should be developed for the country as a whole, not simply the South.

---

[101] This was the time when AACC debated a "Moratorium" (Missionaries Go Home), John Gatu from Church of East Africa, was one of the voices that most influentially this idea

Regionalism was, however, rejected by the Northern politicians when the Commission's recommendations were debated in the Constituent Assembly. They argued that it would endanger national unity[102]. The cause of national unity was clearly stated by the Prime Minister Sadiq al-Mahdi in terms of the Islamization of the South: "The failure of Islam in Southern Sudan would be the failure of the Sudanese Muslims to the international Islamic cause. Islam has a holy mission in Africa and the Southern Sudan in the beginning of that mission"[103]. This was the beginning of the call for an Islamic constitution that remained a priority of Sadiq's vision.

Religion and the identity of the country were thus confirmed as two inseparable issues in terms of Northern policy toward national unity. Assembly representatives of the South and the Nuba Mountains opposed to the Islamic Vision of the state, and argued for a secular system of governance for the whole country. Failing to reach agreement on these issues, the parliament was dissolved in February 1968 and the draft constitution was put aside. New elections were held and two months later, the new parliament convened in attempt to resolve the crisis. The continuous political squabbling led to a military coup in May 1969 that brought General Ja'far Numeiri to power at the head of the so-called May Regime before the 1968 draft constitution could be enacted by the Constituent Assembly[104].

4.10: THE SUDAN COMMUNIST PARTY'S APPROACH TO FEDERALISM

Before Numeiri came to power in 1969, the Sudanese Communist Party (SCP) had advocated a different approach to Southern problem. They had called for regional autonomy for the South as early as 1954 and stood firmly behind their policy ever since. It was adopted by the May Regime in 1969. In their declaration published in *al –uarapa* (Truth/sincerity) on 28th September 1959 they spelt out a plan for the

[102] Abel Alier, Southern Sudan: Too Many Agreement Dishonoured
[103] Mansosur Khalid, 1990, op., p.218
[104] Masour Khallid, 1985, op.cit., pp.5-10

South. The stated that regional autonomy for the South was the only option that would preserve the unity of the country, ad committed themselves to extending this principle to the solution of other regional problems confronting the country. They argued that the Indian, the Soviet Union and Chinese models could be suitable for Sudan as a multi-national state. Contrary to Northern Parties" demand for an Islamic constitution, the SCP argued that Sudan would be stronger under decentralized System in which the various regions could develop their own identities under one constitution with a National Parliament.

In the field of economy they proposed prepaid development projects in the south in order to close the gap between the North and the South and that the wages of Southern employees should be brought to the level of their counter-parts in the North. Opposed to the Missionaries' role in education in the South, they suggested that the government should allocate a greater proportion of educational funds in order to develop Southern education to the same standard on the North.[105] The SCP programme for the South was presented to the 1965 round table conference, but found no acceptance in Northern political parties until Numeiri came to power in 1969.

4.11: NUMEIRI'S POLICY STATEMENT: 1969

The Main objective of the Military coup of 25 May 1969 was to achieve national reconciliation and terminate the long civil war. In its policy statement of June 1969, the government recognized the ethnic and cultural difference between the North and the South, and declared its readiness to grant regional autonomy to the three Southern provinces of Bahr al-Ghazal, Equatoria and Upper Nile.[106] In contrast to the unsuccessful attempts of previous governments to end the conflicts, the new regime promised to solve the imbalance s between the two regions by implementing programs in favour of the South as Allen Reed

---

[105] Gabriel Warburg, op.cit., pp. 155-7

[106] Tristam Belts, "The Southern Sudan: The Cease-fire and after", Report prepared for the Africa Publications Trust, p.1

outlined in his paper presented to Church World Service in January 1971 as follows[107]:

That there would be a continuation and further extension of amnesty law announce in May 1969, and the government agreed to engage in peaceful negotiations with the Anya-Nya movement, and stop the Sudanese army form taking reprisals against Southern civilians[108]. Secondly, that the government would implement policies for the economic and social development of the South,[109] with Southerners given special training so that they could manage the development of their region as a contribution towards the economy of the whole country. In addition, a ministry for Southern Affairs would be created, with Southerners in charge of formulating the programs for the regional autonomy for the South.

While the proposal clearly moved in the direction of acknowledging Sothern demands, it fell short of conceding the principle of federation,

---

[107] Allen Reed, "Southern": Report to Church World Service, 1971, pp.-6 (Geneva Archive)

[108] Allen reported that many atrocities had been committed by government troops in the South. For example, in Upper Nile Province, in November 1970, a force of 80 government soldiers attacked Kur Village. All the houses and grain store were burned, and three people were killed. The report added that in December 1969, the Sudanese army supplied with Egyptian ad Russina jets had resumed bombing civilian targets in all the Southern provinces. The report concluded that southerners at home and in exile had reason to doubt the sincerity of the amnesty offered by the May Regime

[109] The report noted the Anya-nya Movement was providing medical and educational facilities in the controlled areas that they controlled, but that government forces had attempted to destroy For example, in central Equatoria province the Amuri Primary School in Morta area was the Largest primary boarding school that had classes up to primary 4, with more than 400 students. Their teachers were volunteers who had received some training under a Southern Sudanese-run Teaching programme. In the late September and early October 1970 the Sudanese army in conjunction with Libyan paratroopers, Egyptian and Soviet supplied aircrafts, bombed the Morta Area and drove the students out. The civilians fled in large numbers to the neigbouring countries for safety.

demanded at the 1947 Juba and the 1965 Round Table Conferences. Sudanese army aggression against civilian targets in the South also continued. For example, on 23rd July 1970, Sudanese soldiers crossed Sudan-Congo border to the village of Banza where Southern Sudanese refugees were camped; about 60 people meeting for Christian fellowship in the home of a man called Kandolo Modi were tied to the pew and the soldiers opened fire before burning the church on top of them. Of the 27 who died that day, many were children, women and elderly people. Others died later of gun wounds and burns. This and other similar atrocities convinced the South Sudanese that the new government was not seriously concerned to end the violence in the South; it advocated peace one hand and yet continued the carrying out atrocities on the other.

In their struggle to defense civilians in the 1970s, the Anya-nya forces achieved a greater degree of unity. They became more effective fighting force and openly attacked several Sudanese army garrisons in the South. For example, on 11th October 1970, they occupied most of Burmath area, a town between Akobo and Pibor districts in South Sudan. They entered the town killing more than 45 soldiers, collecting 15 automatic weapons, and forcing the Sudanese army to withdraw. A Sudanese convoy from Akobo town that attempted to reinforce the fleeing forces was ambushed. The Anya-Nya destroyed two of Sudanese army trucks and killed more than 40 soldiers. On returning to Akobo the army took revenge by killing South Sudanese intellectuals in the town. They killed more than 80 people. I was among those people who narrowly escaped by leaving Akobo town two days before the massacre took place. Allen Reed described the situation as "a mockery of anything called regional autonomy in the minds of Southern people"[110].

Atrocities such as these had the effect of dissipating any popular confidence in Numeiri's declared policies for the South. The gap between South Sudanese people and the new regime was widening in the late 1960s. At the same time President Numeiri was facing growing opposition within the Revolutionary Command Council (RCC). Northerners feared that the concessions that Numeiri was making

---

[110] Allen Reed, op. cit., pp 6-7

to the South, limited as they were, would enable Southern Politicians and administrators to get real power, and that this would lead them to issue a United Demand for Independence (UDI) that Khartoum would have to suppress by a massive use of force[111]. The Communist party, led by Hashim al-Atta, a member of the Revolutionary Council, staged a coup in July 1971. Numeiri and the rest of the RCC were arrested and a new seven-member RCC was announced. However, regiments loyal to Numeiri suppressed the rebellion. When Numeiri returned to power, his revenge was severe against the Communists[112]. Among those he executed were Babiker el-Nur, the coup leader, Khalek Mahgoub, Major Hamadallah, and Joseph Garang– A South Sudanese.

Moscow protested the execution of these leading Sudanese communists, and TASS, the soviet news agency, reported that: "a massacre is going on in Sudan and a bloody clash is taking place between progressive and nationalist factions, who should have untied to accomplish a great national task"[113]. Because of these events in Sudan, Moscow sent a delegation to Khartoum in a bid to heal the rift,[114] but to no avail. The SCP, like all other parties in Sudan was banned, though they continued to wield considerable influence within Numeiri's leftist alliance[115]. Meanwhile, the Anya-Nya forces were gaining ground in the South.

4.12: THE ANYA NYA MOVEMENT

Anya-Nya was born as an organized force in 1963. It comprised previously isolated groups of local insurgent throughout the South. The process of organization and unifying the fragmented forces took several years due to ethnic and ideological difference among Southern Political leaders[116].

---

[111] ibid., 26-11-1971
[112] Mansour Khalid, 1985, op.cit., pp.21-26
[113] ibid., "Soviet new agency tass", July 27 1971 (WCC Archive
[114] "Soviet new agency tass", July 27 1971, Moscow (WWCC Archive)
[115] John Chadwick, "Daylead " of July 21, Khartoum (WCC Archive)
[116] Philips Bowring, Financial Times, 26/11/1971

In mid-1967, some young South Sudanese politicians led by Mr. Gordon Mortat and Mr. Bari Wanji attempted to bring the exile political groups and the Anya-Nya leaders into one organization. This initiative resulted to the formation of Southern Sudan Provisional Government (SSPG) headed by Mr. Aggrey Jaden as its President. Tribal and leadership contests soon led to the disintegration of the SSPG. In March 1969, a Nile Provisional Government (NPG) was established under leadership of Gordon Mortat, but failed to provide a coherent leadership capable of uniting all the South Sudanese factions. In July 1970 the NPG dissolved in favour of a coalition of political grouping under the Anya-Nya Movement led by Colonel Joseph Lagu. This consisted of the Anyidi Revolutionary Council, a movement based in Central Equatoria, Nile Provincial government of Bahr al Ghazal and Upper Nile Provinces, the Sue (pronounced Sway) River Republic based in Western Equatoria, and the Azania National Liberation front in exile.

Lagu, a former captain in the Sudanese Army, took over the leadership of Anya-Nya in the second half of 1969 before becoming a colonel[117]. It was through his leadership that the organization gained access to supply of weapons. From 1969-1971, gradual unification of the Southern forces was realized and Anya-Nya became as fighting force capable of challenging GoS authority throughout the South. The South Sudan Liberating Movement (SSLM) became unified into Southern resistance body that had sufficient power to negotiate with the Sudan government.

4.13: THE FIRST ECUMENICAL INITIATIVE TO RESOLVE THE CIVIL WAR

The gradation of the civil war in the South was the cause of increasing concern among Sudan's neighbouring states, especially Uganda where many South Sudanese were studying in schools and at Makerere University. Dr. Storrs McCall, a Canadian tutor in Makerere

---

[117] Tim Niblock, Class and Power in Sudan: The Dynamic of Sudanese Politics 1898-1985

University, became involved in advocacy on behalf of the South and formed the Makerere Group that developed contacts with the Anglican Communion took a lead in developing a peace process in Sudan. The Anglican Archbishop of Jerusalem, George Appleton, who had overall responsibility for the Middle East, including Sudan, was in contact with Archbishop Eric Sabiti of the Church of Uganda and Canon Max Warren, General Secretary of the Church Missionary Society, and with two Sudanese Bishops in exile – Eliana Ngalamu and Yeremia Dotiro. These bishops coordinated their initiative with the Makerere Group, and with Bishop Oliver Allison in Khartoum, though the latter kept a low profile because of the vulnerability of his position.

Prompted by this Anglican initiative, the AACC and World Council of Churches (WCC) felt that the time was right, in 1970/71, for a new approach to the government of Sudan. They met with Makerere Group and with two representatives of the Anglican initiative – Bishops Sabiti of Uganda and Appleton of Jerusalem. Kodwo Ankrah, the Africa Secretary for WCC, took the view that South Sudanese should be contacted on equal terms as their counterparts in the North. The AACC General Secretary, Samuel Amissah, on the other hand, maintained the position that the AACC had established in its 1966 "Goodwill Visit": that it was wrong to negotiate on any terms that might lead to the partition of a sovereign African state. This latter view, as we have noted already, was in conformity with the OAU policy that accepted National boundaries drawn in colonial times and opposed the redrawing of the boundaries of independent African states. The two positions were reconciled in the agreement to contact both the GoS and the SSLM, and to encourage both to resolve their differences with the framework of the existing state of Sudan.

Following the visit of the ecumenical team (AACC and WCC) to Khartoum, the initiative was passed to Sudan Council of Churches (SCC), under the General Secretary, Samuel Athi Bwogo and Bishop Augustino Baroni, the Italian Vicar Apostolic of Khartoum. Bwogo was charged with establishing contacts with SSLM and international communities. Baroni strongly encouraged that the Churches' contribution to peace in Sudan should be fully ecumenical, and this opened the door to the participation of the Catholic bishops. In July 1971, Sudan Conference of Catholic Bishops appealed to the Anya Nya to enter dialogue with the GoS. In August, Baroni travelled to Geneva to brief the WCC on the situation in Sudan, and to confirm that all contacts in search for peace would be in the name of all the Churches. It was due to this initiative that successful contacts were made between the GoS and SSLM on one hand and the international community on the other[118].

4.14: CONCLUSION

This chapter has reviewed the estrangement of the South and North of Sudan during the first period of Sudanese independence from 1956 to 1972. It has demonstrated that questions about the place of the South in a united Sudan that were unresolved by the British colonial administration became the major issue of instability in the early history of the new state. Northern policies to secure national Unity through the Arabisation and Islamisation of the South met with stiff resistance from the South Sudanese who, failed to find much understanding or acceptance in the North of their demand for regional autonomy rallied to the option of armed struggle under the banner of the Anya-Nya Movement.

Church-state relations were directly impacted by the North-South conflict. The Missionary Societies Act of 1962 represented a critical moment when the GoS suppressed the historic presence of Christian missions in the South, and insisted on the Africanisation of the Sudanese churches. Initially this left the latter in a vulnerable position in which they were controlled by the state system of licensing. The only alternative for an independent church initiative toward the government lay with the AACC, but its policy of supporting the existing Africa states within their colonial frontiers resulted in a more positive attitude toward the GoS than toward the Southern opposition. Under WCC influence, however, this policy was applied more flexibly in 1970/71 as the AACC and WCC launched a combined initiative toward bot the

---

[118] ibid., p.439

GoS and the SSLM, and - equally as significantly – insisted the Sudan Council of Churches and the Catholic Church in Sudan should carry the initiative forward.

Christian- Muslim relations during this period reflected the political problem. Whereas the North tended to view Christianity as a foreign missionary religion, the South Sudanese Christians regarded Islam as an imperializing force that was being imposed upon them by the North. I have maintained that the Missionary Societies act (1962), despite the ambiguous motivations of the government, served to redress the first part of this problem, by expelling the foreign missionaries and Africanizing the churches. South Sudanese fears that the Government was using Islamization as a policy for uniting the South with North, while justified in terms of the Abboud government, were allayed when President Numeiri seized power and adopted a secular, pluralist Communist Party. It is therefore reasonable to conclude that religion was not a major factor in the early development of the civil war, although it provided a language in which political difference were often expressed.

This may explain why the first ecumenical initiatives toward peace negotiation did not emphasize the need for Christian- Muslim reconciliation, at time when both the Roman Catholic Church as a result of the Second Vatican Council, and in the world Council of Churches, were beginning to develop their programs on Christian- Muslim dialogue. Their approach was ecumenical in the sense of including both Catholics and Protestants, but there was as yet no emphasis on the wider ecumenism of dialogue with other religions in this case Islam in Sudan.

FIVE

THE ECUMENICAL INERVENTION LEADING TO THE ADDIS ABABA PEACE CONFERENCE

5.1: INTRODUCTION

This chapter offers a detailed analysis of the ecumenical peace initiative that was introduced toward the end of the previous chapter. Focusing on some basic issues that shaped the civil war in Sudan, it examines how these were addressed by the AACC/WCC in the proposals that they brought forward as mediators between the GoS and SSLM/*Anya-Nya*. It will also take account of the contribution made by the Sudanese churches themselves, through the Sudan Council of Churches (SCC), and the Roman Catholic Church (RCC) in Sudan. This initiative took place in the late 1960s, and laid the foundation for the negotiations of the full peace treaty in the Addis Ababa Accord of 1972, which will be examined in the second half of this chapter.

It will be shown that the WCC set the Sudan conflict within the wider context of the African continent, and that the procedure it developed for the Sudan negotiations conformed to principles that it articulated for the conflict resolution within the African continent as a whole. This did not ignore the fact that the Sudan situation was an important respects a unique case. But it did mean that the WCC approached the Sudan conflict within the parameters of principles that had been agreed among African states and enshrined in the Charter of the Organization of African Union (OAU).

5.2: THE DYNAMIC OF SUDANESE CONFLICTS

The main question facing the AACC/[WCC delegation in their mission was how the Churches assessed President Numeiri's policy of regional autonomy for the South within a united Sudan, and whether the policy expressed the sincere intentions of the GoS. It was a token of good intent that the Government was willing to reverse General Abboud's decision to declare Friday the official holiday in the South, and to reinstate Sunday as the day of rest while Friday remained the Muslim public holiday in the North. This was seen as a symbolic step toward accepting the cultural and religious pluralism of a united Sudan.

Encouraged by this significant improvement, the WCC undertook a thorough background study of the conflict in Sudan, recognizing that it was unlike other conflicts in Africa. Sudan, it was recognized, presented the challenge of determining the most appropriate geo-cultural relationship between Arabs and Africans, against a long history of colonial division, and fifteen years of civil war at this time this book was being written. This was quite different from the kind of racial problems between white minority regimes and black minority populations that affiliated Southern Africa. However, the WCC recognized that it was essential to find a solution to the problem in the Sudan that was sustainable in relation to continental principles of nation building enshrined in the charter of the OAU.

5.3: THERESA SCHERF'S MIMEOGRAPHED PAPER "THE SUDAN CONFLICT"

Theresa Scherf' was given responsibility for preparing this study, and her findings were published as a mimeographed background paper entitled

The Sudan Conflict: Its History and Development[119]. The paper was aimed to provide the Churches with basic historical information about the situation, to enable the WCC to produce constructive proposals in any future role it might play as mediator. In examining the influence of external agents in the development of the Sudanese conflict, the paper made no attempt to whitewash or justify the negative influences that Christina missionaries and churches had exerted in the whole process. The section on "The Missionaries" raises some serious criticism of missionary attitudes and activities and underlined certain stances and utterances by the missionaries and their societies that were frankly derogatory of the Southern population itself[120]. So the paper concluded that the GoS had objective reasons to curtail missionary activities in the 1962 Missionary Act, and was not motivated, as many missionaries had alleged, by anti-Christian religious persecution *Per se*. This background document prepared the ground for WCC to take an active role in the reconciliatory process of 1972.

Leopold J. Niilus, in a pamphlet entitled Peace in the Sudan, stated: "After both the government representative and SSLM members had read the document (i.e. the Scherf paper), they both recognized the validity and relevance of WCC basic descriptions although both of them had different criticisms to offer[121].

5.4: THE WCC CONCERN ABOUT UNITY AND JUSTICE IN AFRICA

The WCC determined to take the opportunity to understand the motivations and forces that were shaping the African continent. It was appropriate for them to examine in detail the political and economic structures of power that obstructed African aspirations for unity and engulfed the whole continent in bitter and protracted struggles, with the risk of a major world conflict. Consequently, the WCC became

---

[119] Theresa Scherf, The Sudan Conflict: its History and Development, (unpublished Mimeograph), pp. 11-15 (WWCC Archives)
[120] Ibid., pp 11-17
[121] Leopoldo J, Niilus, "Peace in the Sudan" (unpublished paper), March 12, 1973 (WCC Archives), p.10

involved in the Sudan problem as part of its concern for unity in the whole Africa[122].

For Africans, the concept of "the Unity of Africa" was an essential pre-requisite for their survival. Tribalism has to give way to national, regional and continental unity in order that political and economic exploitation and cultural domination could be overcomed. Yet, it was clear that most African Government were failing to achieve these objectives, and were therefore betraying the aspirations of contemporary Africans.[123] The WCC Central Committee meeting in Addis-Ababa January 1971, attempted to tackle this question of unity.

The OAU charter emphasized that it gives "due regard to the charter of the UN and the Universal Declaration of Human Rights." It recognizes that the search for unity and self-determination in Africa is impeded not only by the legacies of the colonial epoch, but also by the interference of the rich and powerful nations in the affairs of Africa. This foreign interference represented the most serious threat to the stability and development of Africa nations, and makes the solution of the existing problems more difficult. Therefore one of the first decisions taken by the heads of the Africa states and government after the establishment of the OAU was to recognize what it termed the "frontiers of peace". This meant that peace among African states required common acceptance of the frontiers drawn by the colonial powers, in place of frontier disputes that would be the cause of endless conflict between states. However, national unity had to be founded on the respect of legitimate human rights, especially of ethnic minority peoples. Such recognition in any field – political, religious or traditional – should be of primary importance.

Accepting this conceptual framework, Kodwo Ankrah (Africa Secretary of WCC) saw the problem of Sudan primarily in terms of tribal conflicts, similar to those that affiliated Nigeria in the 1960s. He argued that the ethnic conflict was caused by developmental superiority

---

[122] Petition presented to United Nation by Southern Sudan Resistance Organisation in 1969 (unpublished document), (WCC Archives-Geneva)
[123] WCC Central Committee, Unity and Human Rights in Africa Today, Addis-Ababa, January, 1971,pp.1-7

of the Northern Sudanese who therefore played the preponderant role in political and socio-economic affairs.

The southern Sudan resistance organizations disputed this view and the principles enshrined in the OAU Charter to which the WCC/AACC were giving uncritical acceptance. In their analysis the Sudanese problem was one of internal imperialism by the Arab Northerners over the African Southerners. In their petition to United Nations (UN) of 1969, they argued that the OAU has a duty to oppose Arab Colonialism in Southern Sudan, just as it supports African struggles against the continuing elements of European colonialism in other parts of continent. They appealed to the right of self-determination as one of the human rights enshrined in UN principles, and pointed out that the OAU charter does not approve the imposition of unity against the wishes of a people. They argued that the OAU was not consistent in the application of its principle about national frontiers. For example, OAU had accepted the separate sovereignty of Senegal and Mali after the breakup of Federation of Mali in 1960 two months after its independence. The petition argued that the union of Arabs and Africans in the Sudan, at the cost of the lives of millions of Southern Sudanese, would stand condemned by all freedom loving people of the world. Imperialism is not a white man's monopoly, and Arab domination of Southern Sudan, it argued, included the political imposition, economic exploitation and social discrimination of one racial group by another[124].

The WCC inquiry set out its priorities that it commended to its member churches: Among others issued aimed to promote the concept of the Inter-independence of peoples through the creation and furthering of a new international ethos; and by urging governments to assist and support the efforts of the free African nations to attain and preserve their full self-determination, independence and unity, also to encourage governments to enact effective legislation against giving support and encouragement to foreign mercenaries.

---

[124] Petition presented by Southern Political Organisation (Azania Liberation Front) to 4th OAU Conference meeting in Kinshasa, Congo, 11th Sept, 1967 (unpublished), (WCC Archives)

5.5: AACC/WCC APPROACHES TO THE CONFLICT

With this framework, the WCC was able to concentrate its attention on the Sudanese situation, working in close co-operation with the AACC. The AACC had shown interest in promoting a peaceful settlement of the North-South Sudan conflicts form the time of its "Goodwill Visit" to Khartoum in 1966[125]. It was now planned for the WCC and AACC to send a joint delegation to the Sudan to review the position of GoS and its willingness to negotiate with the SSLM/*Anya Nya* Movement.

The ecumenical delegation was composed of Messr, Ooner and Ankar of WCC. From the outset they made it clear that they saw themselves as neutral mediators between conflicting parties and not a party to the conflict itself[126]. Their aim was to identify principles on which a peace negotiation could take place. As the first state they met with SSLM representatives and sympathisers in Kampala, Uganda. Here the principle was agreed that reconciliation between the North and South within a united Sudan. This next stage was for the WCC delegation to visit Khartoum at the invitation from the SCC and the GoS (9th – 17th May 1971). Here the focus lay on the urgent need for relief aid for Southerners affected by war. The churches in Sudan expressed their urgent concern for those who were in need of immediate help in inaccessible areas of the Southerners provinces, or who were in refugee camps in neighbouring countries. So it was agreed that such emergency programs could be organized under the Sudanese Churches, concurrently with the search for peace and security.

It was along these lines that the combined efforts of WCC, AACC and the SCC concluded with recommendations for a way forward for peace in the country[127]. It proved sufficient for the GoS to agree to meet with the SSLM, and for the WCC General Secretary to be authorized to make contacts with Sudanese groups and individuals in Ethiopia. Early July 1971, the SSLM delegates speaking on behalf

---

[125] Tim Niblock, op.cit., p. 275
[126] LS. Passmore Sanderson & G.N. Sanderson, <u>Education, Religion and Politics in Southern Sudan,</u> p. 431
[127] Tim Niblock, op.cit., pp. 275-276

of their movement assured Canon Burgess Carr, Secretary General of AACC that they were prepared to negotiate with the GoS on neutral ground.

Political events in Sudan in the form of the coup against President Numeiri and his successful counter-coup, and the subsequent plebiscite that reconfirmed him as President, delayed the second AACC/WCC mission to Khartoum. This eventually took place in between the 14th and 24th October 1971. On this occasion the delegation included Messrs Niilus, Ankrah and Reuchle of the WCC, and Messrs, Kijlstra, Su and Bakasa of the AACC. Before meeting with the GoS, the delegation briefed the Sudan Council of Churches about their contacts with SSLM leaders, and requested the SCC to accompany them to meet the GoS representatives.

On 17th October the delegates met the government ministers at the Ministry of Interior where they presented their report with regards to contacts made with SSLM leaders as requested by the government. They reported that all the Southern leaders whom they had met were agreeable to finding a solution that would satisfy the general interests of the south within the framework of a united Sudan.

In November 1971 the GoS and SSLM held secret talks in Addis-Ababa, Ethiopia hosted by Emperor Haile Selassie. The choice of venue marked a significant concession on the part of the GoS. Earlier it had insisted that negotiations with the SSLM should be held inside Sudan, on grounds that the problem was one of internal national concern, and that to locate a conference outside Sudan would seem to internationalize it. The GoS change of mind on this matter may be seen as its response to the concession that the SSLM had already made in agreeing that the negotiations would proceed on the principle of a united Sudan, and that the SSLM would accept regional autonomy for the South under a new national constitution rather than pressing for full independence.

The negotiations proceeded well. In December 1971 the GoS secretly froze all military activity by the government forces in the South. Confidence was also build up through the tragedy of a Sudanese Airways crash on 23rd December 1971 near Mundri in Equatoria province, an area controlled by *Anya Nya*. The passengers, mainly Northerners, were well looked after by the *Anya Nya* forces and were escorted to Mundri. This sent out a positive message about the stare of discipline and humanitarian concern among *Anya Nya* forces[128].

The SSLM/*Anya Nya* had other reasons for taking a more flexible approach to the negotiations. Events in Uganda deprived them of an important line of military support when General Idi Amin Dada cut diplomatic relations with Israel and expelled all Israeli military advisors from Uganda[129]. This immediately deprived *Anya Nya* of a channel through which Israeli military assistance could reach the South. Furthermore, SSLM had just recovered from internal differences that had weakened it in recent years. Neither SSLM nor *Anya Nya* felt that they were in a position to risk losing the opportunity of negotiating with the GoS.

5.6: THE NEGOTIATIONS

After preliminary consultations with the AACC/WCC delegation, the two conflicting parties agreed to meet face to face in Addis Ababa on 15th February 1972. The Emperor of Ethiopia initially accepted to be in the chair. The Sudan government was represented by Vice-President Abel Alier, Minister of the Interior, Dr. Gaafar Mohammed Ali Bakheit, Minister of Public Service and administrative Reform, Brigaditer Mirghani Suleiman and Colonel Kamal Abashar.

The SSLM delegation included Mr Ezboni Mondiri accompanied by Mading the Garang as official spokesman, Dr, Larence Wol Wol, Angelo Voga, Oliver Albino, Fredrick Magott, Rev Paul Puot and Job Adier.

Among those present as intermediaries were Dr. Leopoldo Nilus and Kodwo Ankrah from the WCC, Canon Burgess Carr form AACC and Samuel Bwogo form SCC.[130]

In the event Rev. Canon Burgess Carr, the Secretary General of

---

[128] Roland Werner, William Anderson and Andrew Wheeler, op.cit., pp. 439 - 440
[129] ibid., p, 277
[130] Addis Ababa Agreement 1972, (Appendix III)

AACC, acted as "Moderator" of the conference when, at the last minute, Emperor Haile Selasie decided not to chair the meeting personally. This caused SSLM delegates to walk out before the conference started. However, after consultations, both delegations agreed that Burgess Carr would convene the meeting as a mediator rather than a chairman. The conference went ahead as planned from 15th to 27th February 1972.

Canon Carr managed the negotiations with wisdom and understanding, appealing to both sides to negotiate with each other as people who shared in a common religious heritage. He drew his opening sermon from both the Old Testament and the *Qur'an*, urging all the negotiators to forget the past and join hand in rebuilding Sudan, as Nehemiah led the Jewish people in rebuilding the devastated wall of Jerusalem. He thus succeeded in transcending the level of mundane politics and brought a religious dimension to the negotiations that appealed to both Muslims and Christians[131].

The negotiations started by re-affirming the pre-condition that Sudan should remain a united country[132]. On this basis, these sub-committees were established to draft political, economic and security proposals that would then be negotiated in plenary for final agreement. But the SSLM was short of personnel to represent them in the three sub-committees, and therefore requested that economic sub-committee to be left out.

The political sub-committee quickly reached an agreement on the terms of the establishment of the regional government. The security sub-committee was also able to provide a framework for ending the conflicts and a process of absorbing the *Anya Nya* forces into the national army and other security organs. Although there was some discussion of economic resources for the development of the South within a national development policy, this vital area did not receive the attention it deserved. Insofar as this was due to the SSLM demand that the economic sub-committee was annulled, it must carry the

---

[131] Roland Werner, William Anderson and Andrew Wheeler, op.cit., pp. 441-442

[132] Douglas H Johnson, 2003, 0p.cit., p.39

responsibility for weakening the process of agreement in this important area, and creating discontent among the people of the South.

When it came to the plenary negotiations, each delegation responded to the positions that the other had outlined in advance of the conference. The SSLM Delegation, in the person of Mr. Ezboni Mondiri, reacted to the document of the GoS as follows: "The document as a whole is not only inadequate but it is a document ill-conceived with a colonial spirit and intended as an Act for running a colony." In particular he objected the fact that it gave the President of Sudan excessive power over regional affairs, in effect reducing the executive for South Sudan the status of a puppet government. This was a re-iteration of the long-standing Southern suspicion of the colonialist intention of the Arab government of the North.

Another member of the SSLM delegations, Mr. Oliver Albino objected to the fact that the government document appeared to "subject the holding of a referendum in the South, in the case where any article for the Regional Constitution is to be amended, to the discretion of the President." "In practice," he concluded, "the document will make Regional Autonomy, or whatever you may call it, an empty shell".

Dr Wol Wol proposed that the way out of these difficulties lay not in redefining the role of the regional government, but in initially defining as precisely as possible the powers of the central government. These, he argued should be limited to essential national functions, and all other powers should be relegated to the regional government; however, the negotiations centered on defining the qualified autonomy of the regional government rather than the extensive powers that the SSLM delegation desired.

The SSLM delegation then proposed that regionalism should be adopted for the whole country as a federal state: a Northern and a Southern region, each with its own regional government and administration, under a single federal government in which both regions would take part. This, they argued, would set the South and North on an equal basis.

But this proposal was rejected by the government delegation. On its behalf Mansour Khalid argued that this lay outside the mandate with which the government delegation had been entrusted, and that regionalism could not be imposed on the North against its wishes.

When the Moderator asked the Sudan delegation to respond to the SSLM, they requested a 30-minutes adjournment to enable them to confer. After the recess, Mr. Abel Alier criticized the SSLM for using rough, crude and abusive language, contrary to their spirit of the conference that was one of mutual understanding and friendliness. He then gave the floor to Dr. Mansur Khalid who responded to the SSLM delegation, and argued that their document was far from being colonial in word or intent rather, it was devised to ensure both the unity of the country and "special interests of the South", a phrase that went back to the Round Table Conference of 1965.

With regards to reverting internal boundaries between North and South to what existed at the time of independence the GoS proposed that such demand to be postponed for later discussion. Whether this meant a referral of the issue after the agreement was signed remained unclear in the conference minutes. However, the statement that follows suggest that the GoS delegation meant People's National Assembly, when they further argued that, "Amendment of any article of the documents produced by the conference would require a vote in the People's National Assembly and Southern Provinces of a Percentage not less a figure to be agreed. Redefinition of powers means the delegation of more powers to the Region, or withdraw of such powers the President may delegate to the Region for a particular purpose when that purpose is fulfilled."

The other most contentious issue during the negotiation was the question of Security Arrangements of the Southern Region. The SSLM proposed two regional armies in addition to the national army to which each region would contribute. This proposal according to Douglas was rejected by the government delegation. In search of an alternative, the SSLM delegates strongly argued that the Southern soldiers should remain in the South to protect the Southern people from the government army. But in end, both sides agreed on the retention of an equal number of Northern soldiers in the South to help allay the fear of the central government that a Southern garrison composed entirely of Anya Nya forces would create potential threat to the unity of the country. It was along these lines, therefore, that the security arrangements were defined in Chapter II, Article I of the Self-Government Act of 1972[133]. It was agreed that the Southern Command should comprise equal numbers of soldier from North and South.

This brief summary of some of the main issues of negotiation between the two parties indicated that each had a different perception of "regional autonomy". For the SSLM it implied a federal status for the South, whereas the GoS delegation thought of it in terms of more limited local government. Thus the GoS offered less than the SSLM hoped for, and this became the basis of Regional Government for the South.

Despite such dissatisfaction on the part of the SSLM, it was the price to be paid for bringing about an end of the war in the South, and they agreed therefore to accept the political compromise in the interest offending the seventeen-year old civil war.

5.7: RATIFICATION OF ADDIS ABABA PEACE AGREEMENT 28 FEBRUARY 1972

The Agreement was signed on the 27th February 1972. His Imperial Majesty Haile Selassie I, Emperor of the Ethiopia, said in his address to the parties involved: "We salute the representatives of the Christian Churches here on this auspicious occasion. They represent the best tradition of the Church, the pursuit of peace and promoting of brotherly relation among their fellow men"[134]. On 28th March 1972, Joseph Lagu on behalf of the SSLM and Mansour Khalid on behalf of the Sudan government rarified the agreement in Addis-Ababa, thereafter known as the Addis Ababa agreement[135].

According to Sanderson, the ecumenical mediators played an important role in the run-up to the ratification of the Agreement.

[133] Addis Ababa Agreement, op.cit., Chapter II, Article I, (Appendix III)
[134] His Imperial Majesty Haile Selassie I addressed to the parties involved in Addis Ababa Peace Conference, 1972, (WCC Archive)
[135] L.S Passmore Sanderson & G.N Sanderson, po.cit. p. 432

They provided financial support for the SSLM delegates to return to Addis Ababa since the Sudan government could not pay their fares. When some of the Southerners tried to have the terms of the Agreement amended prior to ratification, the Anglican and Catholic Churches in Uganda exerted their influence on Southern Sudanese to accept the terms that had been negotiated. The Anglican Archbishop in Jerusalem and the Superior General of the Verona Fathers, both of whom were in Kampala, signed a joint letter to General Joseph Lagu, Begging him to ratify the Agreement[136]. Eventually the Agreement was ratified, thanks again to the religious leaders, although it was recognized that some Southern leader were dissatisfied with its terms.

5.8: CRITIQUE OF THE ADDIS ABABA AGREEMENT

In this final section we must look into the nature of the continuing Southern criticism of the Agreement. Essentially it concerns the constitutional arrangements for regional self-government.

The announcement of cease-fire made was followed by the promulgation of the Self-Government Act 1972 by President Order on 29th March 1972. This included the definition of legislative organs and powers and other matters of principle concerning the South. The constitutional relations of legislative and executive power between the regional and central governments were also laid down in the 1972 Act (Articles 11-15)[137].

The Act guaranteed autonomy for a Southern Region composed of the three provinces of Bahr al-Ghazal, Equatoria and Upper Nile under a regional President appointed by the President of the Republic on recommendation of an elected Southern Regional Assembly. A mechanism of checks and balances was instituted between the two governments involving the exchange of information. Procedures for the removal of members of the regional or national legislation[138].

The agreement also conferred legislative powers upon the People's

---

[136] ibid. p. 432
[137] Ahmad A. Sikainga and M. W. Daly, op.cit., p.5
[138] Addis Ababa Agreement, op.cit., p. 35

Regional Assembly, elected by secret ballot of all citizens residing in Southern Sudan (chapter IV Articles 7, 8 and 9). The powers of the Regional Assembly were, however, restricted to the maintenance of public order, internal security, efficient administration of the regional provinces, and development in cultural, economic and social spheres. Emphasis was placed on regional financial resources, machinery for regional and local administration, traditional laws and customs, prisons, state schools, local languages, and cultures[139]. The power of taxation was to be exercised concurrently by the regional and national legislators. Chapter VII, Article 24 empowered the People's Regional Assembly to levy local duties and taxes in addition to the national duties and taxes decreed by the central government.

The executive powers of the Regional Assembly were stipulated in chapter VI, Article 16 of the Act (see appendix 3). The President of the High Executive Council (HEC) was appointed, and could be removed, by the President of the Republic on recommendation of the People's Regional Assembly. The HEC was responsible for all aspects of governance in the region except defense, foreign affairs, currency and finance, economic and social planning.

The President of the HEC and his cabinet were subject to removal from office by two processes: impeachment and no confidence[140]. The clause of impeachment stated that, "The People's Regional Assembly may, by a three-quarters majority.... Request the President of the Republic to relieve the President or a member of the High Executive Council (HEC) from office. But in the case of the resignation of the President, the whole cabinet resigns[141].

With regard to the relationship between the two legislatures, the Regional Assembly was empowered to prevent the National Assembly from enacting laws that would adversely affect the interest of the South. The checks on the National Assembly were two-fold: the Regional Assembly would request the national parliament to postpone the enactment of any law pertaining to the South until contentious issues

---

[139] Mom Kou Nhial Arou, P. 134

[140] ibid., p.36

[141] Addis Ababa Agreement, op. cit., (Appendix III),Chapter V, Article 13 (ii)

could be resolved: secondly, the Regional Assembly and the power to request the total withdraw of a bill if it were agreed to be against the interests of the people of South.

The weakness of this provision was that a final decision on making the checks effective rested with the President of Republic of the Sudan. Article 23 decreed that "the President, if he thinks fit, shall accede to the request,[142] reality gave the President the right of discretion, the exercise of which depended on the degree of goodwill that the President had towards the South. Moreover, the power to veto was vested in the President rather than the head of HEC. The People's Regional Assembly was powerless to override the veto of the President. However, the constitution allowed the regional assembly to re-introduce the vetoed bill (Article 27 of the self-government Act, 1972). The dilemma facing the regional assembly was what should happen in the event of the President re-vetoing a bill.

The Act guaranteed freedom of movement, citizens' rights, personal liberty, equal opportunities in education, freedom of religion and the use of local languages by ethnic minorities as a means of preserving their cultures. The agreement recognized Arabic as Sudan's official language, and English as the South's principal language to be used in administration and taught in the schools, alongside local languages

Special commissions were established for the repatriation of refugees with the co-operation of United Nations High Commission for Refugees (UNHCR) and host countries. With the cessation of hostilities in the Southern Sudan, the tension caused by the presence of large number of Southern Sudanese refugees in the neighbouring countries began to ease.

Qualified *Anya Nya* veterans were incorporated into a 12,000-man Southern command of the Sudanese army in equal number to Northern officers and men. The process of integration of the *Anya Nya* into the national army was to be completed within five years. However, while the full quota of 6,000 *Anya Nya* officers and men were absorbed into the army, the number of Northern troops in the South was not reduced to 6,000, as stipulated in the Agreement, Many *Anya Nya*

---

[142] ibid., chapter II, Article 2

officers were retired early or purged from the army, and others were transferred to the North before the period specified by the Agreement. This became a matter of growing grievance, and was one of the issues that led to the recurrence of civil war in the 1980s[143].

5.9: CONCLUSION

This chapter has examined the roles of the AACC/WCC in the negotiation of the Agreement, something that has been overlooked in most other studies of this period of Sudanese history. Both parties of the conflict showed their desire for peaceful resolution and were encouraged by the ecumenical involvement. When the Agreement was signed, the mediators left implementation to the Sudanese people without external monitors. While we acknowledge the positive facilitating role of the external ecumenical agencies, external guarantees would have been the key to ensuring the implementation of the peace treaty.

We have noticed that during the negotiation process, the SSLM proposed that the Southern people should be asked to confirm the Agreement through a referendum in order to make it legitimate. The GoS representative did not accept this. This, with hindsight, maybe identified as one of the weaknesses of the Accord that the central government later exploited.

But the greatest weakness of the Agreement was its failure to address the Sharing of natural resources in the South that are so essential to the national economy. In my opinion, the question of wealth sharing has proved to be a major cause of conflict whereas it should have served as the basis for a just peace. The fair allocation of resources could have been the key to working out the political broader issues in the country. The Agreement has been reached and ratified was economically inconclusive.

It is fair to say that the Agreement to some extent accepted cultural and religious pluralism in Sudan that eased the growing grievances between church and state, until the recurrence of the Second civil war in 1983. It also provided a framework for Southern participation in most

---

[143] Douglas H. Johnson, 2003, op.cit., p. 42

public institutions. Was the problem of the South solely, participation, it would have been resolved by the Agreement. However, other issues including, economic, social and cultural developments suggest that the Agreement fell short of resolving disparities.

As such, it was not long before these unresolved problems caused a second civil war to break out in 1983, the search for a resolution to which has continued to very recent past - 2005. It was also clear that the Addis-Ababa covenant was not a comprehensive settlement, as it did not involve large sector of Sudanese political parties, and civil societies, which could have contributed and affirmed their commitments to the peace process. It was because of such weakness the political parties in the north latter pressured Numeiri and abrogated the agreement, as we shall see during Numeiri's second period that follows:

CHAPTER
SIX

SECOND PERIOD OF NUMEIRI'S RULE (1973-1985)

6.1: INTRODUCTION

Part Three of this book reviews the political development of Sudan through what may be broadly identified as the second period of its history as an independent nation. This began with the 1973 Constitution, Promulgated by President Ja'far Numeiri on the basis of the Addis Ababa Accord of 1972 that defined Sudan as a federal republic with a wide measure of autonomy for the South. But due to pressures that will be examined in the next three chapters, this second period of Sudanese political development came to be marked by progressive Islamization of the structures of the state and the constitution, until Sudan was eventually declared to be an Islamic Republic. This process re-opened the conflict between the South and the North, and was marked by resumption of civil war that was only brought to an end under the terms of the Machakos Protocol in January 2005.

This chapter convers the second part of Numeiri presidency, the twelve- year period from the 1973 constitution to the introduction of Islamic Laws over the last two years of Numeiri's rule, from 1983 to 1985, when his government was brought down in a successful coup. It is a period that can be characterized as one of transition from a secular federal to an Islamic state, corresponding with Numeiri's personal conversation form secular pan-Arab socialism to Islamism. This changed the character of the North-South conflict by introducing religion as an ideological factor in the struggle, as the Northern attempt to Islamize the state had direct implications for the South that now began to express its political identity in more definitely secular ideological terms. The theme of "Islamization" in the ideological sense of Islamizing the identity of the state through steps toward the implementation of *Shari'a* law will therefore be the main focus of this part of the book.

6.2: SUDAN'S PERMANENT CONSTITUTION

The 1973 Constitution established Sudan as a secular state that recognized the existence of both Islam and Christianity as the religions of Sudan that were the legitimate sources of moral guidance for the nation, and those whose followers among the Sudanese had the right of religious freedom, a right that was extended to the followers of traditional religions as well[144]. Article 16 defined the place of these religions in the Sudanese state. Article 16 (a) states: "In the Democratic Republic of Sudan, Islam is the religion, and society shall be guided by Islam being the religion of the majority of its people and the state shall endeavor to express its values". Article 116 (b) continued: "Christianity is the religion in the Democratic Republic of Sudan being professed by a large number of its citizens who are guided by Christianity, and the state shall express its values." Recognizing both Islam and Christianity as "heavenly religions", other paragraphs of Article 16 forbade either to be "insulted or held in contempt", or to be "abused" by "political exploitation" and assured "followers of religions and spiritual beliefs, without discrimination.... the rights and freedoms of the citizens guaranteed by the Constitution." The Constitution provided that "Islamic principles should form the basis of legislation,[145]" *Shari'a* was applicable only to Muslims while secular and customary laws were recognized for the non-Muslims in the North and the South.

Article 16 therefore, recognized Sudan as a multi-religious,

---

[144] Ahmad Sikainga, and MW. Daly (eds), op.cit., p. 84
[145] Sudan Government, Permanent Constitution

multi-ethnic state. It was intended to preserve the unity of the country, and opened the way for a constructive relationship between church and state, protection religious and ethnic minorities. In the North however, the Addis Ababa Accord and the 1973 Constitution were seen by Northern political parties (the *Umma*, Democratic Unionist Party/ DUP, and Muslim Brothers) as obstacles to the creating of an Islamic state, and deemed them as an imposition by the military dictatorship without the backing of political consensus in the North[146].

6.3: NORTHERN POLITICAL PARTIES APPROACHES TO ISLAMIZATION (1973 -1977)

Until 1977, Numeiri ruled without participation and support of the main Northern parties who wanted an Islamic constitution, and they combined to form the main political opposition to his rule.

The *Umma* Party constituted the political legacy of the 19th century Mahdist movement, and from 1964 was led by al-Mahdi, the grandson of the *Mahdi,* who also acted as the main theorist of this party's platform[147]. He wanted to develop a modern Islamic constitution on the basis of independent juristic reasoning *(ijitihâd).* He argued that his party had a programme for a modern democratic Islamic society that would guarantee human dignity, liberty and freedom of religion within the context of Islamic law[148]. It was on this basis that he claimed to be a democratic pluralist who would accommodate the perspectives of all the religious and ethnic groups in Sudan. An-Na'im has criticized Sadiq al- Mahdi for failing to show how his theories could be applied in practice, and therefore concludes that his claim to be a democratic pluralist is at best ambiguous. I shall offer my own assessment of Sadiq al-Mahdi when examining the policies of his government between 1986 and 1989.

The Democratic Unionist Party (DUP), whose religious leader is Muhammad Uthman al-Mirghani, was the political organ of

---

[146] Douglas Johnson, 2003, op.cit., p 55

[147] Ahmaad Sikainga and M.W Daly, op.cit., p. 103

[148] Ann Mosely Lesch, op. cit., p66

the *Khatimiyya* Order, traditionally opposed to the *Umma* Party as the Khatimiyya had opposed the Mahdist *Ansâr*. It supported a parliamentary system and sought a mixed economy that would allow private enterprise to flourish. At the same time they asserted that the national constitution should be based on Islamic principles, but were quite flexible as to what this might mean[149].

If the *Umma* and the DUP can be classed as traditional political parties in that they were based more on models of Islam that belonged to the late 19th century and first half of the 20th centuries, two other parties can be classed as ideological since each had a definite conceptual understanding of Islam and the *Sharîa*. The first of these to come into existence, in Sudan, in the 1940s, was the Republican Brothers' Movement led by Mahmud Taha (1910 -1985). It advocated a radically reformist approach to the meaning of Islam in modern Sudan, based on the thinking that Taha set out in his important book, The second Message of Islam, published in 1967. In this, he propounded a new hermeneutical method of interpreting the *Qur'an*, distinguishing between its eternal ethical and spiritual principles that are found in the Meccan chapters, and those of a historically contingent character that belong to the Medinan chapters. The Meccan chapters, revealed over 13 Years period of the Prophet's residence in Mecca, emphasize human equality regardless of social origin, gender or religion, and set forth universal principles of justice. In contrast, the Medinan chapters were revealed over ten years that followed the Prophet's migration to Medina, and address the social and political realities of the time, to enable Muslim community survive. Taha argued that the language of tolerance and persuasion that characterize the Meccan verses changed to the language of violence and discrimination[150]. While the Medinan legislation was necessity for human societies at a relative early stage of social development, the social conditions of the Meccan verses could be applied in ways that would be closer to their original spirit and content. Important among these was the principle of equality of people of faith *(îmân)* in One God, and the obligation that lies upon a Muslim

---

[149] ibid., p. 67
[150] ibid., p.257

state to respect other monotheistic religions. This, he argued, was now possible – without the qualification of "protection" (*dhimma*) that Islamic Law introduced as a social necessity in earlier times – in the multi-religious society of Sudan[151]. This would require a reform of *Sharîa,* but meant that it would be possible to identify Sudan an Islamic state while at the same time giving full religious equality and freedom to the non-Muslims.

In contrast to Republican Brothers' the strongest proponent of the application of the *Sharîa* in its received form was National Islamic Front (NIF). From its inception in 1940s, the ideology of NIF was based on *Salafiyya* teaching as expounded by Hasan al-Banna (d.1949) and other Egyptian Muslims Brothers. Under the leadership of Hasan al-Turabi, its main objective is to transform Sudan into an Islamic state based on strict adherence to present of the first generation of Muslims *(Salaf),* as modeled in the earliest Islamic community of Medina[152]. According to this view, therefore, Medina was not a mere historical contingent of Islamic revelation, but a formative example that represents the ideals of Islam in their purist implementation, and therefore a model for all subsequent Islamic societies.

In the 1960s the Islamic Charter Front (ICF) was informed by a various groups of Muslim Brothers in Sudan. During the early days of Numeiri, the ICF was banned and many of its leaders fled into exile after the signing of the Addis Accord. They were opposed to Numeiri's accommodation with the South and viewed it as a barrier to the establishment of an Islamic State. With the evolution of ICF into the National Islamic Front, its ideology remained unchanged. Regional Concessions to the South were regarded as the main impediment to their national project of Islamising the entire state of Sudan, unity with the South being achieved through Southern acceptance of an Islamic polity. This goal had been sought through a vigorous programme of *al-da`wa al-Isl`âmiyya* ("Islamic Call") that aims to Islamize the South through Muslim missionary activity. Their views on the South were

---

[151] Roland Werner, William Anderson and Andrew Wheeler, op.cit., p.586
[152] Ahmad Sikainga and M.W. Daly, op.cit., p.86

delineated in the Sudan Charter, published in 1987, [153] that I shall examine in a later section of this part of the book. Suffice it to point out at this stage: it was President Numeiri's shift to supporting the NIF's ideological approach to Islamization that caused heightening of tensions between the south and the North, a deterioration of the positive church-state relations that were achieved in the Addis Ababa peace negotiations, and the recurrence of the civil war in 1983.

The Northern traditional *Umma* and DUP parties that the Addis Ababa Accord granted too many concessions to the South and would only foster separatist aspirations. Furthermore, Northern politicians saw the support Numeiri gained in the South as a threat to their return to power. Numeiri did not only have the support of the Southern politicians, but also that of the former Anya Nya officers who had been recruited to the Presidential guard and helped him survived the1976 coup attempt.

Three attempts were made to overthrow Numeiri in January 1973, September 1975 and July 1976. The Northern parties and some regional groups staged the third coup, with support from Libya. They included the National Unionist Party (NUP) led by Hussein al-Hindi, the former finance Minister, the *Umma* Party under Sadiq al-Mahdi, the Islamic Charter Front led by Hassan al-Turabi, the pan-Arab Ba'ath Party, some members from the Democratic Unionist Party (DUP), and the Rev Philip Ghabbush's political movement in the Nuba Mountains. Although each of these coups was crushed, they weakened Numeiri's power, and compounded the economic difficulties that faced due to the mounting foreign debt[154]. Faced by public unrest in Khartoum, he realized that he could not survive on the political support only of the South, and the Communist who had brought him to power in 1969. He therefore, adopted a policy of national reconciliation, the aim of which was to appease the Northern parties and, perhaps, to safeguard his leadership.

---

[153] ibid. p. 87

[154] Ann Mosely Lesch, op.cit., p. 52

6.4: NATIONAL RECONCILIATION (1977-78)

Article 16 of the 1973 constitution, as mentioned earlier, stipulated that the Democratic Republic of Sudan "shall be guided by Islam being the religion of the majority of its people, and the state shall express its values"[155]. Having originally interpreted this in a flexible way that understood Islam broadly in terms of culture, Numeiri now began to accommodate the Northern religious parties by emphasizing the nature of Islam as religion. On this basis he cracked down on the Communists, and sought a reconciliation *(mu`ualapa)* with all the parties that claimed an Islamic identity, He established the Constitution Amendment Committee of 1977, giving it the remit to review the Sudanese constitution according to the principles of Islam[156].

The same year he entered into the Port Sudan Agreement (July 1977) with al-Mahdi's *Umma* Party that allowed political detainees to be released, and about 3,000 political prisoners were set free[157]. An amnesty was agreed for all politicians opposed to the regime. The Sudanese Socialist Union (SSU) – the Highest Political Executive Organ in the previous system) – was re-organized, the state security Act was repealed, and it was agreed that the constitution would be revised in such a way as to allow the opposition parties to participate in the system[158]. Al-Mahdi, al-Turabi and Ghabbush returned from exile and joined the regime.

During the 1978 elections *Umma* and NIF gained significance seats in the People's Assembly. This worried Numeiri who thought that his authority would be undermined. Al-Mahdi was elected a member of the Assembly, and was appointed to SSU's Political Bureau.

Al-Mahdi soon resigned from the SSU on the ground that Numeiri failed to fulfill their agreement. Al-Turabi, on the other hand, chose to cooperate with the government and was thus able to strengthen the NIF organizational base and enhance its economic power both inside the

---

[155] Sudan Government, 1973, op.cit.,

[156] Ann Mosely Lesch, op.cit., p. 52

[157] ibid., p.53

[158] M. W. Daly & Ahmad Sikainga, op.cit., p.20

country and abroad under the wing of government policy[159]. In 1978 he was appointed Attorney General and a member of Parliamentary Committee charged with the review of legal system conforming to Islamic principles. As a leading member of the government he succeeded in consolidating the NIF organization base by executing Numeiri's policies while at the same time Islamizing the organs of the state and of the public life. For example, one of the NIF programs was to instruct the government officials in Islamic ideology with the aim of forming them into "the rightly-guided leadership" (al-giyâda al-râshidâ') emulating that of the Rightly – Guided Caliphs (Al-Khulafa' al-Râshidân) of early Islamic times. NIF then placed these Islamically-trained cadres in key administrative positions in schools, universities, and the armed forces[160]. In this way, the NIF implemented a coherent strategy and gained economic and political power that Numeiri could not undermine.

In the context of implementing Islamic principles, the network of Islamic banks enlisted Islamic cadres and experts in economic institution, promoting NIF to become a major player in the field of finance and business[161]. Islamic institutions took up most investments. The entire Northern banking system was Islamized through the introduction of interest-free Islamic banking practices, independent of the Bank of Sudan. The Faisal Islamic Bank of Sudan established in 1978 followed by Islamic Co-operative Development Bank Tadamum Islamic Bank of Western Sudan, and the Bank of Northern Sudan. In 1984 Islamic Banks were exempted from business and development taxes, which resulted to their success in offering higher returns (around $12 billion in 1984)[162] as compared to conventional banks.

The Christian South, aware about the policies of NIF, viewed the national reconciliation referred to above with skepticism, reasoning that it would have negative implications on non –Muslims. Southerners

[159] The Sudan Human Rights Organisation, Religion and Human Rights: The case of Sudan p. 93
[160] Ann Mosely Lesch, op.cit., p. 53
[161] Khalid M. Turabi's Islamist Venture: Failure and Implications, p. 56
[162] Nazib ayubi, op.cit., p. 182

were convinced that the powers that Numeiri entrusted to the Islamist politicians led by Hassan al-Turabi was effectively putting an end to Addis Ababa Accord, and threatening the regions' rights granted to the South in the 1973 constitution. By 1981 there was no Southerner in the Numeiri cabinet, and the South was thus deprived of a voice to argue their case against the process of establishing an Islamic State[163].

6.5: THE SITUATION IN SOUTH SUDAN (1980 – 1983)

During the process of implementation of Islamization, strengthening ties between Egypt and Sudan compounded the anxiety of Southern political leaders. The government support of Iraq, the discovery of oil in the South, and proposals to redefine the frontier between the North and South were all associated with Numeiri's Islamic policies.

6.6: SOUTHERN FEARS ABOUT ARABISATION

In 1982/83, the relationship of Sudan with some Arabs countries was growing stronger. Southern politicians perceived the strength ties between Sudan, Egypt and Iraq as a move towards allying Sudan as a whole in an Arab and Islamic association of states that would further assimilate the South. The 1982 Egyptian Sudan Charter was met with widespread public opposition in the South. Although the Charter had the support of the President of High Executive Council (HEC), some of the Council members joined students in public demonstrations in Juba, the capital of Southern Regional Government. This charter would allow Egyptians and Northern Sudanese to purchase land in Sudan (South). The charter revived fears in Southerners about Egyptian and Northern Arab colonizing the land along Jonglei canal[164]. It has to be recalled in late 1970s Southern Sudanese protested against the digging of Jonglei canal where 60,000 Egyptians would settle. The digging of the canal and preparation for the settlement of Egyptians and Northerners went on but was halted by the eruption of civil war in 1983.

---

[163] Ann Mosely Lesch, op.cit., p. 53

[164] Douglas H. Johnson, 2003, op.cit., pp. 54&197

6.7: THE DISCOVERY OF OIL IN THE SOUTH AND BOUNDARY DISPUTES

The Southern region's main asset is oil that was discovered soon after the signing of Addis-Ababa Accord and the establishment of regional government. In November 1980 Hasan al-Turabi as Attorney General submitted a bill that proposed a realignment of the North-South) in the Kordofan Region that is part of Northern Sudan. Secondly, the bill would transfer the territories that included districts of copper-rich Hulfra al-Nahas and uranium-rich Kafia Kingi to the North. A clause in the Addis Accord provided for a solution to be reached through referendum in the disputed areas. The citizens from these areas were to choose either to remain in the North or to be relocated to Bahr al-Ghazal Region where they belonged before independence.

This action provoked immediate confrontation between the Southern Regional Government and National Assembly. Southerners united in opposition and face the North unanimously. Hence, the relationship between the North and South deteriorate because Southerners interpreted the shifts of oil area from the South to the North as a means of Arab-Muslim policies to control resources.

However, Numeiri eased the tension when he withdrew boundary bill and reaffirmed the commitment of the government to the provision of the Addis-Ababa Agreement concerning the South's boundary. But he now replaced Southern forces in Bentiu area with Northern troops to monitor and potentially restrain the Southern Regional Government's control of the oil fields, thereby contradicting a clause in the Addis Ababa Accord which stipulated that any natural resources in the South should be controlled by the Regional Government. In addition, the site of the oil refinery was then shifted from Bentiu to Kosti in the North. Southerners were embittered because a refinery in Bentiu would improve the infrastructure, catalyze economic development and provide job opportunity of the South, They concluded that the contest over oil was the key objective that led Numeiri to abrogate the peace agreement and Attorney General Hassan al-Turabi to introduce the boundary bill.

6.8: NUMEIRI'S "CONVERSION" FROM PAN- ARAB SOCIALISM TO ISLAMIZATION

It was not easy to explain why Numeiri shifted from socialism and Arabism to become an Islamist. Daly and Sikainga asserted that the Islamic reforms introduced by Numeiri between 1977 and 1983 may be seen as the result of the need for him to adapt to the religious sensitivities of the Northern Muslims[165]. Niblock suggested that Numeiri's intention was to outmaneuver the Muslim Brothers who were in favour of the full implementation of the *Shari̱_'a*[166]. Johnson takes the view that Numeiri was simply trying to find a new power base at a time when his socialist economic policies were failing, and he was under increasing political pressures from the North, with growing disenchantment with his policies in the South[167].

However, Lesch argues that Numeiri experienced a genuine personal conversion that gave him a new appreciation of the religious values of Islam that made him change his own way of life. In Islam, alcohol is not permitted. Numeiri as a young army officer had been drinking even when he became the President of the Republic. He suddenly left drinking and advised his cabinet Ministers to do so and not to gamble either but to commit themselves to the Islamic principles. Secondly, after Numeiri recovered from a heart operation he published pamphlets as a form of confession that endorsed Islamic social and political codes. He then came out openly advocating Islam and pointed out that the Muslims community and ceased to be true believers. Therefore, reviving Islam would bring the unity of the country and

---

[165] M.W. Daly & A Sikinga, op.cit.,p. 20

[166] Tim Niblock, " The Background to the change of Government in 1985", Peter Woodward (ed.) Sudan After Numeiri,p.62

[167] Sudan's National Product declined in 1978, with annual inflation rate of about 60%, the foreign debts ($3billion in 1978, rising to $ 7 billion in 1983), See Herve Bleuchot and Derek Hopwood Ithaca press, 1991, p.260, Douglas Johnson, 2003, op.cit., pp.43-44 Nazib ayubi, op.cit., cit., p. 109, and Kail C. Ellis,op.cit., p. 269

ensure economic prosperity, he argued. According to the observers, Numeiri's conversion was insignificant for these developments.

It seems fair to conclude, therefore, that Numeiri's conversion was caused by both religious and political factors. His personal change of heart was accompanied by a change of vision for the nation that he ruled. This enabled him to take the political lead from the Northern political parties, both those of a traditional character and those of more ideological orientation, and identify the Islamization process with his own person, this giving him a new religion-political legitimacy that protected him from his Muslims critics.

6.9: THE PROCESS OF APPLICATION OF SHARI`A LAW (1980-1983)

The post-1973 shift toward a policy of Islamizing the structure of the Sudanese state reached its climax with the introduction of *Sharî`a* law into the national constitution. To begin with, as we have seen in previous sections of this and other chapters, there had been little more that general acknowledgement of Islam as the source of "values" that should inform the constitution. Previous governments called for a return to Islamic principles in terms of the constitution and legal system, but relatively little was achieved in this regard until the 1980s when the Islamization process was accelerated[168]. The Islamic revolution in Iran in 1979 encouraged a general advance of ideological Islamism, and Sudan did not escape its influence[169].

In 1980 Numeiri took the first step to bringing the legal system into conformity with the *Sharî`a* by decreeing the unification of the civil and *Sharî`a*. By this decree, judges were required to apply both sets of legal codes. This was followed in September 1983 by a Presidential Order that stated: "*Sharî`a* will be the sole guiding principle behind the law of the Sudan". The new Islamic penal and commercial codes were reported to have been taken from the recommendations of the Committee headed by al-Turabi who revised the Islamic legal system

---

[168] Tim Niblock, op.cit., pp. 61-2

[169] ibid., p. 62

(It has been alleged that these codes were drafted secretly by a small group of Islamist). The new codes instituted *hudûd* punishments for crimes against God (blasphemy and apostasy), against morality (adultery, prostitution, drunkenness), and against property (theft) – the punishments to include the option of execution, lashing and amputation in addition to fines and jail sentences[170]. In October 1983 the first such punishments were implemented[171]. Although, in theory, non-Muslims were exempted from all Shari`a laws, there were no alternatives laws that were introduced for the non-Muslims. Muslim judges ran the courts and therefore the question of exemption was not applied.

6.10: PUBLIC AND CHURCH RESPONSES TO ISLAMIC CODES

The new penal codes (September laws) were not widely supported by the majority of Northern Muslims and were the cause of strong protestation in the South. The communists who were working under ground at that time because of fear of persecution, together with the Ba'th party[172] activists denounced the decrees, as did other liberal Muslims. Al-Mahdi denounced the decrees, as did other liberal Muslims Al-Mahdi denounced the decrees during prayers at the Mahdi's tomb in Omdurman, and the *Umma* Party denounced the decrees on the charge that they transformed Islam into a punitive religion and served only to protect an unjust regime. The DUP headed by Uthman al- Mirghani

---

[170] Al-Agab A. Al-Teraifi, " Regionalism in Sudan: characteristics, problems and prospects", in Peter Woodward (ed.), Sudan After Numeiri p. 104

[171] Ann Lesch, op.cit *(hudûd* punishments specified under Shari`a carried out in 1983 included: twenty six men convicted of liquor offenses were publicly lashed forty time each, two young men had their hands cut off on 9th December of stealing a car. More than fifty people had one or more limbs amputated and thousand were sentenced to flogging for theft, brewing or drinking alcohol, adultery, prostitution and political crimes such as agitating and spreading false romours *hudûd* penalties applied to Christians and adherents of African religions and to Muslims. An Italina priest was flogged for storing wine for communion in his home)

[172] Small party in the North originated from Syria and well established in Iraq

also argued that the September decrees distorted Islam. Individual Muslims and trade unions also opposed institution of these laws[173].

The heads of the Episcopal the Evangelical, Presbyterian Churches and the Sudan Council of Churches submitted a joint petition to the government outlining their dissatisfaction with the new laws. Their document emphasized to importance of religious tolerance based on 1972 Addis Ababa Accord, and the 1973 constitution, and argued that the application of Islamic laws would turn non-Muslim Sudanese to second- class citizens[174], and deny them the guarantees that were invested by the 1973 constitution in the South as a self-governing region.

As noted earlier in this chapter, the NIF was the only political party that was cooperating with the regime. Although al-al-Turabi was said to be critical about some decrees, he played a lie-low policy to allow his party to gain ground in the system.

In September 1984 the Zakat and Taxation Act was promulgated with the purpose of replacing the existing fiscal system with an Islamic one. Zakat is levied on various agricultural produce, animals and on profits from trade, capital and property[175]. Zakat has specific areas laid down by the *Qur'an* in which individual Muslim can spend it. The individual may decide to spend his share as encouraged by handing their donations to the state[176]. As we have mentioned earlier in this chapter, NIF created Islamic institutions in which the entire banking system were Islamized in 1978 with the aim to control the economy. So in 1980s *Da'wa Islâmioyya* under the control of NIF cadres were established and Muslims Zakat was pouring into these Islamic agencies for Proselytization.

In 1984 Numeiri decreed the following amendments: that military and civilian officials were required by laws to swear *baya* (allegiance) to the President as the *Imâm* and *Amîr al-Mu'minîn,* the "Leader of Faithful" – a title that classical Islamic usage had confined to the *Caliph.*

---

[173] Nazib Ayubi, op.ciy., p. 55

[174] Ann Mosely Lesch, op.cit., p., P.55

[175] Al-Agab A. Al-Terafi, op.cit., p. 104

[176] ibid., p. 104

This was intended to ennoble Numeiri's Presidency with religious significance in the leadership of an Islamic state. Also in line with classical Islam, it was proposed to establish *Shûra* (Consultative Council) in place of the elected assembly, with the majority of its members being appointed by the *Imâm*. They would have no parliamentary immunity or the right to question or impeach the President. The draft amendments thus threatened to nullify the provisions in the 1973 constitution, including those that guaranteed non-discrimination on the ground of religion and beliefs, ad that made it possible for non-Muslims to hold higher political positions.

The proposed legislation confirmed Southern fears that the national reconciliation would lead to the undermining of the Addis Ababa Accord and the 1973 constitution. The people's outcry was answered on July 11 when 105 of the 151 members of the People's Assembly insisted on postponing the debate about the amendments[177]. Southern MPs, Church leaders and students protested against the proposed bill. Both former President of High Executive Council and second Vice Presidents of the Republic (Abel Alier and Joseph Lagu) put their political differences aside and confronted Numeiri. They argued that the proposed amendments would undermine the Addis Ababa Accord and religious tolerance instituted under 1973 constitution discussed above. Faced with such broad opposition, Numeiri withdrew the proposed amendments mentioned in the preceding paragraph.

For Numeiri to proceed with the implementation of his policies he needed to show to individual members of opposition that he was in control and had the tools to silence any critics. In 1984 he turned his attention to small ideological and regional groups. The leading Communist figure, Ibrahim Nagud, and the women rights activist, Fatma Ahmad, were charged with treason but were acquitted. On the regional level, Rev Philip Ghabbush from Nuba Mountains was arrested together with 207 followers and charged with conspiracy against the state. Numeiri was aware of the implications if he execute Ghabbush and his men. The Nuba Soldiers formed a sizeable number within the Sudanese army, and fearing possible mutiny, he showed clemency. He

---

[177] Ann Mosely Lesch, op.cit., p. 56

then turned to the Republican Brothers who were more critical about the way he was implementing Islamic principles. Although, Taha had approved of Numeiri coup of 1969, with its secular agenda, he was opposed to the introduction of the September Islamic laws in 1983. His radical political ideas led to his final arrest on charges of apostasy, and he was executed on 18th January 1985. His death provoked and angered the nation and became a symbol of the repression of the regime that played a part in bringing down President Numeiri in April the same year. The Islamic laws remained theoretically in force, awaiting the decision of the incoming democratically elected government in April 1986.

6.11: CONCLUSION

In this chapter, I have analyzed the first stage in the process of Islamization over the last twelve years of Numeiri's rule. It has been shown that the shift of policy from the 1973 constitution to the introduction of the Islamic Laws in 1983 reflected both the personal conversion of Numeiri form a secular to religious worldview, and pressures form the Northern political parties. In the event, however, the implementation of *hudûd* laws failed to carry the consensual support of the Muslim community or its traditional parties, and only the NIF gave its approval. The result was that Numeiri was even more isolated politically after 1983 than he had been after 1973, and it was not long before his government fell. But having introduced the Islamic laws, he left a legacy that no subsequent Muslim political leader was willing to rescind: while the laws may have been unpopular in themselves, they symbolized that Islam was to be enshrined in the Sudanese constitution a s the normative source of legislative guidance, firming up what had been stated less clearly in the 1973 constitution. The impact of this development of church-state relations in evident: the church would henceforth be dealing with an ideologically-motivated Islamic government, rather than one that was orientated to secular Arab nationalism. The implications of this change will be examined in later chapters.

SEVEN

MILITARY AND PARLIAMENTARY PERIODS (1985-1989)

7.1: INTRODUCTION

This chapter reviews the four-year transitional period from the end of the Numeiri regime and its replacement by the military government of General Swar al-Dahab (1985-86) to the collapse of the parliamentary period of Sadiq al-Mahdi's Premiership (1986-1989) that was characterized by a political alliance between Sadiq's government and NIF. It will examine the Sudan Political Charter (1987) as the basis of their alliance.

7.2: GENERAL SWAR AL-DAHAB (1985-86)

The fall of Numeiri, brought in a government led by al-Gizouli Dafa'alla as the Prime Minister and General Swar Al-Dahab, Chairman of Transitional Military Council (TMC)[178]. Political parties and trade unions were represented in the Council of Ministers. The Southern

---

[178] Abdullahi Ab-Na'im, " Peaceful Coexistence at Risk", in Kail C Ellis (ed), The Vatican, Islam and the and the middle East, 1987, p. 270

People's Liberation Movement was invited to join the government[179]. There were great expectations among the Sudanese public that the new government would return to a pluralist constitution of 1973 and to resolve the issue of the Islamic laws.

One of the demands of the popular uprising against Numeiri was the cancellation of Islamic laws that had been introduced from September 1983. However, the Chairman of TMC, Swar al-Dahab, moved in the opposite direction, and disbanded all the institutions instituted through public consent, which included the 1973 constitution and political organizations. He decided to retain *Shari`a* laws *pro tem,* and to allow the issue to be decided by an elected government that would take power after April 1986.[180] This decision was not merely one of political expedience. Swar al-Dahab is quoted as having said: "No Muslim leader could possibly abrogate Islamic laws and survive politically" [181]. As an-Na'im has argued: "Whatever Muslims in the North may think of Numeiri's policies to implement *Shari`a*, they will find it difficult to argue for its abrogation. Northern Muslims have a religious duty to implement Islamic law and traditionally *Shari`a* is the majority view of Islamic law... The inability of the government after Numeiri to repeal the laws was an advantage to the proponents of *Shari`a*". He contends that the traditionalist and ideological parties would always agree to maintain *Shari`a* as the source of legislation when they come to power after a year of transitional government, he did not repeal the *Shari`a* government, although he had argued strongly against them at the time of their institution.

While still in opposition, Al-Mahdi advocated the separation of religion and state – a position that he had first established in the 1960s when his uncle and he each took separate responsibility for religion and politics respectively. It was consistent with the division

[179] Gizouli Dafaala Prime Minister "Letter " to John Garang, 10 November 1985, in John Garang The call for Democracy in Sudan, Mansour Khalid (ed.) pp. 94-100
[180] Kamal Osman Salih, "The fading Democracy," in Peter Woodward (ed), Sudan After Nemeiri, p. Nemeiri
[181] M W. Daly & A. Sikainga, op.cit., p 84

of powers that he subsequently opposed Numeiri's introduction of the Islamic laws. In 1986 the separation of religion and state had been agreed in principle in the so-called Koka Dam Accord that was drawn up by the factions opposed to Numeiri's Islamization Policies. This called for the abrogation of the Islamic laws, and the abolition of all political and military treaties with foreign countries that impinged on the sovereignty of Sudan; the state of emergency could then be lifted, a cease-fire declared between the North and the South, and a National Constitutional Conference could be convened in Khartoum[182].

As will be seen later in this chapter, the terms of this Accord that promised reconciliation between the North and South were progressively ignored by Sadiq al-Mahdi's government. This was the reason why the SPLM declined the invitation to join the transitional government, and to demand instead the separation of religious institution form the state[183]. They further argued that the transitional government failed to create a favourable atmosphere for political parties to reach a consensus.

7.3: SADIQ AL-MAHDI ERA (1986-1989)

When al-Mahdi came to power in 1986, he made an early declaration of his intention to repeal the *Sharî_a* law and replace with alternative of a "sound" Islamic code. This presaged a shift of the position that he had previously held in opposition to at least a revised position that he held in government. On the one hand he had pledged to repeal September laws; on the other the NIF were opposed to such abrogation unless and until an acceptable Islamic substitute could be found. Treading a path through this political minefield al-Mahdi declared: "We wish to establish Islam as the source of legislation in Sudan because of its Muslim Majority[184].

The government compiled several national charters under the guidance of Sadiq's Attorney General at the time, Abdel Mahmoud Salih, designed to draw up alternative laws. The National Concord

---

[182] ibid., pp. 216 - 218
[183] Tim Niblock, op.cit p.62
[184] Douglas H. Johnson, 2003, op.cit p. 79

Committee established in November 1987 was charged to produce alternative Islamic Codes to replace the 1983 September laws. The guiding principle to the committee's work was: "Muslims should have the right to pass laws that satisfy their Islamic aspirations"[185]. In his public pronouncement Sadiq argued that 95% of the penal laws were satisfactory to the nation, and that only 5% were yet to be agreed upon.

After the formation of the "national unity government" in 1988, the *Shari_'a* issue again became contentious in parliament when the NIF insisted on its full implementation as a condition of its (NIF's) participation in the new coalition[186]. NIF absolutism on this issue was both an expression of its ideology, and evidence of its growing influence over the two traditional parties. After the fall of Numeiri, NIF was able to use its operational and financial resources to achieve a significant success in the national election of April 1986, in which it became the third major party in parliament. Their electoral success was due to serious flaws in the laws and regulations governing the elections. The fact that NIF had financial and administrative advantages that other parties did not have during the election campaign was evidence of running the show.

As National Islamic Front became the third largest party in the Constituent Assembly (1986-1989), it continued to advance its programs as a junior partner in the al-Mahdi's coalition government. It exerted maximum pressure to keep the issue of *Shari_'a* at the top of the government's agenda, and succeeded in pressuring the other coalition parties to agree that Islam was no longer a matter of personal faith but the mainspring of constitutional and political life[187]. This was expressed by the Charter of National Accord signed by the three major parties and other smaller ones, including some factions from the Southern parties and Nuba based Sudanese National party[188]. The Charter's first document contained issues that were agreed upon by

[185] John Garang, op.cit., p. 149
[186] Tim Niblock, op.cit., p 62
[187] John Garang, op.cit., p. 148
[188] Tim Niblock, op.cit., p. 55

all parties, while the second document dealt with differences yet to be resolved.

Hassan al-Turabi, leader of NIF, now became the Attorney General and Minister of Justice,[189] charged with drafting a new legal code based on Islam. This was completed in August 1988 and referred to the Council of Ministers for deliberations. The Council of Ministers made alterations on the draft and came up with a dual legal system. The aim was to repeal September Laws and replace them with a modified *Shari̇_'a* law that would be applied in the Muslim North; while other regions, the South in particular, would have a secular code that was not based on the *Shari̇_'a* and did not include *Shari̇_'a* laws[190].

Sudanese lawyers association rejected the draft proposal on the grounds that a dual legal system would encourage separatist tendencies. Instead they proposed a single secular legal code, which in their view would not divide the population on the basis of ethnicity, religion or culture. This met with the approval of the Southern parties, the National Salvation Alliance and the Communist Party, all of which favoured a secular legal system against *Shari̇_'a* law[191]. This included the SPLM that made the abrogation of *Shari'a* law one of their preconditions for a political settlement in the Sudan.

The country was therefore completely divided over the issue. The majority of *Umma* party, some DUP members and NIF wanted to retain *Shari̇_'a* as the sole legal system. The other group comprising of southern political parties, some other regional parties, also the liberal wing of DUP united in support of secular law. In the meantime, the September laws had neither been repealed, nor were they or alternative laws being implemented. Chaos ensued, and the government was paralyzed by Sadiq's political inconsistency.

Al-Mahdi's role during the transitional period can be explained on two accounts: Firstly, as pointed out already, he had to satisfy a range of conflicting views among the Northern parties, and in this situation he came to rely increasingly on the view that Islam provides the main

[189] ibid., p. 55
[190] ibid., p. 63
[191] ibid.,p. 63

source of guidance for the state. This, secondly, affected his relations with the SPLM leader, John Garang, with whom he had met in Addis Ababa to review the Koka Dam Accord. Instead of fulfilling the terms of the agreement, that included the abrogation of the Islamic laws, he requested a fresh dialogue with the SPLM. The latter saw this as a change of attitude, and evidence that the *Shari_'a* laws had become a symbol of identity for Muslims to sustain their power and their culture.

In this situation, the South's attitude toward al-Mahdi returned tone of distrust that saw him in the traditional role of a Northern leader whose policy was to colonize the South through the imposition of Islam and Arab culture. They noted his exploitation of existing differences among the pastoral and agricultural tribes, and the formation of a tribal militia among Baqqara people who supported the *Umma* Party against their Dinka neighbours and other Southern tribes within their reach. This was intended to complicate the civil war by spreading conflict among the Southern peoples along racial and cultural lines.

Al-Mahdi also encouraged the settlement of Islamic scholars (*fugahâ*) and merchants in the South, and intermarriage between Arabs and the Indigenous Africans in the expectation that many of the latter would eventually adopt Islam, and become assimilated into Arab genealogies, customs and culture. This would be a peaceful process in which social transformation, cultural and ethnic assimilation would be achieved without forceful conversion. He advocated the spread of Islam and Arabic language in the South and declared that the dominant feature of the Sudan in Islamic revival.[192] All this implied that Southern Sudanese have no culture of their own, and must be assimilated into the Arabic and Islamic culture of the Arab North.

As a consequence the three years of al-Mahdi's government saw an intensification of the conflict between the South and the North. Failing to come up with a sustainable political option, he continued to seek a military victory that would bring SPLM to negotiating table. The Sudan government received military support variously form Egypt, USA, Iraq and Libya, and the SPLM looked to Ethiopia for support. This internationalized the Civil war, and polarized it as a struggle

---

[192] ibid., p. 83

between an Ethiopia on the other.[193] As Southerners began to think of the war as *a jihâd* against them, the Northerners on the other hand, perceived Southern struggle as Christian crusade against Sudan. The prospect for a peaceful settlement faded away, and the civil war began to take on a distinctly religious character.

7.4: CONCLUSION

In this chapter, I have reviewed the four-year transitional period from the end of the Numeiri regime to the collapse of the parliamentary period of Sadiq al-Mahdi's Premiership (1986-1989) that was characterized by a political alliance between Sadiq's government and National Islamic Front. In my opinion, the continuing ambiguity about the *Shari`a* laws and the deepening problem with the South we have noted were the result of al-Mahdi's indecisiveness and inconsistency. He proved unable to assert himself over his Northern political rivals, and ended up in compromises and undermined his initially promising relationship with the SPLM in the South. Although this ambiguity had negative consequences on the civil war that increasingly came to be viewed in religious terms, the evidence of this chapter suggests that this was not so much the result of a define religious policy on the part of the government, but rather a consequence of its inability to find a durable political way forward. Al-Mahdi's change of attitude in 1988 cannot be compared, therefore, with Numeiri's change of mind some years earlier. It was less an affirmative expression of Islamism than an inability to find a way of dealing with the NIF. But if it is correct to interpret al-Mahdi's shift of ground as the result of political pressures, it also shows how Christian-Muslim relations in Sudan was vulnerable to political tides.

In the event, al-Mahdi increased military intervention in the South did not succeed in bringing the SPLM into negotiation. Early in 1988 the army issued Sadiq with ultimatum, criticizing him of failure in handling the war in the South. In response, Sadiq formed

---

[193] Douglas H. Johnson, "North - South Issues", in Peter Woodward (ed.), Sudan After Numeiri, p. 134

a new coalition with DUP to revive peace process with SPLM. NIF refused any terms that would undermine the vision of an Islamic state. They abandoned the coalition and made common cause with Islamist Muslim officers in the army who staged a coup against al-Mahdi in June 1989.

CHAPTER
EIGHT

ISLAMISATION UNDER THE NATIONAL SALVATION REVOLUTION OF GENERAL OMAR AL-BASHIR

8.1: INTRODUCTION

This chapter discusses the final stages in the process of Islamization that are identified with the military regime of General al-Bashir who led the coup against al-Mahdi in 1989, and has ruled Sudan for thirty two years (32). It will be shown that the new regime, from the outset, was determined to press on with ideological reform of Sudan as an Islamic state, and that, to achieve this end, the military leadership depended heavily on the guidance of the National Islamic Front in the formation and implementation of policy. This resulted in the promulgation of a new constitution in 1998.

The chapter will examine in particular the policy of re-organizing the federal structures of the state, its educational policy, and the 1998 Constitution. This will lead to an analysis of constitutional position of Christians in the Islamic state, and the relationship between church and state under these new conditions.

8.2: OMAR AL-BASHIR (1989 – 2020)

Before coming to power as head of state, General Al-Bashir was a Sudanese military officer with no clear political background. The NIF leader, Hassan al-Turabi described him as a committed Muslim believer rather than a traditional Muslim politician, and as a man of the people rather than a member of the political elite. As such al-Turabi saw him as a symbol of Sudanese personality who could bring the Sudanese to Islam.[194] According to Lesch, he was suspected by the Sudan Military Intelligence of having sympathies for the NIF as early as 1985, and was therefore transferred to the South Sudan to fight against the Southern People's Liberation Army (SPLA)[195]. It was during a brief return to Khartoum *en route* to Cairo for military training that he executed his coup with a group of military confidants and NIF supporters on 30th June 1989.

The fall of al-Mahdi returned Sudan to military rule under what was called the National Salvation Revolution (NSR). From the very beginning Bashir made it clear that the new government would be based on Islam that, as the religion of the majority of the Sudanese people, was the essential basis for the country's nationalism and the source of principles upon which the nation's legal, political and economic systems would be defined. Arabic, the language of the Qur'an would have precedence over indigenous languages and English as the official language of the state[196]. The September laws would be preserved. The government's war effort against the SPLA would stepped up, now under the ideology *of Jihâd,* and greater efforts would be made to propagate Islam in Sudan. In all these policy issues Bashir made no secret of the fact that he would keep a close relationship with the NIF, and would rely on NIF cadres, in addition to the national army, to implement the and programs that would transform Sudan into an Islamic state [197]. It

---

[194] Mohamed "E. Hamdi, The Making of an Islamic Political Leader: Conversion with Hassan al-Turabi, p.59

[195] Ann Mosely Lesch, op.cit., pp. 114-115

[196] Ann M. Lesch, op.cit., p. 113

[197] Nazib op.cit., p. 38

is for this reason that the National Salvation Revolution government became synonymous with the NIF.

8.3: NIF FEDERAL STRUCTURES AND POWERS

NIF had long opposed the Southern demand for a federal system on grounds that it would weaken the unity of the state, and impede the process of Arabisation and Islamization on which, according to its view, the unity of the state should be based. It was for this reason that the NIF criticized Numeiri for granting regional autonomy for the South, under its own regional government in Juba, in the 1973 constitution. Under this constitutional arrangement the three traditional Southern provinces – Bhar el Gazal, Equatoria and Upper Nile and three other newly created – had their own administrations under a provincial commissioner, and the commissioners were accountable to the regional government in Juba. The NIF feared that this would militate against its ambitions for Sudan to be governed as a single Islamic state. When al-Turabi became the Attorney General charged with revising the constitutional arrangements, he used his influence to maximize the authority of the central government and undercut the actual autonomy of the regions[198]. This resulted in the dissolution of the Juba government in 1983, and the administrative reorientation of the regional administrations to the central government in Khartoum. Three Governors were appointed for Bahr al-Ghazzal, Equatoria, and Upper Nile in place of the former Southern regional administration, but their powers were reduced.

Al-Bashir pressed this policy further by abolishing the three-province structure of the South and dividing the region in ten states, each under the authority of a *Wali*- a term drawn from traditional Islamic polity – who, in most cases, were Muslims appointed by the military government. This revised federal system was extended to the North. Because of the situation of civil war, in which the SPLM was the actual government of much of the South, only four states – Bahr al –Ghazal, Upper Nile, Bahr al-Jebel and Jonglei – functioned in

---

[198] M. W. Daly & Ahmad Sikainga, op.cit., 1993, p.88

accordance with these new arrangements. The other *walis* were merely nominal appointments of persons based in Khartoum where they served the interests of the NIF government. In September 1993 al-Bashir replaced *walis* with military officers, and made further changes in January 1995 in which governors in the South had less power than their colleagues in the North who controlled finances and set policies for the economy, education, information under Islamic principles. Transferring Southerners to the North and posting NIF's cadres in the South enabled the government to promote Arabisation and Islamization

This raises the issue of the place of Islamic law under the NIF government. Consonant with the principle of centralization, national laws prevailed over regional laws. Since 1983, Islamic principles were defined the operation of the state in which Muslims formed the majority of the population. Thus, in February 1991, each of the provinces came under Islamic laws in all aspects of public affairs.[199] In terms of penal law the Southern states were theoretically under the terms of the 1987 Sudan Charter that states:

> The legislative authority of any region predominantly inhabited by non-Muslims can take exception to the general operation of the national law, with Respect to any rule of criminal or penal nature derived directly and Solely form a text in the *Shari`a* contrary to the local culture. The said authority can instead opt for a different rule based on the customs or religion prevailing in the area...The general presumption otherwise, is for (*Shari`a)* law to be effective country-wide over all persons and religion.[200]

A Council of Native Administration was established that recognized the authority of traditional leaders over their non-Muslims peoples. But no such provision was, or could be made for Christians since they do not have an equivalent code of Christian laws. As a result they were

---

[199] Ann Mosely Lesch,. Op.cit., p. 126

[200] ibid., p. 126

included under Islamic law, and were only exempted from certain laws, including some of the *hudûd* laws that were intended for Muslims on the basis of particular *Qur'anic* injunctions. For example, Christians were allowed to drink alcoholic liquor in the privacy of their home, but not publicly, and the production of alcoholic drinks was forbidden, But Christians were liable to the Islamic punishment of amputation for crimes of theft, and were punished under other regulation of Islamic law. Similarly Islamic legal prescriptions regarding the status of women were applied to all women, irrespective of their religion and all Sudanese women were required to dress according to accepted Islamic customs.

The disparity between the GoS attitude toward non-Muslims whom it identified as "native" and its policy toward Christians tends to suggest that the NIF concept of Islamization allowed for ethnic differences, but was at best ambiguous in terms of religious pluralism. Ironically, traditionalist leaders who were normally identified in classical Islamic legal texts as *kuffàr* or "unbelievers" had more power under the basis of their being representatives of ethnic rather than religious groups, and under the new arrangements the GoS sought to create new structures within the local communities that would be loyal to it, by recognizing new tribes and have their leaders incorporated into political relationship directly with the central authority. Douglas interprets this as a shift away from the "participatory federalism" of the 1973 constitution, in favour of "ethnic federalism" in which small communities operate independently of each other in political arenas that are controlled by the central government.

8.4: NIF EDUCATIONAL POLICY

Education was, as we have seen in earlier chapters, a critical instrument in the implementation of government policy. Since the period of president Abboud's government policy advocated the philosophy one language, one religion, and one nation. This was strongly supported by the NIF government. The Ministry of Education became one of the main arenas of NIF activities, all officials being replaced if they were not ready to support NIF's objectives. In 1995, the Minister of

Education, Mr. Kabashour Kuku, stated that it was the policy of the government to educate all students according to the teaching of Islam, through Arabic as the medium of instruction.[201]

The language policy put non-Muslim students at a disadvantage, due to the fact that their mother tongues were not recognized as official languages. Thus, it was difficult for non-Muslim students to pass the required entrance examinations for admission to government schools. Consequently, most Christian students who could not pass their exams find themselves inferior to their Muslim colleagues. To remedy this situation, the government claimed, it was necessary to appoint Arabic-speaking Northerners into most teaching positions. The appointment of NIF sympathizers meant that the Arabic language requirement became a vehicle for the spreading of Islamic teaching throughout the school system.

The confusion of Arabic and Islam is evident in the problem of the religious exam that is required of students for graduation from secondary schools. Muslims students, of course, have no difficulties in passing an exam on Islam in the Arabic language. For the followers of traditional African religions, the practice is that they are given their certificates if they meet a minimal standard of Arabic. For Christians to pass the exam in religion, it was required that they are taught Christianity in Arabic, a condition which was rarely met by those whose educational backgrounds were in English. In order to meet these requirements, the Catholic Church established a four- year Arabic-language training college that graduated its first batch of students in April 1996[202].

The negative impact of this educational system on non-Christians cannot be over-estimated. The relative lack of Christians who are yet able to meet government qualifications for the teaching profession means that qualified Muslim teachers fill the positions. The varied demands of government-prescribed syllabus have relegated the teaching

---

[201] ibid., p. 126
[202] ibid., p. 213

of Christian faith to a marginalized position, and in practice little Christianity is taught in the public schools[203].

It is against this background that Southerners, especially Christians, feel that they are being confronted by the Arabic language as a tool for assimilation which they experience as an oppression that is aimed to eradicate their own cultural identities. This is not to fall into the mistaken generalization that Arabic can never be used by Christians. Sudanese Christian acknowledged that Arabic has been and remains an important medium of Middle Eastern Christianity since the 8th-9th centuries. Increasingly Sudanese Christians themselves are beginning to speak Arabic as *a lingua franca* of Sudan, but they do so under the apprehension of coercion, that they have no alternative, and that it is part of a larger policy of the present government to impose one religion on all the peoples of Sudan, and eradicate the cultural traditions and values of the minority ethnic communities. This is an example of the situation that Frantz Fanon had described as "the antagonistic identities of political alienation and cultural discrimination[204], that requires constitutional arrangements.

8.5: THE 1998 CONSTITUTION

Against this background we can now turn to the new constitution that the national Assembly introduced in March 1998. It is important to analyze the text carefully in order to distinguish between what it states and what Sudanese Muslims and Christians often interpret as meaning, although the ambiguity is part of the problematic that will also be addressed in this section.

The Preamble of the Constitution makes clear that it is conceived and written within a religious perspective, since it invokes "the Name of God, the Compassionate, the Merciful" and speaks of God as creator and giver of life and freedom, and "the legislator of right guidance for

---

[203] Joseph Cardinal Cardeiro, " The Christian Minority in an Islamic state: the case of Parkistan", In Kail C Ellis (ed.), The Vatican, Islam, and the Middle East, P. 285

[204] Frantz Fanon, Black Skin, White Masks, Foreword/xix

the communities." The phrases placed between inverted commas are clearly Islamic in nature, and although here is no explicit mention of Islam in the preamble, its reference to "the renewing efforts of the National Salvation Revolution " must read in light of the Islamization policy that has been discussed in previous sections of this chapter.

The only explicit reference to Islam is found in the first paragraph of Part One of the Constitution that defines the nature of the state: "The Sudan is a comprehensive homeland where ethnicities and cultures harmonize, and religions are tolerant toward each other, where Islam is the religion of the majority of the people, and Christianity and customary beliefs are professed by a considerable number of the population". This falls short of defining Sudan as an Islamic State, and strictly speaking only recognizes Islam descriptively as "the religion of the majority of the people", whereas the 1973 Constitution prescribed that "society shall be guided by Islam being the religion of the majority of its people." Yet the fact that the harmonization of ethnicities and cultures, and tolerance among religions, are sought in the public arena "where Islam is the religion of the majority of its people" implies that harmony and tolerance are to be pursued in Islamic terms. The paragraph also says less than the 1973 Constitution about Christianity and traditional beliefs; whereas the 1973 constitution recognized Christianity as a "heavenly religion" and traditional religions as containing "noble aspects of spiritual beliefs", the 1998 constitution speaks of them simply as being "professed by a considerable number of the population".

Paragraph 4 addresses the principle of governorship and sovereignty. "Governorship in the State is for God the creator of mankind; and sovereignty is for the successor people of the Sudan, to be practiced as the worship of God, and assumption of trust, building of homeland, spreading of justice, freedom and *shûra,* and all shall be regulated by the constitution and the law." While Islam is not mentioned, the Islamic implications are again clear. Governorship (*wilâya*) rests with God, and the people of Sudan are God's "successor" (*khilâfa*), a more democratized version of the classical institution of Caliphate, in which the *Qur'anic* principle of *shûra* or "consultation" is the constituted mechanism for governance.

The constitution specifically instates two Islamic duties within in the functioning of the state, in terms of the defence and the economy. Paragraph 7 dealing with the "Defence of the Homeland", stipulates that "defence of the homeland is an honour, and *Jihâd* for its cause is a duty." As generations of Islamic jurist have taught, *Jihâd* may only be legitimately fought in defence of *Dâr al –Islâm* – i.e. territory that can be considered "the Domain of Islam" due to its being administered under Islamic law. Those who lose their lives in the cause of *jihâd* are recognized as martyrs, and it is to be noted that this term is used in Paragraph 7 of the constitution: "The State cares also for the fighters injured in wars, and for the families of the martyrs." The second Islamic duty that is constituted as a function of the state is prescribed in Paragraph 10: *Zakât* is a financial duty which the state collects, and the law regulates the manner of its collecting expenditure and administration." This is, in fact, the closest the constitution comes to implying that *Sharî`a* is the national law, *Zakât* being one of the five pillars of Islam and therefore an obligation under Islamic law that State is religiously bound to administer. In addition to *Zakât*, Paragraph 10 of the constitution recognizes and encourages voluntary alms giving, and the Islamic system of *Awgâf* (religious endowments). For example, properties bound for religious purposes, are therefore exempted from taxation. In contrast to these Islamic elements the constitution dictates the economy, whereby Paragraph 10 also refers to other "taxes, rates and duties being regulated by the law fairly."

Beyond these references to Islamic duties that are to be incorporated in the constitutional functioning of the state, the 1998 constitution makes a single reference to the sources of Islam in the paragraph dealing with "religiousness" reference "Employees (Paragraph 18): "Employees of the State and public life shall employ it (religiousness) in the worship of God, The Muslims shall adhere to the Book (i.e. the *Qur'an*) and observe such spirit in the plans and laws, policies and official work of the political, economic, social and cultural fields, to prompt public life to such objectives, and direct them towards justice and uprightness, and toward the favour of God in the Hereafter". The intent of this passage clear. "Religiousness" defines the character of public life in the state, the worship of God to be the intention of all the public servant of the state[205]. For Muslims this explicitly entails adherence to the *Qur'an* ad *Hadith*, the two immutable sources of Islamic law *(Sharî'a)* and religion *(Dîn)*. This being the only reference to religion in the paragraph it is fair to read the following statement, "all shall maintain the intents of religion", as meaning that in terms of public life, all state employees – whether Muslim or non-Muslim –will observe the *Sharî'a* in the conduct of their duties.

From this analysis of Part One of the 1998 constitution that sets out its guiding principles, it may be concluded that, while falling short of defining Sudan as an Islamic state, the constitution has an Islamizing intent. Its intent is that the public spirit of Islam, with the two immutable sources of Islamic law being recognized as the framework of "religiousness" within which the state should operate. As the constitution states at the conclusion of its first part in Paragraph 19: "The guiding principles are general objectives with which the State organs and the employees shall work and be guided. There are no limits controlled by constitutional justice. They are principles by which the executive organ shall be guided in its projects and policies, and which the legislative organ promotes in its legislations, recommendations and controlling, and towards which all who are in the service of the state shall work".

It should be noted that the 1998 constitution makes no explicit mention of *Sharî'a* law. It does, however, contain references to it, as has already been seen in terms of *Zakât* and *Awgâf* in relation to the economy. There is another important reference to *Sharî'a* law in Paragraph 33 (a) that deal with "Immunity from the Death Penalty except for just cause" where it is stated : " no penalty of death shall be passed except as retribution (*Qiûâû*), or as punishment for offences of serious danger, according to law". *Qiûâû* or "retribution" is a category of criminal law in the *Sharî_'a*, dealing with crimes that the State has

[205] The National Assembly, The Republic of the Sudan, Constitution Bill, 1998, pp.14

the obligation to punish with the object of deterrence. Islamic law recognizes three categories of such crimes: the *hudûd* offences that carry prescribed and mandatory penalties that were discussed in a previous chapter of this book; the *Qiûâû* offences that concern crimes against a person such as murder, wounding and assault, for which there are prescribed punishments that are not mandatory, and can be waived by the next of kin of the injured person in return for financial compensation (*diya*); the third category *Ta`zîr* are offences for which prescribed punishments fall within the discretion of the judge. The constitution makes no reference to the *hudud* punishments that were the cause of public controversy when they were originally introduced by president Numeiri. The explicit reference to *Qiûâû*, however,, makes it clear that the constitution's intention is to apply *Shari`a* criminal law in such a way as recognized prescribed punishments, while allowing for discretion in their application. Thus, the death penalty applies for cases of murder and assault, but under the rules of *Qiûâû* it may be waived if the family of the injured person opt for compensation.

Within this Islamizing framework for the public life of Sudan, the constitution upholds the right of freedom of belief and worship, and thought an expression for all Sudanese citizens. Paragraph 24 states: "Every person shall have the freedom of conscience and religious belief, and shall have the right to display his religion or creed, and propagate the through worship or education or practising the rites or ceremonies, and no one shall be coerced to profess a faith which he does not believe in, or practice the rites which he does not freely accept, and this without hurting the feelings of others, or the public order as detailed by law." In similar spirit Paragraph 25 states: "The citizens shall be guaranteed freedom of seeking any learning or professing any doctrine or thought without coercion ad shall be guaranteed freedom of expression, reception of information, and of publication and of the press, without prejudice to security, public order, safety or public manners, as detailed by law".[206]

---

[206] ibid., pp. 5-8

8.6: CHURCH-STATE RELATIONS (1998 – 2005)

Turning to the impact of the Islamizing policies of the NIF government on church-state relations, it is clear that the latter have been characterized by mutual suspicion and distrust. From the perspective of the church leaders, the carefully- worded principles of the 1998 constitution seem designed to give the government a wide measure of freedom to pursue its Islamization policies without formally declaring Sudan to be an Islamic Republic. They therefore assess the constitution in light of what the government and government-approved bodies actually say and do.

The church leaders feel acute sensitivity about the application of *Shari`a* law. They noted, for example, that the ideological leader of the NIF, Hasan a-Turabi, declared publicly in 1993 that "the county is…. an Islamic republic for all effective purposes regarding the implementation of Islamic injunctions in the political, economic, social and cultural fields. At present, Islam is ruling in Sudan: Islamic values prevail in society, and Islamic injunctions are being implemented in all fields." The church leaders interpret this in light of the NIF Sudan Charter of 1987 that speaks as follows regarding *Shari`a* as the general source of legislation: " It expresses the will of the democratic majority and conforms to the values of scriptural religions…. (Muslims) have the right, by virtue of their religious choice, of their democratic weight, and of natural justice to practice the values and rules of their religion to their full range – in personal, familial, social, or political affairs… *Shari_a* should be effective country wide over all person and regions, except in regions predominantly inhabited by non-Muslim who take exception to any rule of criminal or penal nature derived directly and solely from a test in the *Shari_`a* contrary to local custom." This implies that non-Muslim may only exempt themselves from *Shari`a* law in particular cases, and that in general terms they must accept to live under *Shari_`a* regulations. *Turabi's* assertion that the *Shari`a* represents the values of all scriptural religions in contradicted by the legal opinion (*fatwa*) issued by a conference of Islamic legal scholars in 1983 that declared non-Muslims to be "heathens" (*kuffâr*) who stand in need of "the Islamic call" (*da_wa*), and that it is "the duty of Islam to fight and kill them" if they resist. It is in light of such statements – the significance of which must be set in the context of the civil war – that church leaders accuse the government of ambiguity" on the one hand it assures non-Muslims that their rights will be upheld under the Sudanese constitution, while on the other it allows its own representatives and formal bodies of Islamic jurist to issued statements that prejudice non-Muslim communities and put their very existence into question. President al-Bashir himself added to the public perception of his government's intentions when he compared the National Salvation Revolution with the Mahdist Revolution with the assurance that the former would continue "for as long as the Sudanese people stuck to the principles upheld by the Mahdist Revolution which had called for the victory of the religion of truth"[207].

On its part, however, the government argued that Christianity has been growing in most parts of Sudan during the 1990s. Christian churches and denominations are well established and well represented in Khartoum and in the heart of Islamic Northern Sudan, as well as in the South. This includes two cathedrals the St Matthew's Catholic Cathedral and the Anglican Al Saints' Cathedral. The Catholic Church is also a major landowner in Khartoum itself. The government claims that more than five hundred new churches were established in the Khartoum state in the first four years of its accession to power, though it should be noted that this was due, at least in part, to the influx of refugees from Southern Sudan escaping from the government's military incursion in the civil war. The Catholic Church has reported, for example, that over six thousand adults were baptized in one Catholic Church in Khartoum on Easter night alone in 1995.[208] The Episcopal Church of the Sudan has four hundred clergy serving two hundred and seventy five churches across Sudan.[209] The Jesus Fellowship Church and Dawn Ministries claim that, in 1996, 3.21 million people saw the Jesus film, based on Luke's Gospel, after which 1.62 million people professed

---

[207] Human rights Watch/Africa, op. cit., p. 195

[208] The Sudan Foundation, op., cit,pp. 8-9

[209] Source from the Internet: " The Anglican Communion, the Inter-Anglican Information"' 19th February 1997, s HH:/www.qust.org.uk/tour/sudan/html

to "show great interest in Christianity"[210]. This evangelical mission also stated that "most churches are growing", and, following a pastors' conference in May 1996, have decided to work together more closely in systematically evangelizing the country. The government takes these sorts of statistics as evidence that freedom of worship clearly exists.

In February 1993 Pope John Paul II visited the Sudan at the invitation of the government. His open-air mass in Khartoum gathered more than half a million people, and marked a moment of triumph for both the Christian community and the government. The former saw it as evidence of international awareness of the situation of the Christians in Sudan, and the government took it as a friendly gesture towards its policies. On the basis of this event, Turabi took the lead the following year in convening an inter-faith conference between Christians and Muslims. In this forum, president al-Bashir used the Organisation of Alien Voluntary Act (OAVA) of 1988 to repeal the 1962 Missionary Act.[211] It is to be recalled that it was under the Missionary Act (1962) that the Abboud government expelled all Christian missionaries, and pressured the churches in Sudan to accelerate Africanisation of their leadership. The fact that the Missionary Act could now be repealed provided some evidence that the government saw this objective as having been achieved. On the other hand, it angered the Sudanese Christian leaders by decreeing, under the Provisional Order of October 4, 1994, that churches should be registered under exactly the same regulations as pertained for foreign non-governmental organization (NGOs). Under this law existing churches were required to register with the Commissioner of Social Planning, who would have the authority to issue or withhold their contracts; new churches were required to register separately from their mother churches, and were treated as independent

---

[210] Source from the Internet: "Dawn Friday fax," 1996 Number 20,Dawn Ministries, 7899, Lexington Drive, Suite, 200B, Colarado Springs, Coo80920, USA and Jesus Fellowship Church (Jesus Army) At http:/www.jesus.org.uk/dawn/dawnabut.html.

[211] Samuel N. ADOR, "Islam", Sudan Council of Churches, Khartoum, (unpublished paper) 11/6/2000

entities. [212] The Catholic and Episcopal churches both denounced the Provisional Order. The Catholic Church condemned it as "the most comprehensive thorough and far reaching attempt to terminate the life and activities of the Church", while the Episcopal Church described it as "repugnant and irrelevant to the evangelistic mission of the Church.

The inter-faith conference was overshadowed by accusation in respect of this government policy, and was an occasion also for Sudanese Church leaders to voice their concerns to the government in regards to the abuse of religion in Sudan, and to call for equality between Muslims and Christians. This initiative opened communication between the government and the various Church leaders with the aim to improve Christian-Muslim relations. The Episcopal Bishop of Rumbek joined the government in the Ministry of Foreign Affairs. But the intended dialogue did not develop, and each party continued to harbor suspicions regarding the intentions of the other. It was in this atmosphere that the Archbishop of Canterbury, Dr. George Carey, in 1995 declined a government invitation to visit Khartoum, and instead visited Southern Sudan identify with the suffering of the Christians in the civil war. This led to a deterioration of relations between the Anglican Church and the Sudanese government, and the rupture of diplomatic relations between the British government and the Republic of Sudan.

As tension between churches and the state increased, security forces were used to arrest and summon church leaders as the government deemed necessary. For example, in 1996 two Catholic priests were arrested in Dongola and charged with preaching on a Sunday service against Islam; they were later released. The Sudan Interior Church (SIC) Gideon theological building in Malut Southern Sudan was taken by the government on grounds that it was needed as a clinic, while it was actually used as a place for attending to the medical needs of government soldiers. The Roman Catholic Church Club was confiscated and turned into the government party's conference center. As Harris has observed, these were examples of seemingly gratuitous actions on the part of government officials, intended to violate the rights of Sudanese Christians and their leaders. Harris went on to

---

[212] Human rights Watch/Africa,op.cit., p. 209

cite the worse incidents of 1998-1999, when Father Hillary Boma, Chancellor of the Archdiocese of Khartoum, Father Lino Sebit, a Parish priest and twenty others were charged with attempted sabotage. Three of the accused according to unnamed sources died in custody.[213] These were but a few examples of local discrimination against churches and Christian leaders that confirmed Christian suspicions regarding the actual intentions of the government in its determination to Islamize Sudan.

8.7: CONCLUSION

The analysis that I have given in this chapter on the process of Islamization under the leadership of president of General al-Bashir, with particular reference to the 1998 constitution, leads to the conclusion that Sudan was being governed as if it were an Islamic state, although this is not explicitly acknowledged in the constitution. The latter says less that the government intends, although it includes coded references to an Islamic polity that permit the government to proceed as if Sudan were an Islamic state. The ambiguity that results has complicated the nature and conduct of church-state relations in contemporary Sudan, and the ambiguities have been aggravated by military conflicts of the civil war.

In this situation, the Sudanese churches have generally adopted a defensive position in respect of the government. It has been quick to make negative criticism, but has been reluctant to engage in critical dialogue with the government. To this degree, in my opinion the churches have failed to evolve alternative policies to those of the government, as we shall see in the next chapter have allowed themselves to become identified with the SPLM.

As Harris argued, "Christians are allowed much more freedom in Northern Sudan than in other Muslim countries such as Saudi Arabia where it is even against the law for Christians to worship together in

---

[213] Lillian Craig Harris, op.cit., p. 187

their own homes"[214]. Given the war situation, it is understandable that the Sudanese churches have given most of their energy and resources to supporting people in need, especially among the Internal Displaced Persons who have moved from the South to the IDP camps in the North. But while the churches have been very active in meeting the needs of their own peoples, they have been less concerned to engage the GoS, except by criticizing its policies. There has been a tendency for the churches to liken the government to Islamic regimes as exist in Iran, or formerly in Taliban-controlled Afghanistan, whereas the ambiguities to which I have referred to earlier in this book show that the Sudanese government, while committed Islamization, continues to allow a significant measure of freedom for the Sudanese churches. It is true that in any society there are always individuals who may abuse their positions and to victimize the helpless in order to enforce their intended policies and the government of Sudan cannot escape this criticism. But there is no clear policy as such to persecute the Church in Sudan.

---

[214] Lillina Craig Harris, in Joy and in Sorrow: Travel among Sudanese Christians, p. 17

NINE

SEARCHING FOR A VIABLE PEACE PROCESS

9.1: INTRODUCTION

The aim of this chapter is to review the political search for a peace settlement between the Government of Sudan and the SPLM. Looking at this challenge from the perspective of the South, the analysis offered in this chapter begins with the SPLM declaration in 1994 of its "solution modalities". These set out the policy lines on which SPLM was prepared to negotiate with other political parties in Sudan, including the GoS. Over the next two decades the search for a peace process continued in fits and starts. Contending views over the unity of Sudan, arguments over the right of self-determination, the relationship of religion and state, political suspicious and suspected conspiracies, and dispute over the development of natural resources – especially oil and water – combined to retard the process. Following the events of 11th September 2001, the United States began to take a constructive interest in finding peace in Sudan, partly to solve the danger of Sudan continuing to provide support for anti- American terrorism. This resulted in the Machakos initiative that brought the GoS and SPLM to the negotiation table under the auspices of the Inter-Governmental Authority of Development (IGADD) in East Africa. A peace treaty was signed at the beginning of 2005, on the basis of which a new constitutional framework was then worked out for Sudan.

It is not my intention to go into the details of any part of this long process, though, I shall return to the Machakos Agreement in the final chapter of this book. This chapter simply provides a brief overview of the process, to complete the analysis of the independent history of Sudan that I have offered in Part Three, and to provide a framework for the theological discussion that will follow in Part Four.

9.2: SPLM "SOLUTION MODALITIES" TO SUDAN CONFLICTS (1994 – 2003)

The federalist approach to the political constitution of Sudan that was endorsed in the 1972 Addis-Ababa Accord acknowledges the regional diversity of the country and the ethnic and religious pluralism of its peoples. It was on this basis that the 1973 constitution prohibited discrimination on the ground of religion, race, language or gender. It stressed Sudan's dual Arab and African identities and called for respect for Islam, Christianity and "noble Spiritual beliefs."

Following the president Numeiri"s annulment of the 1972 Accord and his step toward Islamizing the 1973 constitution, both of which contributed directly to the resumption of civil war in 1983, the SPLM proposed an approach to the Sudanese constitution that differed from both the Addis Accord and the GoS. They rejected the concept of fixed religion, linguistic or ethnic majorities and minorities. Against a religiously-defined state they called for a secular polity that would embrace a pluralist political system, arguing that the concept of a permanent Muslim majority automatically "isolates large segments of population form the political forces and therefore denies them basic rights and threatens the unity of the country[215]. The SPLM model would blend various languages into a unique pattern in which no single element would have hegemony, and the plurality of cultures and beliefs would be respected.

To achieve this end, the SPLM proposed a set of "solution

---

[215] Ann Mosely Lesch, op.cit., p.23

modalities" for the Sudan conflict. These included Political Settlement (PS), Armed Struggle (AS) and Popular Negotiations (PN). These approaches apply to all liberation movements but vary according their situations.

With regards to peace programs the SPLM proposed three simultaneous tracks. Firstly, it accepted that there should be a dialogue with the GoS, aimed at finding a Negotiated Political Settlement. These negotiations took place through the mediation of IGAD, the Inter-Governmental Agency for Drought and Desertification, and were thus known as the IGAD peace process. Secondly, the SPLM entered into membership of the National Democratic Alliance (NDA), and association of mainly Northern political parties and military groups opposed to the NIFE regime. The NDA advocated a return to the pluralist vision of Sudan bases on the 1972 Accord and 1973 constitution, and the right of self-determination for the South. The SPLM therefore, considered the NDA as a potential alternative government that might replace the National Islamic Front.

In the Koka Dam Accord of 1986, the SLPM and DUP reached an agreement on pluralist model. This was re-affirmed when the NDA launched its military coup against Numeiri in 1989, and again in Asmara Accord of 1995 that endorsed the right for self-determination for the people of the South. That provision was important as it created a new mutual understanding between the North and the South, at least among opponents of the NIF government, under which the Northerners acknowledged Southern fears that reached back to the 1947 Juba conference. Muslim signatories of the Asmara Accord accepted that the right for self-determination would be a way to bolster unity, and agreed: "If the North does not abided by the agreed upon programs during the transitional period, then the South can exercise the right for self-determination and can terminate the union." Although the NDA and SPLM failed to reach a consensus on the inclusion of other marginalized areas such as Nuba Mountains and Ingessena Hills, the 1995 Accord recognized the ethnic pluralist model as the only viable option for the survival of Sudan as united state. Secular pluralism was articulated as the ideological alternative to the NIF model of a state in which unity was coerced under the imposition of a single religious identity in which civil society would be restricted, and all political life conformed to an Islamic image.

The third major SPLM policy is Peace Through Development (PTD). This applied to the areas that, in the civil war, were under SPLM control, the regions that were called the "New Sudan" including Bahr al-Ghazal, Equatoria, Upper Nile, South Kordofan and Southern Blue Nile. Together these regions sustained roughly one third of the total population of Sudan, some 10 million out of the national total of 32 million[216] at the time. It was clearly the responsibility of the SPLM to provide a wide range of social services for this sizeable population, whose needs were immediate and could not be left until peace had been achieved.

9.3: THE DEVELOPMENT OF THE PEACE PROCESS BETWEEN THE GOS AND SPLM

As soon as they come to power in 1989, the NIF government opened consultative meetings with Southerners within those areas of the South that were still under GoS control. This came to be identified as the "Peace Within" policy, and was conducted with a break-away faction of the SPLAM/A, known as the Nasir Faction (NF). This resulted in the Frankfurt Declaration of January 1992, in which the GoS formally acknowledged the right of the Southern peoples for self-determination. This was the first time that any central government had formally acknowledged this right since the creation of Sudan as an independent state.

SLPM responded to this Declaration by proposing a number of options, including the reconstruction of a united Sudan on the basis of a confederation of sovereign states[217]. But at the first Abuja Conference, May-June 1992, the Nigerian government and the OAU observers pressured the SPLM and the NF to accept self-determination

---

[216] Sudan People Liberation Movement, "Solution Modalities in the Sudan conflicts"(unpublished), (1994 -2002), p.2
[217] Douglas H. Johnson, 2003, op. cit., p. 174

as their common objective in negotiation with the GoS. This had the positive result of uniting the Southern groups despite their ideological differences. On the other hand, the government delegation now rejected the principle of self – determination which they had earlier accepted in 1992 with the Nasir faction. That raised the question of government seriousness to peace process. The Nigerian government continued to try to take the negotiation forward as the second Abuja conference in May 1993. But the deadlock over the issues of religion and state remained unresolved and the negotiation failed.

In 1993 a new peace initiation was launched by IGAD involving the states that bordering Sudan-Eritrea, Ethiopia, Uganda and Kenya-each of which was being adversely affected by the war. A declaration of principles (DoP) Drafted by Ethiopia and revised by Eritrea, proposed self-determination for the South through a referendum, or a secular government for a united Sudan. The DoP was adopted by the IGAD mediators as the bases for negotiations between GoS and SPLM and other Southern factions that were latter on included in the peace process at the time.

IGAD summoned the parties to the conflict to a round table discussion in 1994. The talks broke up, as the Sudan government rejected the proposed right to self-determination, and insisted that it had the constitutional right, as well as the religious duty, to Islamize the whole of the Sudan. Clearly the GoS placed its reliance on an eventual military victory over the SPLA,[218] while in the meantime exploiting internal divisions which had weakened the SPLM. It was not until 1997, when the government military position was precarious, that it accepted the DoP as one of many bases on which dialogue could take place.

In 1999 Egypt and Libya advanced another proposal for peace in Sudan that differed from the DoP. Both countries had a vision for Arab unity and wanted to form a union with the Sudan. This would have given them a powerful voice as three Arab states on the African continent both among the Arab states and the OAU. Following this line of thought, it was clear that Egypt and Libya agreed with GoS

---

[218] ibid., p.174

in resisting any settlement between the North and the South that might result in separation. In addition, Egypt's dependence on Nile waters gave it further reason to support the unity of Sudan, for fear that cessation of the South would increase the number of independent African states through which Nile flows.

The Egyptian-Libyan proposal contained three provisions: a cease-fire, the unity of Sudan, and an end to hostile propaganda between the NDA and GoS. NDA leadership accepted the proposal and attempts were made to incorporate it to IGADD peace process, despite the fact that its rejection of the principle of self-determination was at odds with the DoP that had already been widely accepted by all parties except the GoS. The SPLM was therefore ambiguous about Egyptian-Libyan initiative and eventually rejected it. This provoked anger among the other NDA members who split into rival factions.

By 2001 Egypt and Libya put forward a revised proposal that contained nine points. According to these the unity of Sudan remained sacrosanct, but concessions were made in terms of citizenship rights and decentralization policy. As with the previous proposal, however, the new one fell short of dealing with the central issues of religion and state, and self-determination as set out in DOP.

In the face of the repeated failure of African and Arab initiatives to develop a sustainable peace process, the United States became actively involved in 2002. It had already been exerting hostile political and economic pressure on the Sudan government through the late 1990s. The presence of Osama Bin Laden in Sudan between 1991 and 1996, and the involvement of Sudan in terrorist activities persuaded the US to add the Sudan to the list of terrorist states. The US government was also sensitive to domestic Christian and anti-slavery lobbies that were well represented in congress and support the cause of Christians in the South of Sudan[219]. The beginning of the development of oil resources in south also drew attention of the international community, especially the US, to the Sudan situation. France, Germany and later the United Kingdom now persuaded the US to develop a more constructive

---

[219] Duglas H. Johnson, 2003, op.cit

policy toward the Sudan, and at the same time pressured the SPLM to negotiate with Sudan government.

The United States (US) intervention marked a turning point in search for peace in Sudan. The events of September 11, 2001, and the war against terrorism brought the US government to recognize the urgency of the need for a settlement of the civil war. Furthermore, in the light of September 11, 2001, the government of Sudan decided to cooperate with US in the war against terrorism. It was able to provide intelligence that was vital to US security networks. President Bush appointed Senator Danforth as his special envoy for peace in Sudan. The senator initiated series of consultative meetings in early 2002 that produced developments that were conducive to a resumption of the IGAD peace process. The peace talks were resumed in June 2002 at Machakos, Kenya.

The Machakos peace process has involved facilitators from Britain, Norway and US. The Machakos protocol, signed on July 2002, set out a framework for peace building that produced a new optimism. Give and take was a positive recognition of each party's seriousness on the issue of self-determination and religious state[220]. On the other hand, the Sudan government conceded the right to self-determination for South; on the other the SPLM withdrew its demand for the secularization of the whole of Sudan. The option for unity, which is part of the deal, was yet to be detailed together with other issues in the proceeding rounds of talks.

Parallel to the Machakos peace talks, the Sudan government and the SSLM, headed by Dr. Wal Duany, signed a political charter on 21st July 2002 that recognized the right to self-determination for the South, and called for a comprehensive peace settlement that would include other Sudanese forces such as the South Sudan Democratic Forum, which were not part of the Machakos peace process.

The Machakos initiative came to a conclusion with Naivasha peace Agreement of January 2005, drawn up between the GoS and SPLM. This retains the system of plural states as defined in the

[220] GoS and SPLM, Machakos Protocol – Framework for negotiations to resolve Sudanese conflicts (unpublished), July 2002

1998 constitution. In addition, it restores decentralized power to a Southern Sudanese government (SPLM) as was provided by the 1973 constitution, with the difference that the Southern government has increased economic and military powers, and shared responsibility in all the powers reserved to the central government. Under this arrangement the South will operate a secular system, while the North retains its Islamic orientation. Non-Muslims who choose to remain in the North will therefore remain under *Sharî_'a* Law, but this will have no competence in the South, except for the personal affairs for Muslim who choose to live there. The Principle of self-determination for the South is accepted in the provision that is made for a referendum in the South after six and a half years.

9.4: THE ANALYSIS OF SUDAN COUNCIL OF CHURCHES/NEW SUDAN COUNCIL OF CHURCHES TOWARD THE PEACE PROCESS

In this section we examine the contribution of Sudanese churches to the peace process, with special reference to the document issued in March 2002 entitled "*let My People choose the Right to self-determination for the Southern people and other marginalized Areas*" commonly referred to as the Right to self-determination (RSD) document.

The RSD was issued in the names of all the member churches of both the Sudan Council of Churches (SCC) and the New Sudan Council of Church (CNSCC). The SCC came into existence in 1972, following the Addis Ababa Accord, and, with the exception of the All Africa Conference of Churches, it is the most ecumenically representative body in Africa. Its member churches include; Roman Catholic Church (RCC), Episcopal Church of the Sudan (ECS), Presbyterian Church of the Sudan (PCoS), Sudan Presbyterian Evangelical Church (SPEC), Coptic Orthodox Church (COC), Ethiopian Orthodox Church (EOC) Greek Orthodox Church (GOC), Armenian Apostolic Church (AAC), Sudan Pentecostal Church (SPC), Sudan Interior Church (SIC), African Inland Church (AIC), and Sudan Church of Christ (SCC). With the resumption of the civil war in 1983, the churches in the SPLM-controlled areas of Southern Sudan were isolated from the SCC in Khartoum, and as a result they formed the New Sudan Council of Churches (NSCC) in 1989, based in Nairobi. The NSCC includes the Roman Catholic Church, the Episcopal Church, the Presbyterian Church, the African Inland Church, the Sudan Interior mission, and the Pentecostal churches. Despite the logistical difficulties of being based in different countries, and not being allowed to meet either in Khartoum or in SPLM-controlled areas, the two councils have succeeded in maintaining an effective dialogue between themselves and have met in various parts of Africa and Europe. It was through this process of consultation that they jointly produced the RSD document as their contribution to peace process that has been discussed in the earlier sections of this chapter.

The SCC/NSCC set their advocacy of the right of self-determination in context of the struggle against injustice that has marred the history of independent Sudan, at the cost of immense human suffering in the South. It is important to note, however, that the SCC/NSCC does not propose a resolution of these problems in terms of separating the South from the rest of Sudan. On the contrary, it argues that "In a country where justice prevails, there will be no incentive or reason for separation or fragmentation." It notes, however, that Southern peoples have paid dearly for maintaining national unity in the past, and that the only ground for unity in the future is justice for all. Thus, RSD advocates a peace process that will liberate marginalized peoples from all aspects of oppression that cause them suffering. The document cites South Africa and Namibia as examples of African countries where conflicts has been resolved without national partition. On the other hand, it rejects the policy of using the principles of *Uti Possidetis* - i.e. the retention of pre-independence colonial borders – as a reason for suppressing RSD among peoples who have been excluded from national decision-making, as has been the case with the Southern Sudanese from the national decision-making, as has been the case with the Southern Sudanese from the national independence. Citing the case of the Eritrean war, the document points out that "under certain conditions that principle (i.e. *Uti Possidetis*) could be ignored".

After reviewing historical steps toward self-determination, the

RSD document recognizes that there is a difference between statement and action: "Claiming RSD is one thing, and an important thing at that. However, working for RSD in a systematic, programmatic and consistent manner is quite another. The South is today called upon to pursue the latter course in terms of developing a strategy that combines "a Vision, Mission and programs". The SCC/NSCC notes that a greater degree of public awareness now reflects the essential elements of RSD in terms of humans' rights, the rule of law, humanitarian principles, good governance, democracy, etc. than at any time in the history of the Sudanese Republic. It emphasizes that the churches are ready to play their role alongside other institutions of civil society to develop educational programs aimed to promote regional and international support for RSD: "The church should work with civil society and civil authority to promote good governance in which justice and human rights are respected".

Fundamental to the SCC/NSCC approach is that RSD must be exercised by the people - "our suffering people" – rather than choices and decisions being made for them by distant elites. To quote from the RSD document: "We believe that nobody is wise or knowledgeable enough to make choices for them (i.e. the marginalized peoples). The historical evidence is clear enough. The elites on the previous occasions concluded Agreements on their behalf. Systems have been imposed on them (i.e. marginalized) but they have not lasted. Current attempts to impose decisions from above are not the correct recipe for a just and lasting peace. The SCC/NSCC therefore opts for a "people–to-people" an approach that works from the bottom up, rather than top down, and will prepare the people to exercise the right of self-determination in the enactment of a referendum law[221].

The RSD document is broadly in line with the SPLM policy and its approach to peace making. Therefore, there have not been tensions or conflicts between the SCC/NSCC and SPLM, as there have between the churches and the GoS. This is not to deny that there are

---

[221] Paulino Lukudu and Joseph Marona, " Let My People Choose" The Statement of the Sudanese Churches on the Right of Self-Determination for Southern Sudan and other Marginalised Areas, p. 2-4

no differences of opinions between the SCC/NSCC and the SPLM. The RSD document emphasized that peace making must be rooted in the active participation of local communities and civil society, and thus be constructed "from the bottom up", whereas SPLM/A as a military movement needed to develop an administrative culture that comes from the people themselves. This would dissolve another latent tension between the SPLM's ideological secularity and the religious cultures of the Southern Sudanese peoples. It may be concluded, therefore, that the SCC/NSCC support the SPLM's approach to the peace process in terms of the political future of the South, but wants to develop a more contextual approach to sustainable peace building.

9.5: CONCLUSION

This chapter brought our review of Sudanese political history since national independence in 1956 up to date with the signing of the Naivasha Peace Agreement of 2005. It has shown that that the problems facing independent Sudan were, in many respects, a continuation of the unfinished business of the Anglo-Egyptian Condominium. Successive central governments have attempted to build the unity of Sudan on policies of Arabisation and Islamisation. These have been consistently resisted by the South Sudanese people in favor of self-determination, federalism and secularism. Neither the North nor the South has been willing to break the unity of Sudan, but it has been extremely difficult to find a way of living together. In the absence of political solutions to this problems, civil wars have continued with only a brief respite between 1972 and 1983 until the cease fire of 2002, and the then Naivasha Peace Accord.

As we have already noted that the Addis Ababa Agreement failed on Account of Numeiri's decision to adopt an Islamization policy under pressure from the NIF. This critical decision, that re-ignite the civil war, demonstrates that Sudanese political decisions have been made at the levels of ideology and political parties, with little or no reference to grass root communities and civil society organizations. This failure raises questions about the nature of Comprehensive Peace Agreement

(CPA) negotiated under the terms of Machakos Protocol that again has been negotiated exclusively at the level of the GoS and SPLM. However, as distinct from the 1972 Accord, its sustainability will depend on popular assent since a referendum has been promised for the people of the South. A critical question, therefore, for the future of Sudan was the degree to which South Sudanese would give or withhold their consent to live in a united Sudan. This will depend on many factors, among which development of a sustainable civil society will be essential.

In Sudanese society, in which religion plays such an important factor, the building of civil society cannot exclude the role of religion. Even the SPLM, which is now developing into the government of Southern Sudan, accepts that religion has important role to play in secular state. It is to the challenge of articulating a religious approach to peace building in Sudan that we turn to, in Part Four.

CHAPTER
TEN

TOWARD A CUK (PEOPLE'S) CONTEXTUAL THEOLOGY

10.1: INTRODUCTION

Part One to Three of this book have examined the historical development of Sudan form the Anglo-Egyptian Condominium up to 2005, as the framework in which church-state relations have been examined from the perspective of Christian-Muslim relations. The problem that has been examined is that of finding a durable political solution to historic conflicts between the Southern and Northern regions of Sudan that, for the greater part of Sudan's existence as an independent state, have been the cause of civil war, excepting a period of peace from 1972 to 1983. The peace arrangements of those years proved unsustainable, partly due to the central government's resumption of an aggressive policy Islamization, and partly due to the failure of the political elites of the North and the South to create a culture of peace-building that involved the general populations. The Naivasha Peace Agreement of 2005 gave Sudan a new opportunity of building a durable peace and presents the Sudanese with the question: will the Naivasha Accord suffer the same fate as the Addis Ababa Agreement or will the peoples of the Sudan this time find ways of sustaining peace by building a culture of reconciliation between the North and the South?

It is to this question that we turn in Part Four of the book, in which it will be argued that a lasting peace in Sudan needs to include the dimension of inter-religious reconciliation and co-operation among Muslims, Christians and those who adhere to the traditional religions of the Nilotic Africans of Southern Sudan. The aim of this final part of the book is to propose a basis for Christian-Muslim relations that is rooted in the religious realities of the peoples of the Sudan, and find its contextual integrity by developing indigenous African concepts of the peace and inter-religious understanding. The Roman Catholic theologian, Hans Kung, famously observed: "there will be no peace among nations until there is peace among religions[222]. My intention here, is to apply this maxim to the challenge of post-Naivasha Sudan, and propose a contextual foundation for an indigenous Christian-Muslim dialogue for reconciliation and peace-building in the Sudan.

The discussion in Part Four builds on the Right of Self-Determination (RSD) Document of the Sudan Council of Churches and the New Sudan Council of Churches that was analyzed in the previous chapter. The statements calls for a strategy of peace- making that comprises the three elements of "Vision, Mission and programs". Part Four will therefore be structured in two chapters: the first will elaborate the vision of Sudanese contextual theology that draws of the resources of Sudan's three religions traditions – indigenous African, Christian, and Muslim – and integrates Christian and Islamic understanding of mission and *Da`wa:* the second will address the important issue of peace-making programs, based on some empirical examples of practical Christian-Muslim dialogue.

10.2: TOWARD A SUDANESE CONTEXTUAL THEOLOGY

I begin by making the case for a contextual theology that addresses the political realities and cultural needs of the South Sudanese people. The historical parts of this book have shown that the regions and peoples that now comprise South Sudan have endured nearly two centuries of exploitation and colonization from the *Turkiya* period of

---

[222] Paul F. Knitter, No Other Names? A critical Survey of Christian Attitudes Toward the World Religions 2003, p. 126

the Turco-Egyptians, followed by the *Mahdīya* and the Anglo-Egyptian Condominium up to 1956, when the governance of independent Sudan was handed to the Arab Muslim Northern Sudanese who continued to rule the South through policies of Arabisation and Islamization that Southerners experienced as a form of internal colonialism. It is against this background that a contextual theology for Sudan has to reaffirm the cultural and social values of Southern Sudan as well as those of the North, and must address the need for a durable peace following the five decades of civil war, within the framework of religiously-plural state.

First and foremost is the need to restore the human dignity of the Southern peoples, who have been oppressed, enslaved economically deprived, and politically excluded from participating in the building of a modern constitutional Sudanese state. Secondly, contextual theology must retrieve and re-affirm cultural values and ways of life that have been eroded by the imposition of other cultural-religious systems: i.e Islam that has been progressively imposed by the Northerners since the time of the Funj Sultanate, and Christianity that was introduced by the Western missionaries during the Anglo-Egyptian Condominium in the first half of the 20th Century. Finally, Southerners need to gain the rights of self-determination (RSD) enshrined in various UN declarations. These elements are embraced in the RSD document of the Sudan Council of Churches (SCC) and the New Sudan Council of churches but the document itself does not include a theological perspective. It is this omission that I seek to rectify in chapter.

The foregoing study of the history of Sudan shows that religion is an inalienable part of Sudanese culture; and Sudanese society is religiously plural, comprising traditional religion, Islam and Christianity. Contextual Sudanese theology (whether traditional, Muslim or Christian) not only has to take account of this plurality of religions, but also has to engage it in creative ways. In particular, contextual theology has to resolve three problems in the religious history of Sudan.

Firstly, it must deal with the historical fact that Islam and Christianity were each introduced by outsiders – Arab Muslims and Western Christian missionaries – neither of whom understood and respected the religious traditions of the indigenous Nilotic African peoples (Bari, Dinka, Nuer, Shilluk, etc.), and assumed that their own forms of Islam and Christianity had a universal validity that could be imposed on indigenous peoples. Neither Arab Islam nor Western Christianity was disposed to acknowledging the validity of the other, or of African traditional religion, in a religiously plural society. Religious pluralism, will be argued in this chapter, as a condition of a durable contextual theology in Sudan.

Secondly the political analysis of Sudan's history shows that Islam and Christianity have, in different periods of Sudanese history, been manipulated by ruling political elites for their own purposes. In the period of Anglo-Egyptian Condominium, Western Christian missionaries worked hand-in-hand with the colonial administration in the separate development of the South, and used Christianity as a tool of regional development. This created a legacy of mistrust among Northern Muslims, who perceived the missionaries as being hostile to Sudanese independence and united Sudan. It was this that led General Abound to introduce the 1963 Missionary Act that expelled foreign missionaries, and forced the Sudanese churches to Africanize in the sense of taking responsibility for themselves. From the perspective of contextual theology, however, this did not improve the situation, but simply changed the religion that was being imposed on the South, opening the region to the progressive Islamization as the Government's means of controlling the peoples and the resources of the South. In each case religion has been used for political ends. It will be argued that Contextual theology has to rescue the religions of Sudan from such abuses, and from the negative competition against each other that such political manipulation has aggravated, if not caused.

Thirdly, contextual theology has to deal with the reality that there are increasingly large numbers of Sudanese who at the time, recognizing the dangers of co-opting religion into the service of the state, have turned to the alternative of a secular state on the Western model that privatizes religion to the sphere of the individual. Evidence of this can be found among some Northern Muslims and in the South it has become the operational ideology of the SPLM in its advocacy of secularism as the constitutional basis of the so called New Sudan.

A contextual theology for Sudan should not seek to turn the clock back on the growth of secularity in Sudanese culture, but needs to take advantage of the freedom that secularity offers for new kinds of religious identity and co-operation in a society in which religions are equal and equally respected.

Politicized religion and ideological secularism combine to place Sudanese contextual theology on the horns of a dilemma. Religion, on the one hand, is an inseparable part of indigenous culture, but has been clearly exploited as a means of control and destruction.

Secularism, on the other, has been pursued as an ideological alternative to religion, and while it seeks to rescue the state from politicized religion, it does so at the threat to the religious values that are deeply rooted in Sudanese cultures. Contextual theology therefore needs to articulate an understanding of religion that (1) affirms indigenous religious values, (2) accepts that Christianity and Islam are both represented by large sections of the national population, (3) opposes the political exploitation of religion(s), (4) resists the erosion of religious values under the impact of militarized secular ideology, (5) offers a way to peace through reconciliation, that gives priority to real human needs ("people –to-people"), and (6) develops constitution theory and structures from bottom up, rather than from top down.

The top-down approach to the unity of the Sudanese peoples in a single state has been exemplified in the constitutional history of Sudan since independence. Successive governments have attempted to impose policies of unification through the national constitution backed up by military force.

While accepting that a political, constitutional approach to national unity in Sudan is necessary, this book argues that it needs to be complemented by inter-religious support that engages the people, if diplomatic and political solutions are to be sustained. The aim of this chapter, therefore, is to propose the building blocks of a contextual theology that draws on the faith traditions of the three religions –traditional African, Islam and Christianity. The starting point is the concept of "covenant" that is found in all three religious traditions – a covenant that binds people to the Almighty and to each other.

10.3: COVENANT THEOLOGY OF THE NUER

The present author comes from the Nuer people, and it is from the perspective of the Nuer traditions that this chapter is written. In the context of the political history of Sudan where the different ethnic groups that make up the national population have been torn apart through the long decades of civil war, Nuer culture offers an inclusive understanding of the "people". The Nuer language has two words for "people". *Cuk*, (singular *cok)* means "peoples" in the inclusive sense in contrast to the word *Naath* that denotes "people" in the particular sense of the Nuer themselves. As the latter term is used by the Nuer to identify themselves separately from others, and to infer sense of ethnic distinction,[223] *cok/cuk* denotes the wider human community to which they belong, all of whom – including the Nuer – it likens to small black ants in terms of their relationship with the almighty power of *Kuoth* (God). The metaphor serves to make an important point in the Nuer worldview: although differences between different ethnic, linguistic, social or religious groups are significant from a horizontal human perspective, they are insignificant in a vertical perspective, seen, as it were, form the perspective of God. The Nuer expression, *kɔndial labnɛ gaat Kuoth* (" we are all like little ants in the sight of God")[224] explains that the Nuer see ants as helpless, and is the same way the Nuer believe that God sees the whole humanity in their diversity without distinction. Another Nuer expression state that human beings are "foolish in the sight of God" (*Naath kɛ däär wang Kouth).*

This brings us to the Nuer understanding of *Kuoth.* The Nuer believe that God is the Creator (*cäärk)* of all that exists. *Cäärk* is also the word that the Nuer language uses for "creation". The fact that Creator and creation are denoted by the same word is of great significance in Nuer belief. Creation does not spring form nothing (*ex nihilo),* but is

---

[223] P. P. Howell, <u>A Manual of Nuer Law</u>, p.7
[224] E. Evans – Pritchard, <u>Nuer Religion</u>, pp. 11-12

understood to come from God, as an extension of God's own reality. This means that creation itself is infused by God's being, and this is expressed through the Nuer belief in a spiritual cosmology, creation being full of spirits that are understood as being part of *Kuoth*. The Nuer understanding of *Kuoth* includes the whole range of spiritual beings: ancestral spirits, household spirits, talking spirits, sky spirits, and earth spirits[225]. It is through theses spiritual intermediaries that are inseparable form *Kuoth* himself that creation is sustained, and it is to the spirits as intermediaries, therefore, that the Nuer turn when they address *Kuoth* in worship. God is found everywhere, in every culture, and meets individuals in his own ways. God's power therefore extends to all peoples (*cuk*), God protects all people, and God embraces every human being in justice and equality. To express the individual quality of human experience of God, the Nuer language uses the Word *Raan* meaning "person as distinct from "people"[226]. As God relates equally to all "peoples" *(Cuk),* every person (*Raan*) has a direct relationship with God.

It is as a consequence of this Nuer understanding of God that the Nuer believe in equality of all human beings. Nuer religion treats all human beings equally, and insists that all human beings respect each other. Each person is responsible and accountable to God, the guardian of morality, for his/her actions.

Nuer religion expresses the relationship between God and the people through the concept of "covenant" (*Nguöt/Ngut*) that denotes an inviolable bond both between the creator and all creation, and between all peoples[227]. *Nguöt/Ngut* is made known through revelation and prophet- hood in Nuer belief. The Nuer concept of prophets is both particular and universal because the Nuer accepts that all these prophets are genuine messengers from God. Prophets may receive revelations in a variety of ways including dreams. However the revelations are received,

---

[225] Douglas H Johnson, 1994, op.cit., p. 105-106
[226] E. E Evans – Pritchard, po.cit., p. 7
[227] Wal Duany, Wal Duany, Neither Palaces Nor Prisons: The constitution of Order Among the Nuer, p.46

they are considered to be authentic and valid for the particular people among from whom a prophet comes.

The role of the prophet is to make clear to the people what *Nguöt*, or covenant, requires of them of their moral lives. *Nguöt* means rules and regulations (laws) that the Nuer apply across all aspects of their lives, as communities and individual. For example the Nuer customary laws are referred to as *Nguöt Fangak* (a district where all Nuer met for the first time in 1943 to discuss and formulated their Customary Laws). This includes rules that are agreed and applied by the Nuer to punish the wrong doers who have broken the covenant, and rituals by which those who have committed evil can restore themselves to covenantal relationship with God and their communities. In this respect *Nguöt* (literally "to cut") regulate sacrifices that are to be made to *Kuoth* as means of moral and spiritual restitution.

It follows that *Nguöt* are especially important in terms of conflict resolution and reconciliation, providing an agreed body of rituals that bind people together in their relationship with God. This is evident in the importance of the late 19th century Prophet Ngundɛng who stands in the Nuer tradition as the great prophet of peace and reconciliation. Before Ngundɛng, the Nuer prophets and priests were mainly concerned with the welfare of the Nuer community in particular. Some of the prophets carried out raids on other communities that had caused instability with their neighbours. However, when Ngundɛng came he instituted principles of compensation that were intended to reduce conflicts and created harmony among the people. For example he forbade young men to carry spears to dances place, and urged the Nuer to stop raiding their neighbours, thus, reducing instability. Secondly, he involved representatives of the Nuer and their neighboring tribes in the building of a pyramid-shaped mound as a symbol of peace building. The shrines of the spirits and divinities of all the tribes were brought to the Mound, as a sign of curtailing the escalation of the conflicts among the Nuer and their neighboring communities. Those who brought mud and ashes to maintain the Mound became part of a moral community that extended beyond the Nuer society. As Johnson has shown in his discussion of Ngundɛng sacrifices, they were intended to have universal effect, ensuring the wellbeing not just of the Nuer but of all the neighboring *cuk* (communities). In this way the building of the Mound helped Ngundɛng to expand his influence beyond his ethnic and social limits[228]. The Dinka, Annuak and other people came to the Mound, and by adhering to Ngundɛng's teaching, they combined faithfulness to their own particular traditions with acceptance of a universal order. Ngundɛng received revelations mostly by night and he related these revelations to the people in form; of songs, unlike ordinary songs or poems, which men construct for themselves when herding in the grazing grounds, To this day these spiritual songs are memorized and used for prayers by the Nuer and their neighbours, The singing of hymns to the spirits of God are essential in keeping with the religious character of the rites and enhance the community wellbeing[229].

The Nuer use the traditional system of reconciliation that involves two important functionaries known as *Kuär Muon* ("Earthly Custodian") and *Wud Hok* ("Cattle Custodian"). They mediate between parties in dispute, the one having responsibility for conflicts that pertain to the earth, while the other deals with issues of ownership. *Kuär Muon* has priestly power derived from a divinity referred to as *Kuoth Rieng* ("God of the flesh"), while *Kuär Muon's* responsibilities are to control the earth and its productivity and to promote the welfare of those who live on and by the soil. He is also responsible to mediate between disputants in conflicts concerning rights in land, grazing, and water, and cases of homicide – the latter being understood as polluting the soil with blood.

This explains why *Kuär Muon* has an essential role in the ritual of atonement and reconciliation among the Nuer customs. He has no political authority to compel the warring parties to come to agreement, and commands no military force that can coerce parties in conflict against their will. His ability to reconcile derives solely from his moral and spiritual authority. The *Kuär Muon's* authority derives from his association with the land, and extends to all the people because they

---

[228] Douglas H Johnson, 1994, op.cit., p. 105
[229] E. Evans – Pritchard, op.cit. p. 123

depend equally on all that the land produces. By reason with the association with the land, *Kuär Muon* has the ability to curse and ban people, and traditionally uses these powers to intervene, For instance, he can interpose himself between the contestants in an actual fight and draw a line on earth, which no ordinary person would dare to pass[230].

The implementation of reconciliation involved the restoration of the traditional system of justice under both the spiritual and community leaders. The elders and community custodians are responsible for the enforcement of *Nguöt* within their covenant, and the creation of specialized youth groups known as *Bunaam* to safeguard the covenant. *Bunaam* is a newly established institution in the Nuer governing system mainly in the eastern Nuer, but plays a very important role in conflict resolution. Religious and community leaders take the role of explaining to the community the changes that have taken place.

One other important element in connection with the Nuer religious beliefs that have bearing on the covenant is the oath, which is also sworn before the *Kuär Muon.* There are two forms of oath in the Nuer traditional system: *kueg kuil* or *käp tang* ("to hold the spear-shaft") which is used in a variety of circumstances, while *mäth* ('to drink") is the form often employed in cases of homicide. The taking of an oath is collective process by the accused party. In the former ceremony both the accuser and the accused are expected to take part. In the latter, were there is no known accused, those suspected and all their kinsmen are required to participate and shoulder the responsibility[231].

Reconciliation according to the Nuer *Nguöt* can therefore be said to comprise five elements: First, the desire of disputants to resolve their differences; second, the authority of the mediator; third, the search for agreement through full and free discussion among the disputants; and fourth, the willingness of all parties to give way to the chiefs, elders and opinion leaders without loss of dignity; and oaths[232].

Against this background, I want to propose the term *"Cuk"* Theology" to express the religious insights of the Nuer people and

---

[230] ibid., p. 43
[231] ibid., p. 219
[232] ibid., p. 28

other Nilotic African communities who follow the peace-making teaching of the Prophet Ngundɛng. It provides the foundation for a contextual theology of reconciliation that affirms the religious pluralism of Sudan, accepting all religions as valid, without ignoring the particular characteristics of each. *Cuk* Theology is not concerned with comparative religion, but with the search of humanity dignity that respects the ethical values of all peoples, with the aim of resolving injustice and religious exploitation.

Since *Cuk* Theology turns on the issue of covenant (*Nguöt*), it offers a basis of common understanding with Islam and Christianity in Sudan, these religions also having concepts of covenant at the heart of their theologies. In the following sections, therefore, we shall examine the understanding of covenant among Muslims and Christians in Sudan

10.4: COVENANT IN ISLAM (MITHÂQ; `AHD)

The *Qur'an* uses two words for "covenant": *Mithâq* (from *Wathiqa* = to trust), denoting a "trust" between two or more parties, and `ahd (from `ahida = to bind), meaning a "contract" that binds the parties. While the two terms occur about equally in the *Qur'an*, and are often used interchangeably in Muslim writings, a distinction can be drawn between them.

Mithâq is the more comprehensive of the two terms. It is used in relation to God, and denotes the covenant that God initiates. It occurs twice in the *Qur'an* to denote the concept of God's primordial "covenant" with all prophets: "When God made covenant with Prophets, He said, "Behold that which I have given you of the Scripture and knowledge... Do you agree, and will you take up My burden?" They answered, we agree.' God said, "Then bear ye witness. I shall be a witness with you" (3:81; 33:7). `Ahd is used more in relation to the particular with whom God creates covenant by sending prophets to them – for example, by Abraham (2:124) – where the focus is more evidently upon human response to God's covenant in terms of obedience to its laws.

It is therefore seems legitimate to understand *Mithâq* as denoting

God's initiative of establishing a relationship of "trust" with all human communities through the concept of prophets sent to them as witnesses of God's truth. This correlates with the *Qur'anic* statement that humankind accepted the "trust" (*amâna*)[233] that God offered but which the heavens the earth and the mountains refused (33:72/3). If *Mithâq* emphasizes the divine initiative in covenant making, `*ahd* tends to emphasize the human response of obedience to God through observance of the laws that give ethical substance to God's covenant.

According to the *Qur'an* it is through the prophets, with who God established His primordial covenant, that covenants with particular people are struck, and ethical principles are established in the form of moral laws that the people agree to follow. The *Qur'an* teaches that God has sent prophets to every human community among the descendants of Adam, and that no human community has passed away without a prophet having come to it, bringing divine revelation and establishing a covenant between the God and the people. If this corresponds with the Nuer, belief that *kuoth* calls up prophets from every people, the Qur'an also, like the Nuer, teaches that all the prophets receive genuine divine revelation because all revelation comes exclusively from God. It follows, therefore, that the *Qur'an* also, believes that all the revelations received by the prophets convey essentially the same message: *Islâm*, or "peace" in the active sense of "making peace" through active "submission" or "surrender" to the will of god as revealed through the messages of the prophets. "Seek they (i.e. the prophets and the peoples to whom they are sent) other than the religion of God, when unto God submitted whatsoever is in the heavens and the earth?" (3:83). The Prophet Muhammad is held to be the final prophet, "the seal of the Prophets" (33:40). It is through Muhammad, therefore, that Muslims believe that God renewed His covenant for a final time, restating what had been contained in all previous covenants, and it is to this covenant that Muslim commit themselves in living faithful lives of obedience to God.

In terms of how this final covenant could be understood in relation to the challenges of reconciliation and peace-building in Sudan, it is

---

[233] M. R. BB, J. H. Kramers, E Elevi-Provencal, J. Schacht, Encyclopedia of Islam, p. 255

important to pay attention to the exegetical procedure and conclusions of the Sudanese Muslim religious thinker, Mahmud Taha, who has already been mentioned in terms of his opposition to Numeiri's policy was an expression of the very different way in which he (Taha) interpreted the Qur'an. In his book The Second Message of Islam he delineated a new approach to Medina periods of Muhammad's ministry. The former, he argued set out principles of Islam, and of God's covenant with human kind: peace, justice, equality, human freedom, and human dignity. By the same argument, the *Medinan* verses applied *Meccan* principles to the degree that was possible, but this could only be achieved in part since the fuller realization of the *Meccan* principles required a higher stage of social evolution of human community. Having made this distinction, Taha asserted that *Meccan* verses, in terms of their legal authority if not their moral significance, on grounds that revelations that belong to the later years of Muhammad's ministry abrogate those that came earlier. As a result the *Shari_a* was based on the *Medinan* revelations, and thus, gave greater authority to that which was historically contingent over that which has eternal value. This was, he argued, the wrong way round, and had led the *Shari'a* to under-represent the *Qur'anic* values of equality, religious freedom and human dignity. To rectify this he proposed that the *Meccan* verses should not be considered to have been abrogated in terms of their legal authority; rather;, their legal authority was temporally suspended until such time as human society had evolved to the state in which they could be implemented in accordance with human and social will. This is what he means by "the Second Message of Islam": the "first message" was the attempt to implement the eternal principles of the *Meccan* revelations in the historical conditions of earlier Muslim societies, from Medina onwards; the "second message" is the full implementation of the *Meccan* revelations that is possible now that modern society has evolved to a stage in which it is possible to implement *Qur'anic* ideals as social realities.

The reason that Taha opposed Numeiri was that he (Taha) believed that Numeiri was implementing a *Shari_a* was outdated because it was based on *Medinan* rather than *Meccan* principles. It was time to move from the "first" (based on the *Medinan* revelations) to the

Second Message based on the *Meccan* vision of Islam. He argued that many of the *Medinan* verses have "become irrelevant for the new era" of the 20th century, and should be laid aside, to allow the Second Message to emerge as "the basis of the legislation" in a modern Muslim society[234]. This should, he argued, include positive regard for Biblical scriptures, both Old Testament and New Testament, in which the same principles of justice, kindness and peaceful co-existence can be found, together with the rejection of violence and coercion as legitimate means of spreading religion. Taha disputed that slavery, private property, inequality between sexes, polygamy, divorce, the wearing of veil and segregation of women were any sense original to Islam[235]. He advocated a socialist economy in which no one should be allowed to own anything that permits the exploitation of the resources or labour of others. Economic equality was the basis on which political and social equality could be established. The former implies a democratic system of in which each individual is respected for having free will, and the latter entails the absence of discrimination on the ground of race or faith. By this argument, Islam justifies a pluralist system of governance and a socialist form of economy for Sudan.

From the point of view of searching for a religiously-based approach to reconciliation and peace-building in the Sudan, it has to be regretted that the Numeiri government not only turned a deaf ear to Taha's teaching, but treated it as apostasy for which he was executed. This is a tragic example of what may happen when religion is recruited into the service of a political regime. Taha's ideas have survived, however, through his disciples among the Republic Brothers. In the challenging conditions of the so- called New Sudan, the reformist ideas of Mahmud Taha merit renewed attention.

10.5: COVENANT IN CHRISTIANITY (BERIT AND DAITHIKE)

The Biblical concept of *Berît*, "covenant", is derived from the Hebrew words *barâ, meaning* "to create", and *Barâh*, "to cut". *Berît*, is an active

---

[234] Mahmud Taha, op. cit., p 258
[235] ibid., pp. 132 -2145

noun, from the *hiphîl* form of the verb that indicates that covenant is an active concept that belongs to the creative action of God. It is important to note that *barâ*, "to create", also carries the connotation of "to eat together". This may be the origin of the word, which explains the idea that creation is the action by which God establishes intimacy with humankind, on the analogy of eating with them.

The first covenant in the Bible was established between God and every living creature following the Flood. God established an eternal relationship with Noah, and assured him: I now establish my covenant with you and with every living creature that was…never again will there be a flood to destroy the earth" (Genesis Chapter 9: Verses 9-10 NLT Version). This first covenant was marked by the symbol of the rainbow – a sign of relationship between God and Noah, between God and every creature that lives on earth. Noah stepped out of the boat onto an earth devoid of human life. But God gave him a reassuring promise. This covenant between God and Noah had three parts: Never again will a flood do such destruction; as long as the earth remains, he seasons will always come as expected; and that a rainbow will be visible when it rains as a sign to all that God will keep his promises. The earth will order and seasons are still preserved, and rainbows still remind us of God's faithfulness to his word.

God's covenant with Abram/Abraham (Genesis Chapter 17 NLT Version) renewed the essence of the Noahic covenant: it was to be an eternal covenant between god and Abraham, and with Abraham's descendants through the generations (Chapter 17 Verse 9 NLT Version). But this covenant introduced the idea of selection, in that the covenant will be passed on through Isaac and his descendants: "But My covenant will be confirmed with Isaac, who will be born to you and Sarah about this time next year." (Genesis Chapter 17 Verse 21 NLT Version). However, this selection was not intended to exclude Ishmael whom God promised to bless and make fruitful: "As for Ishmael, I will surely bless him also as you have asked. I will make him fruitful and multiply his descendants. He will become the father of 12 princess, and I will make him a great nation" (Genesis Chapter 17 Verse 20 NLT Version).

The idea is, therefore, that Isaac bears the responsibility of covenant on behalf of all, with the intent that all should be included in its embrace.

Covenant becomes the key concept in establishing the Biblical identity and responsibility of Israel. Exodus Chapter 19 gives the dramatic setting, and chapters 20 to 23 set out the actual covenant between God and the Israelites. Chapter 24 shows the covenant being confirmed. The Ten Commandments represent the ethical core of God's covenant with Israel. The rest of the Old Testament (OT) can be read as a commentary upon them·

Within this broad framework of the OT concept of "covenant" as expressing God's relationship with creation and humankind, other parts of the OT frequently invoke covenant as the model of human relationships within Israel. The necessity of reestablishing relation of peace among human beings and between humanity and God is based in the Hebrew notion of *Shalóm* that signifies peace in a broad sense of harmony of people with nature and with God. For example, Laban proposed a covenant with Jacob in order to restore mutual trust between them (Genesis. Chapter 31Verses 44 -55). A cairn was built to record the events: an appeal was made to God as a witness; an oath was taken, and relatives invited to a sacral meal. The details of the story serve to set the theological principles of covenant in the social context of the emerging identity of Israel. It is significant that the reconciliation between Jacob and his uncle Laban preceded Jacob's experience of wrestling with God at Jabbok, as result of which he was renamed Israel.

The prophetic books of the Old Testament offer a repeated reflection on the nature of God's ancient covenant with Israel. Interpreting it as the symbol of God's love, the prophets constantly call for a renewal of covenant in terms of its being internalized as something that should be written on the heart of the believer, a spiritual relationship that expresses both human repentance and divine forgiveness, and open a new life of righteousness for the believer (Jeremiah Chapter 31Verse 31). The Prophet Isaiah emphasized the universal nature of the covenant, as an intimate relationship with God that Israel was called to share with all the nations, rather than keep to itself (Isaiah Chapter 49 Verse 6).

The New Testament presents Jesus as the fulfillment of the

prophetic hopes for a renewed covenant. Covenant is now understood less in terms of a legal code, and more as a life lived in self-less service of God. Jesus' Beatitudes, recorded in the Sermon on the Mount, set the standards of the New Covenant (Matthew Chapter 5 Verses 1-12, Luke Chapter 6 Verse 20 -26 NLT Version). "The beatitudes can be understood in four ways: They are code of ethics for disciples and a standard of conduct for all believers. Second, they contrast kingdom values of what is eternal and what is temporary. Third, they contrast the superficial "faith" of the Pharisees with the real faith that Christ demands and fourth, they show how the Old Testament will be fulfilled in the new Kingdom. The beatitudes are not multiple choice, taking what people want and leave what they don't, they must be taken as a whole. They describe what we should be as followers of Christ and are associated with two great commandments: "Love the Lord your God with all your heart and with all your soul and with all your mind" and second, "Love your neighbor as yourself" (Matthew Chapter 22 Verse 37-39 NIV Version). This was the simple way in which Jesus taught the essence of life in the New Covenant.

In the context of religious pluralism such as exists in Sudan, one of the issues that contemporary Christian theologians are addressing it that of relating the New Covenant in Jesus Christ to the existence of other religions[236]. The approaches that they adopt in dealing with this issue have been categorized under three heading: exclusivism, inclusivism and pluralism.

The first opinion holds that the explicit knowledge of Jesus Christ and membership of the Church are required if one is to become part of the New Covenant. This maintains the classic axiom that "there is no salvation outside the church" (*extra ecclesiam nulla salus*) It may be true that the exclusivist paradigm is mainly held by Protestant of the evangelical tradition; yet the concrete attitudes of missionaries

---

[236] Dupuis J., "Religious Plurality and the Christological Debate" a paper presented in Baar, Switzerland, (9-15 January 1990) at a symposium sponsored by the "Dialogue with Living Faith" section of the World Council of Churches (unpublished), pp.1-3

belonging to various churches would seem more often than not to betray a similar theological stand.

The second approach seeks to combine the New Testament affirmations of the universal salvific will of God, on the one hand, and of the finality of Jesus Christ as Saviour on the other. It understands the mystery of Jesus Christ and of his Spirit as being present everywhere, and operative outside the boundaries of the Church, both in the life of individual persons and in the religious traditions. The inclusivist paradigm, while being proposed by a large number of Roman Catholic theologians, is not their exclusive preserve, and finds its parallel in 19 and 20th century Protestant thought.

The third opinion holds that God has manifested and revealed himself in various ways to different peoples in their respective traditions. This is pluralist approach that relatives the finality of Jesus Christ in terms of Christian faith and experience, but urges that other religions have their own ways of expressing ultimate concerns, and all are equally valid.

Thus, for the exclusivist position Jesus Christ and the Church are the necessary way to salvation: for the inclusivist the truth of Jesus Christ embraces the truths found in other faiths; and according to the pluralist approach, Jesus is the way for Christian while other religions have their own ways to the Truth. What is common to each of these approaches is that they consider the issue of religious pluralism from the sole perspective of Jesus Christ - i.e. from a Christological position based on metaphysical assumptions about the nature of Christ. In recent years this approach has been challenged, especially by Christians from Southern cultures that question the relevance in their own contexts of the Graeco-Roman metaphysics on which traditional Christology is built. They argue that the understanding of whom Jesus Christ was/ is cannot be separated from what he taught and how he lived. They start form the position that Jesus, in the Synoptic Gospels, spoke less about himself than about the Kingdom of God, the term that he most frequently used to designate the central theme of his mission: "The Kingdom of God is near! Repent of your sins and believe the Good News" (Mark Chapter Verse 15 NLT Version). At its heart the Gospel is concerned with the Kingdom of God, and this gives priority to ethical rather than metaphysical issues[237]. This, therefore, should be the perspective through which Christians seek to address the question of religious pluralism: "Seek the Kingdom of God above all else and live righteously, and he will give you everything you need" (Matthew Chapter 6 Verse 33 NLT Version). This verse tells us that we should put God first in our lives, to fill our thoughts with his desire taking his character for our pattern and to serve him and obey him in everything we do.

This returns us to the importance of the Sermon on the Mount and the Beatitudes (Matthew Chapter 5: verses 3-12). The Beatitudes not only describe the types of the people to be seen in the kingdom, but also the nature of their happiness within. The Sermon goes on to set new ethical standards which are higher than those provided in the old covenants set in the kingdom, but also the nature of their happiness within. The Sermon goes on to set new ethical standards which are higher than those provided in the old covenants set in the Torah (law) of Moses. The righteousness (*dikaisune*) of the New Covenant exceeds that of the Scribes and the Pharisees. The Greek word *basileia* (*mamlaka* in Hebrew), is less accurately translated as "kingdom" which denotes a static sense of place or institution, and should better be rendered as "reign" in the dynamic sense of the creative and salvific power of God. Participation in the kingdom of God (*basileia tou Theou*) should not therefore be limited in its meaning to imply only those who are members of the church in an institutional sense. It includes all who allow their lives to be infused by the "reign" of God that transforms their being, their culture and their society.

---

[237] I.M.C. Obinwa, "the Kingdom of Heaven and Its Ethical Implications as reflected in the Sermon of the Mount", in African Journal of Biblical Studies, Vol VII N. 2, October 1992 p.83

10.6: COVENANT AND ITS IMPLICATIONS FOR CHRISTIAN MISSION AND ISLAMIC DA'WA

The discussion of "covenant" in the respective understanding of Nuer religion, Islam and Christianity has shown that in each of the religious traditions of Sudan covenant conveys the concept of a binding relationship between God and creation. In this primary sense it belongs to the order of creation itself, and includes everything, animate and inanimate, that God has created. It is therefore universal, and includes all the peoples of the earth. Whether God is named as *Kuoth, Yahweh* or *Allah*, His covenant with creation is an expression of His love and mercy to all that He creates. This is referred to by Christians as grace, and by Muslims as *ni'ma,* and in Nuer, each term denoting that which is freely given by God, to which human beings can freely respond in faith. Faith, in the sense of active acceptance of covenant relationship that Gods creates, entails moral obedience to God. All three religious traditions of Sudan accept that human beings are therefore moral beings, and need to live according to a moral order. They also agree that this order is revealed by God through prophets, and that the teaching and lives of prophets establishes an exemplary pattern in which covenant responsibility toward God can be implemented. The moral dimension of covenant relationship with God in the three religious traditions also addresses the problem of human disobedience that breaks the covenant relationship. Confession, repentance, forgiveness and reconciliation are recognized spiritually, ethically and ritually in the three traditions, and each hits procedures to re-establishing the covenant relationship when it is infringed. Each religious tradition particularizes its covenantal relationship with God in terms of its own faith and moral responsibilities. This is more pronounced in Christianity and Islam, Christians tending to emphasize the elective nature of the inheritance of God's covenant with Abraham through Isaac, Israel and the "New Israel" in Jesus Christ, while Muslims affirm the finality of Muhammad. While this often produces exclusivist theologies among Christians and Muslims, we have shown that both the Bible and the Qur'an set this particularism within the wider understanding of God's universal covenant with the whole of nature and humankind. The Biblical understanding of the Kingdom of God, as expounded today particularly by Christian theologians from the Southern hemisphere, offers a creative understanding of how the meaning of God's covenant ad kingdom in the Sudan.

On the problems that Christianity and Islam have faced in their respective histories in Sudan is that of competitive mission, that continued to be a problem to resolve. This section of the discussion must therefore address this problem, and ask the question: is it possible to reconcile Christian and Islamic *Da`wa* with the understanding of God's covenant and kingdom that has been elaborated in the previous section?

The Roman Catholic theologian, Paul Knitter, has tackled this question in respect of Christian mission. "If the mission of Jesus was the kingdom of God," He argues, "it cannot be otherwise for the mission of the church". The church and the kingdom must not be identified as the same thing on an identical basis' they are related, but not co-terminous. The kingdom is more extensive than the church. The purpose of the church is to serve the kingdom not the other way round[238]. Therefore, the church leaves out its true nature when it is kingdom-centered, not ecclesio-centered.

This according to Knitter is not to deny the importance of missionary goals, but only to keep them in proper perspective. If Christians come to understand the role of the church as service of the kingdom, and affirm the absolute value of the kingdom over the value of the church, and live up to the church as a means of serving the kingdom, then they will have to be wary of traditional theological language about the kingdom in the world being "ordered" toward the church, or about the church being "necessary" for the kingdom. In place of these traditional views Christians should now see the church as a servant of the kingdom, and be opened to engage creatively with other religions that bring their own ethical and spiritual insights into the task of extending the kingdom on earth. Mission in the cause of the kingdom necessarily involves dialogue with other faiths. Looking

---

[238] Paul F. Knitter, op.cit., 1995, p. 108

upon other religions, as potential agents of the Kingdom, Christians are not trying to "include" them neatly in an already clearly and definitely defined project and vision. While Christians feel that they have a universally meaningful and decisive grasp of what the kingdom is to include, they also admit that there can be other meaningful, urgent, decisive contributions to the ever greater realization of a new way of being human and living together. Therefore, when Christians look upon others as agents of the kingdom, they do not view others as assistants but as co-workers.

The reign of God was for Jesus, and remains for his community today, a dynamic symbol that can never be pinned down in a precise definition. As Knitter pointed out there has been growing consensus among scripture scholars that one of the essential characteristics of the Kingdom preached by Jesus was its worldly equality. Seeking the Kingdom of God is to seek the well-being of human kind in this world. Promoting human well-being requires social transformation, development, political liberation ad in some instances revolution. Action on behalf of justice, and participation in the transformation of the world are constitutive dimensions of preaching the gospel. Transformation in this sense involves both the political and the spiritual dimensions of human identity. It is necessary to set aside false polarities that separate spiritual mission and social service. Nor is it sufficient to change individual humans in order to realize peace: there needs also to be a transformation of the institutions of power that control people's lives. Mission must be concerned equally with spiritual renewal and political change.

The kingdom of God therefore might be defined as the new order of human society in which God's power of love, justice, mercy and forgiveness transform the lives of human beings and empower them to build institutions of governance and polity that sustain human equality regardless of ethnic, ideological or religions difference. Such a kingdom is both socio-political and spiritual, and its realization brings about human development and harmony with God.

Turning to the Islamic aspect of this challenge, it should first be noted that the Arabic word that Muslim use in this context– *Dawa*, – expressed the sense of "call" or "invitation" that comes from the verb *dââ* to call"; the active participle *daî* (plural *du_â* means "one who calls or invites"[239]. The Arabic concept of *Dawa*, therefore mission as "sending". The verb *dâ_â* occurs frequently in the *Qur'an*. Most frequently its subject is God who calls to "the Domain of peace" (*dâr al –Islâm)*, and guides whom He pleases to the straight path. Other occasions the subject is the prophets who invite people to believe with their Lord. The subject can also be the people of faith themselves, who call upon God making their sincere religion unto Him, but in this case the calling denotes prayer[240].

A key verse in the *Qur'an* lays down the obligation of *Dawa*, *in* relation to the Muslim community: "Let their spring form you a community who invited to goodness, who enjoin what it right and forbid what is wrong; they are the ones who attain felicity" (3:104). Some Muslim commentator interpret this to mean that "inviting to goodness" is the collective responsibility as a whole. It is the latter interpretation that, since the late 19th century, has justified the development of *Dawa*, organization in Islam, an example in Sudan being the Muslim Brothers. Their understanding of "enjoining what is right and forbidding what is wrong" tends to express particular ideological interpretations of Islam.

The contemporary Muslim interpreter of *Dawa*, Jamal Mohammed Al-Surraj, in his article "Equality and Justice in Islam", argues that Islam has, throughout its history, emphasizes justice and equality. From

---

[239] The sources for Da`wa and mission are taken from the work of Prof. D... Kerr's Article: "Islamic Da 'wa and Christian Mission: "Towards A comparative Analysis", in International Review of Mission, Vol LXXIX No 353, April 2000. Kerr is a specialist in Christian Muslim relations and Director of Centre for Study of Christianity in the Non-Western World (CSCNWW), University of Edinburgh, Scotland United Kingdom, Badru D. Katergga and Dvaid W. Shenk Islam and Christianity, first published in 1980, Byron And cooley, Christian and Muslim Together, An Exploration by the Presbyterians, published by the Geneva Press 1987, the Work of Mahmud Taha, The Second Message of Islam first Faith, Published in 1967 and m icharel Parker Gurdians of the Ark: A Sudanese Pilgrimage of Faith, Presented at The Church in Sudan, February, 1967

[240] David D. Kerr. Op.cit., p. 51

early Islamic times he cites the example of ‘Umar Ibn al Khattab, the second Caliph in Islam. The governor's son and a Coptic were involved in a horse race that the Copt won. The bitter defeat made the ‘Amr's son furious and he therefore flogged the Copt and said: "Take this, and damn the descendant of the ignoble." The Copt complained against this humiliation to the *Caliph* himself. The Governor and his son were summoned to *Medina*, and when the Caliph had heard the case, he ordered the Copt to flog the Governor's son the same way he had been flogged. The Caliph then ordered the Copt to beat the Governor, saying "are you enslaving people whose mothers bore them free?" The Copt however refused to beat the Governor on the grounds that it was not he, but his son, who had aggrieved him. This story is cited by al-Surraj to exemplify the justice and non-discrimination that the original Rightly- Guided Caliphs intended to characterize a Muslim state, and he offers it as a standard for the respect that Muslim should show Christians in the course of Islamic *Dawa*, [241].

In the contemporary discussion of Islamic *Dawa*, great emphasis I placed on the *Qur'anic* verses that states: "Those who believe (in the *Qur'an),* and those who follow the Jewish (scripture), and the Christians and the Sabians[242] and who believe in God and the last Day, and work righteousness, they shall have their reward: no fear shall come upon then, neither shall they grieve" (2:62). Two interpretations of Islamic *Dawa* in relation to religious pluralism are derived from this verse. One accepts that religious pluralism is a phenomenon of history but argues that it does not negate the duty of *Dawa* to "invite" all religions to

---

[241] Jamal Mohammed Al –Surraj, "Equality and Justice in Islam", Sudan Vision, Vol. 2 Issue No. 267, 19/6/04

[242] A. Yusuf Ali, op.cit., p.33 (The Sabians were: (a) The Pseudo-Sabians of Harran who attracted Khalifa mamun – al- Rashid in 830 A.D, by their long hair and peculiar dresses. They adopted the name as it mentioned in the Qur'an in order to claim the privileges of the People of the Book. (b) The Sabians played an important part in the history of early Arabia and are known through their inscriptions in an alphabet allied to the Phoenicians and the Babylonians. Their kingdom was in Yemen religion in South Arabia about 800 BC. They worshiped the planets and stars (Moon, Sun, and Venus).

confessional acceptance of Islam: since other religions include people of good faith and conduct, however, Islamic *Dawa* should observe the *Qur'anic* instruction "to call unto the way of the Lord with wisdom, fair exhortations, and reason with them in a better way[243]. A second interpretation given by the late Professor Isma'il *al- Farugi* in his presentation on *Dawa* at the 1976 WCC colloquium on "Christian Mission and Islamic *Dawa*. *Dawa* according *al-faruqi,* ecumenical par excellence in that it accepts that all religious traditions are *dejure,* for they are based on a common source, the religion of God, which God implanted equally in all human beings. The *Qur'an* call this *din al fitra,* or "the religion of nature". *Al Faruqi* therefore advocated an understanding that draws Muslims and non-Muslims into dialogue of mutual self-criticism that he likes to" a domestic relationship between kin." Within this relationship, *Dawa* invites an ecumenical cooperative critique of other religions rather than its invasion by a new truth." According to this view Muslims should co-operate with Christians and others in struggle for what is good and just for all humankind, and in establishing a just social order against all kinds of injustice[244].

Mahmud Taha advocated the same kind of approach to *Da_wa* in Sudan. He held the person and teaching of Jesus in great respect. His knowledge of the Christian scriptures occasionally enabled him to quote from the Bible in his *Second Message of Islam* especially the Sermon on the Mount. To Taha Jesus taught and practiced ethical ideals that are also to be found in the eternal principles of the *Meccan* teaching of the *Qur'an*[245].

Taha believed in the notion of "oneness" of all believers and encouraged his followers to seek contact and dialogue with people of other faiths. It is on this basis that he, and his Republican Brothers, advocated a peaceful solution to the Sudanese conflicts. In this way he justified *Dawa* and religious pluralism, and insisted on the *Qur'anic* dictum: *lasta alaihim bi-Mussaitir* "you are not to dictate them[246].

---

[243] David D. Kerr, op.cit., p. 161
[244] Christian W. Troll, S.J., op.cit
[245] Mahmud Taha, op.cit., p. 11
[246] ibid., p.11

10.7: CONCLUSION

My aim in this chapter has been to explore the resources of the religious traditions of Sudan that can contribute to the task of reconciliation and peace-building for the future. It is evident from the early parts of this book that the main focus of a political approach to unity among the diverse peoples of Sudan has been the constitution. As the 1972 Addis Ababa Peace Agreement to the 1973 Constitution and that the 2005 Naivasha Peace Agreement has been formulated within the 1998 Constitution. The argument of this chapter is that the former agreements failed because they had insufficient grounding in popular support and partly because the Numeiri government shifted from a pluralist to amore exclusively Islamist religious policy. The future of the latter (Naivasha Peace Agreement) remains in the balance, and begs the question: will it attract popular support, and build confidence among Sudan's multi-religious population?.

In the interest of contributing to a positive answer to this question, I have proposed in this chapter that constitutional stability at a political level needs to be founded upon, and complemented by a religious commitment to the unity of all the Sudanese people in Sudan. This, in my view is possible on the basis of the value of "covenant" that is to be found in the three religious traditions. As God's covenant with human kind is part of the order of creating and binds all human beings together in relationship with Himself, so there needs to be a covenant with God between all Sudanese as part of the creation of the New Sudan. As God makes covenant with different peoples in particular ways, so the different religious traditions of Sudan must be respected in their diversities. My discussion of the Nuer, Islamic and Christian understandings of covenantal responsibility has shown that each lays importance on peace and reconciliation. In the same way, the different religious communities of Sudan can affirm their respective covenantal traditions, and at the same time embrace peace and reconciliation among themselves. Rather than allowing the course of Sudan's development as an independent State to continue along the projection of one religion attempting to impose itself on the others, this chapter proposes that the understanding of the "reign" of God in a non-territorial" kingdom" offers a way of both reserving religious values, and the freedom to express them, in the New Sudan. It has been shown that Christian mission and Islamic *Da`wa* can be interpreted in ways that support and sustain this vision, and can thus be liberated form negative forms of competition that have laid them open to political exploitation.

CHAPTER

ELEVEN

INTER-RELGIOUS RECONCILIATION
AND PEACE-BUILDING

11.1: INTRODUCTION

The previous chapter laid out a conceptual approach to reconciliation and peace-building based on the notion of "covenant" that is found in the three religious traditions of Sudan. As the aim of that chapter was to build on the Right of Self-Determination (RSD) statement of the Sudan and New Sudan Councils of Churches, this final chapter responds to the RSD emphasis on the need for a "programme" that can put vision into action. Three examples of Christian-Muslim dialogue for reconciliation and peace-building will be examined. The first two are empirically based instances of successful initiatives in Christian-Muslim dialogue that have been undertaken in situations of conflict, in Nigeria and in Sudan. The third, borrowed from Pakistan, elaborates an understanding of dialogue that is appropriate for Sudan as well, and serves as a conceptual conclusion to the chapter.

Each of the cases that will be examined is concerned with peace and reconciliation. The Hebrew word *Shalom* and the Greek *eirene,* like the Arabic word *salam*, and of human society. The Apostle Paul connected the individual and social dimensions of these terms in the emphasis that he gives in his letter to the meaning to communal peace-indicating it as opposed to strife and perceived reconciliation (*katallage*) that Christ has brought between people that were traditionally antagonistic toward each other – in his case, the Jews and Gentiles. The new relationship of peace and reconciliation produces a new community (*koinonia*) between formerly hostile peoples who, through forgiveness, are set free for a new human relationship (Ephesians Chapter 2 Verses 14-17). Peace thus, comes to mean a comprehensive reconciliation event concerning God and human beings to one another through Christ[247].

Paul provides a new insight into his perception of peace among the communities by pointing to the reality of power structures that hinders human efforts towards peace, having their root causes in the "principalities and powers" and the spiritual hosts of wickedness in the heavenly place (Ephesians Chapter 6 Verse15-16). He goes on to suggest that Christian life is a struggle in partnership with God against these spiritual powers that frustrate peace in human community. Through this struggle the church extends itself in love and service for all (II Corinthians Chapter 5 Verses 18-19; Ephesians Chapter 4 Verse12). The Christian community therefore, established by reconciliation and for reconciliation, is intended to model in its own life what reconciliation means in actual practice[248].

The realization of peace in the New Testament provides the motivation for the development of human community in which Christians and Muslims are called upon to engage in a power encounter against those unjust structures that thwart human efforts towards peace and development.

11.2: A NIGERIAN EXAMPLE: CHRISTIAN-MUSLIM RECONCILIATION AND PEACE-BUILDING IN WUSASA

Nigeria, like Sudan, is an African nation that has been torn apart by religious conflicts between Muslims and Christians. In 1987 the

---

[247] Onwu N., " Biblical Perspective for Peace, Development and Reconstruction: Its Socio -Religious implications for the Churches in Africa", in Isabel Phiri, Kenneth Ross and James Cox, *The Role of Christianity in Development, Peace and Reconstruction. (eds.) Kolbe Press, p. 36*
[248] Ibid., p. 36

tension between the adherents of these faiths resulted in a serious crisis that had left dissension among the communities. The village of Wusasa, near Zaria in Kaduna State, suffered direct conflict between the two religions. One of its Christian leaders, Josiah Atkins Idowu-Fearon, initiated a process of reconciliation that he later wrote up in a Doctorate of Ministry thesis entitled: *Reconciliation of a Religiously – Divided Community through Inter-faith Dialogue*[249].

A group of Christians and Muslims in Wusasa organized a joint project with the purpose of studying their scriptures – the *Qur'an* and the Bible – together in search for healing of the violence that had inflicted and destroyed the village. The groups related their scriptures through a combination of memorization; life experiences and explaining selected passages from the *Qur'an* and the Bible. They invited each other to participate in their religious ceremonies. These were occasions where communities of different faiths gathered together and shared fellowship as one community who have learned their scriptures in ways that gave direct personal meaning in their lives[250].

The goal was to effect reconciliation through the use of scriptures, by selecting relevant topics such as love, goodness, and justice only to mention a few. The texts relevant to these are selected from the *Qur'an* and the Bible as a basis for group discussion, with questions being posed, stories told, life experiences and illustrations shared to help people discover the spiritual resources for reconciliation in their respective traditions of faith. The theologies they used were not concerned with the conversion from one religion to another, but a genuine opportunity for dialogue of their social concern and security.

The author of this enquiry, Idowu-Fearon, has drawn a number of observations from the experiment. When the programme was implemented after the 1987 religious conflict, the community was able to settle its differences, and restore peace and harmony among the Christians and Muslims, so that religious fanaticism was no longer

---

[249] Josiah Atkins Idowu – Fearon, Reconciliation a Religiously – Divide Community through inter-Faith Dialogue: An experiment in Wusasa – Saria of Nigeria, Hartford Seminary
[250] Ibid., p. 50

a part of their experience. Muslims felt free to come to the church during occasions such as funerals, christening, weddings and special thanksgivings. They recognized that Christianity is similar in some ways to Islam and that the *Qur'an* acknowledges Christians, too, realized that Islam is not a religion of hatred, as they had previously perceived before interacting with Muslims. They began to respect Muslims as people who practice their daily prayers regularly according to the *Qur'an*, and they constitute a peaceful loving part of the *Wusasa* community.

The Participants identified three important areas of life where peace should be nourished: peace in the mind, peace in the home, and peace in nation. Both believers considered peace in mind as the most important, and reasoned that the latter two were reflections of the former. They emphasized that the absent of the three were responsible for the lack of peace in their village in 1987, that resulted in deviating from the path of truth as taught in the scriptures[251]. The final ingredient among others was justice that the participants perceived as a gift from God to humankind.

From this programme, the Nigerian Muslims and Christians learned much from each other, and were able to resolve the strained relationship among their communities. The village chief gave land for the continuation of this experiment in other ways that have increased the social health of Wusasa

11.3: EXPERIENCE OF WOMEN'S ACTION GROUP FOR PEACE AND DEVELOPMENT IN SUDAN

The Sudanese conflicts as discussed in the proceeding chapters, have multiple causes that involved historical dimensions for which the blame is shared by leadership both past and present. But the responsibility lies with the Sudanese people to bring peace through dialogue, a tool of which could only be effective if it takes roots from the bottom rather than top down scenarios. The Sudanese Women's Action Group

---

[251] ibid., p.58

(WAG) has developed a model for healing and reconciliation from which lessons can be learned.

WAG was founded early in 1996 by a group of Sudanese Christian and Muslim women who identified principles that enabled them to enter dialogue about peace and development in Sudan. The technique was to build bridges between various regions that have been affected by negative emotions and by feelings of anger and pain that arise from war, displacement, social prejudice, religious dogma and cultural transition[252]. The aim was to make an impact on the community that eventually women could gain a greater role in peace and development processes.

The WAG's first experience for dialogue was one-day workshop held in Khartoum, August 1996, during which the women told their stories and listened to what Lillian Harris described as painful experiences. There were tears, Amazement and at the end there was joy. They listened to one another and exchanged information listening to each other they began to recognize themselves as sisters of one nation who have experiences to contribute towards peace and reconciliation.

Their "listening to loss" dialogue was supplemented by the "dialogue of service" in which women from different background volunteered to work together for the welfare of their communities. This principle was developed during their second workshop that took place in October 1996 at Ahfat University under the theme "The differences that unite us" – the term that became the WAG motto. In this seminar the women had the opportunity to identify the issues that divide the Sudanese people such as *jihad*, human rights, etc. They were concerned about what Sudanese women have in common. That commonness bound them together to share ideas that eventually enabled them provides services to their communities. In these discussions WAG discovered power tools for reconciliation and development. It is a ground for mutual understanding, sharing of ideas and experiences where the gift of compassionate listening, acceptance and forgiveness are the end

---

[252] Lillian Craig Harris, "Christian and Muslim Women in Dialogue", in Stuart E Brown, (ed.), Seeking an open Society: Inter-faith relations and Dialogue in Sudan Today, p. 92

results; as opposed to negotiations or debate where each party would want to win the argument.

11.4: A PAKISTANI APPROACH TO CHRISTIAN-MUSLIM DIALOGUE

These two examples of dialogue are significant in that they show what is possible at the grass-roots level. If dialogue is to be sustained between Christians and Muslims, it must reflect the reality of their lives, by addressing the issues that cause conflict between them, and finding resources in their religious practice that can help redress these problems. To listen to each other, to read scriptures together, to undertake social action for the common good are simple but successful ways of initiating dialogue for reconciliation and peace building.

It is on this basis that the Pakistani Christian theologian, Charles Amjad-Ali, has developed an approach to dialogue through which Christians and Muslims are able to address the issues that confront them both in the modern state of Pakistan. He criticizes dialogue in the forms in which he sees it to have developed in the West. First, as an early manifestation of the study of other religions, dialogue was pursued as a form of debate between Christians and Muslims. Dialogue then came to be proposed as a gentler vision of mission, a more subtle way of seeking conversion. Other religions were treated as *praeparatio evangelica* and dialogue was seen as a way of bringing them to Christ through their own religions. According to Ali this worked well with religions, which came before Christianity. But the position of Islam was difficult to uphold. Finally, came the concern with various approaches that appealed to common ideational transcendence based on metaphysical concepts such as "the same God under different names", "common humanity'" and so on[253].

Ali dismisses these as Western approaches to dialogue that have little relevance in a situation like Pakistan. Dialogue, he proposes, should tackle issues of national reconstruction through peoples' own

---

[253] Charles Amjad – Ali, (ed.), Developing Christian Theology in the Context of Islam, p.1

wisdoms that seek mutual understanding and solidarity. He defines dialogue as "a process of discourse in which the communities involved go through their own respective *logos* to come to some common understanding of certain social and political problems"[254]; rather than looking for abstract concepts on which different religions might agree – a process that he defines as "metalogue" – dialogue should engage the reality in which people of religions actually live[255].

Ali further states that, Christian –Muslim dialogue in Pakistan needs to overcome two major problems. The first is the close association of Christian mission with the western imperial power. Related to this is the fact that Christians in Pakistan, as in most other Muslim countries, are seen by Muslims as the product of the missionary enterprise, and are not allowed to develop any ecclesial or theological independence from the West.

The second problem, related to the first, is the fact that Christians in Muslim countries adopt the theological epistemology of Western Christian theology that was developed in the historically mono-religious cultures of Western society. This theological epistemology has been the determinative basis for all theology, the religiously pluralistic context that was originally that of Christianity in Asia and Africa, having been lost.

Dialogue therefore carries a double challenge for Christians in Pakistan. It challenges them to accept the socio-cultural environment of the Pakistani state as their proper home, and to engage in dialogue with Muslims in order to understand the religion that is followed by the majority of the population. But this does not imply conceding to Muslims over issues that are of fundamental importance to Christianity. Rather, it is to develop an indigenous epistemology whereby Christianity can speak in terms that Muslim comprehend. This, in turn, will enable Pakistani Christians to speak through (*dial*) their Christian revelation (*logos*) to the issues that confront Muslims and Christians alike in the search for a just and egalitarian society[256].

---

[254] ibid., p. 2.
[255] Ibid., p. 3
[256] ibid., p.5

Amjad Ali's understanding of dialogue has much relevance to the challenge that Christians face in Sudan. In my view, it offers a way forward that will enable Christians to contribute to national dialogue in Sudan, in ways that will command respect by Muslims. It creates a way of linking the constructive local experiences of dialogue to the national level, and of ensuring that the latter is rooted in the empirical experience of the former.

11.5: CONSTITUTIONAL IMPLICATIONS OF POST-MACHAKOS SUDAN

The different covenantal arrangements discussed in chapter nine, have similarities that can prepare the people of Sudan to move from a culture of war to culture of peace using each other's tradition as a base for Christian-Muslim relations in the New Sudan. This requires careful planning and confidence building to avoid falling back to the violence that has marred the history of independent Sudan.

The Machakos Protocol of 2002 has proposed compromises that resulted in the signing of the Naivasha Peace Accord between the GoS and SPLM. However, the Protocol felt short to resolving some central issues that would remain problems during the interim period. The issue of national capital was proposed in the draft framework for resolution of outstanding issues arising out of the elaboration of the Machakos Protocol, remains contentious. The SPLM demanded that a neutral capital where all ethnic and religious groups could meet on common ground, free of the *Shari_a* be established as the national capital. The *Umma* and DUP parties both with religious constituencies in the North supported the SPLM's idea of enclave capital; arguing that religious neutrality in the national capital would foster dialogue and peaceful coexistence among religions[257]. This would mean that the SPLM's western secularized model could serve as a basis for the constitution of that enclave capital. The GoS objected to SPLM demand and viewed it as a major departure from the Machakos framework. They argued that

---

[257] DUP,SPLM and UMMA parties, meeting in Cairo, May 2003, (unpublished material)

the Machakos Protocol has settled the issue of the national capital in a manner that does not allow further discussion'[258]. The GoS viewed the SPLM's demand for a *"Shari`a*-free city" as a step toward secular rules that cannot be applicable in the northern Muslim communities in the North. This hardened the negotiations, and although an agreement has been reached (Naivasha agreement, below), this tension continued to be a problem and could affect the out-come of the referendum. This scenario could lay the groundwork for an independent southern state, as it may encourage most Southerners to propagate for secession in the forthcoming referendum in 2011.

The other contentious issue relates to *Shari`a* law, which has not been satisfactorily prescribed in the Protocol. It has to be recalled that when *Shari`a* was imposed on Sudanese people by president Numeiri in 1983 and later implemented step by step by president al-Bashir, there were no alternative laws developed to safeguard the interests of non-Muslims. As noted in my analysis of 1998 Sudan constitution in chapter seven section (3.7.4) that there is no mentioned of *Shari_a* nor declaration of Sudan as an Islamic state. Yet, the elements of Islamic laws were intelligently inserted in the constitution to allow the public life of Sudanese, governance, defence and economy be conducted in the spirit if Islam. And, this enabled NIF's leadership to implement *Shari_a* through republican decrees and for the first time *Shari_a* became a major concern in Sudanese politics.

During the interim period of six and half years there will be many Southern Christians living in the North and many Muslims living in the Southern Sudan. Although the *Shari_a* will have no competence in the south, constitutional protection of these religious communities is essential. In order to avoid this conflict to happen, the current working constitutional committee should considers this issue in their proposal to the constitutional conference and its subsequent presentation to the national Assembly.

Building confidence and trust between Christians and Muslims after a long history of civil wars remains a challenge in post-Machakos

---

[258] Justice Africa, " Prospect for Peace in Sudan'" Briefing July – August 2003 (unpublished literature)

Sudan. Healing of wounds that have been inflicted by both parties during the conflicts requires patience and mechanism under which the process of reconciliation can be conducted. The issue such as human rights abuses in which both the Islamic government and the SPLM in the South has been involved is left untouched in the Machakos Protocol. A reference can be made to the South African experience of "Truth and reconciliation Commission" aimed to heal the wounds that were wreaked during the apartheid era. The Spirit of forgiveness and reconciliation enabled the South Africa to resolve their internal conflict and created harmony among the white and the black South Africans through the fact-finding committee. A model that could useful to the Sudanese, using theology resources analyzed in chapter nine as basis of future dialogical processes of national reconstruction and reconciliation between Christians and Muslims in Sudan. Despite these unresolved issues, the two parties finally concluded a treaty.

11.6: THE COMPREHENSIVE PEACE AGREEMENT (CPA)

The Comprehensive Peace Agreement signed on 9th January 2005, between the Government of Sudan and Sudan people's Liberation Movement (SPLM) addressed most contentious issues. Underlining the agreement was the Machakos Protocol that substantially ended the question of religion and state. It has recognized the importance of the religion in Sudan and unlike the Addis Ababa covenant, the Naivasha accord has provided for, among other things division of Sudan's national wealth sharing of oil revenues between the north and the south, power sharing and autonomy for the South for a transitional period of six and half years.

The formation of Government of National Unity (GoNU) on 20th September 2005 and the signing of the CPA referred to above have fostered a sense of stability in Sudan during the interim period. The government of national unity that is now governing the nation during this period leading up to the referendum would be crucial and essential to test the creditability of Sudanese political leaders to pursue as the matter of policy for justice that would bring about national reconciliation unity and community self-governance as an essential goal of Sudanese approach to peace

There is an optimism shared by both Christians and Muslims communities in Sudan that this agreement may bring a holistic, just and sustainable peace. Their hope is based on the safeguard that the members of the African Union, the IGAD and the international community have invested a great deal during the negotiations periods, and may see to it that the agreement is implemented.

The challenge however, is for Christians and Muslims in Sudan to accept their socio-cultural environment of the Sudanese state as their nation, and to engage in dialogue with each other in order to understand their religious traditions and to speak this through their (logos) to the issues that confront Muslims and Christians in Sudan. It is this understanding of dialogue that Amjad Ali considers to have much relevance to the challenge of diverse people such as that found in the Sudan. As I have already noted, this may offer a way forward to enable both Christians and Muslims contribute to the national reconstruction through their local experiences of dialogue.

As the two organization – National Congress Party (NCP) and SPLM – focus on the implementation of the agreement there will be challenges such as confidence – building measures and building blocks for a post-conflict, economic recovery and reconstruction programs essential for peace maintenance. It will also be essential to establish an inclusive political process that guarantees participation of all Sudanese citizens in the selection of their governments, to enable them to formulate and adopt a new constitutional order that would promote religious pluralism and guarantee people's rights as well as basic universal principles of liberty and freedom.

11.7: CONCLUSION

The Machakos Protocol recognized the importance of the religions of Sudan in terms of the pluralist society that it envisaged. The Machakos process, however, has not engaged the religious communities and their leaders, or the institutions of civil society. This is a weakness in the process, indicating that it has again been negotiated between political elites with insufficient involvement of the people. In defense of the peace agreement, its provision for a referendum in the South after the six and half years interim period is intended to give the people the opportunity of expressing their voices. It is essential, therefore, that steps be taken over these next six and half years to develop programs and thinking among the people that will enable them to make a responsible decision.

It is here that Christian-Muslim dialogue has its most important role. Part four of this book has argued that Christian-Muslim dialogue in Sudan, if it is to be rooted in the lives of the people, must also include the traditional African religionists as partners. *Cuk* theology, as delineated in Chapter Nine, can be a constructive partner in a three-way religious dialogue in the Sudan. In part, this dialogue will serve to help traditionalist, Christians and Muslims to come to a better common understanding of the character and resources of their respective religious traditions. The example of Wusasa in Northern Nigeria offers a model that could be applied in Sudan. As this helps them grow in mutual understanding and trust, so it opens the way to what is commonly termed "social dialogue", or "dialogue of action", in which they address common social issues. The Women's Action Group is an example of what has already been achieved in Sudan, and again offers a way forward. The great challenge, however, is to bring the insights that each of the three religious have in respect of peace and reconciliation to the larger discussion of the social, economic and political development of the Sudan. This is the challenge that Charles Amjad Ali raises from his experience of Pakistan, and it needs to be applied in the Sudan.

This, in my opinion, is what needs to be done as the next state of the SCC/NSCC Right of Self-Determination process. What this may involve in terms of programmatic activity lies outside the scope of this book. It is my hope, however, that the preceding chapters may serve to give the people of South Sudan a clearer understanding of the history that has brought them thus far, and of the opportunities that present themselves for a new approach to religious pluralism in the Sudan that complements and deepens the promise of the Naivasha

Peace Agreement, while leaving the South to decide their future in a referendum.

11.8: CONCLUSIONS OF THE BOOK

This book has analyzed and examined Christian-Muslims relations in Sudan through the perspective of church-state relations from the pre-independence period of the Anglo-Egyptian Condominium (1898-1956), through to after the Sudanese independence (1956-2005). Christian mission activities and the planting of indigenous church in Sudan took root following the defeat of *Mahdist* revolt in 1898. The Missionaries allied with British colonial power in that their concerted and overtly expressed efforts to halt the advancement of Islam in the south until the fragile unity between the north and south and independence in 1956. I have given plenty of leveled against Christian Missionaries that culminated to their expulsion in 1964 resulted to deterioration between church and state.

The military hostilities in modern Sudan started in 1955 lasted until 1972 and flared up again in 1983, these have their roots causes in the historical past that go back to the time of Arab traders' penetration into the south in the first half of the 19th century. This created mistrust of the Arab Muslims as the cause behind the generalized resistance of the Southern Africans to embrace Islam. The Arabized northern tribes, on the other hand, reciprocated with generalized prejudice attitude of contempt towards the population of the south Sudan. We have also noticed other reasons were rooted in unresolved political and economic issues that go back to the early days before and after independence.

The policies of the colonial and successive Sudanese governments have been to deploy Christianity and Islam for political reasons. *Cuk* (people's) theology that could have been a sure way to guide Christian Muslim relations has been concurrently denied to take root.

This book has shown that Arab Muslims, African Christians and indigenous religious communities have inherent capacities that offer potential for effectiveness in reconciliation and peace-building processes. The experience of Sudanese Christian and Muslim women for example, discussed in chapter ten shows that Sudanese people can resolve their problems through traditions where Christians and Muslims would find themselves engaged in dialogue to establish peaceful religious co-existence. In this context it means that the issues that divide the communities are shared in a deeper union of mutual openness even though there would remain differences of perceptions unresolved.

The questions of building on empirical inter-religious peace-making in Sudan has some theological challenges that required dialogical and constant consciousness of religious pluralism in the 21st century.

The theory, that I advocate here, is *Cuk* or covenantal theology of the Nuer that is rooted in people's traditions. This theory is linked with Amjad-Ali's method discussed in chapter ten; that tackles the issues of national reconstruction through people's own wisdoms; a process of discourse in which the communities involved go through their own respective logos to realize peace, and development. The Nuer concept of many "names one God' suggest that the Sudanese communities can co-exist through their covenantal theologies that bind them together. The Political future of Sudan lies on the combined resources of Christian, Muslim and traditional African religionists discussed in chapter nine, whether the country remained united or not.

The model of the Sudanese Churches – "peoples to peoples" that addresses the actual problems at local levels could form the basis on which to build regional and national reconciliation, from "the bottom up". In my view, the "bottom up" approach in not only aimed to resolve the conflicts of political and armed groups in the Sudan, but, equally important internally in the South, where Muslims and Christians live together in most towns and cities, as it is nationally in terms of national reconciliation between the Christian South and the Muslim North.

A constructive approach to Christian-Muslim relations is essential for building constitutional arrangements that promotes religious pluralism as basic principles of liberty and freedom that may ensure smooth implementation of peace agreement.

The Naivasha peace Accord of January 2005 brings a 'New Hope" to the people of Sudan. It is hoped that a just social order for progressive socio-economic and political co-operation of the Arab Muslim North and Christian South Sudan is sustained.

BIBLIOGRAPHY

(A) ARCHIVAL MATERIAL

(i) Church Missionary Society Archives, Birmingham University: Africa Committee, Sudan Mission Reports, G3 A 10/0

Cook A R., "Letter" to Archdeacon Gwnne, Nov.17, 1905", Sudan Mission 1905-1934

De Saram B., CMS Africa Secretary "Confidential letter" to Sir Kenneth Crubb, CMS President. Shaw Archibald "Notes" at Malek Southern Sudan April 27, 1910

(ii) World Council of Churches Archives, Geneva: Churches Commission for International Affairs (CCIA) Papers

B.A.R, Religious Liberty in the Sudan, CCIA/18x/7, July 1963 Nillus J, Leopold, "Peace in the Sudan", March 12,1973, (Unpublished Paper).

Petition Presented by Southern Political Organisation (Azania Liberation Front) to 4th OAU

Conference Meeting in Kinshasa, Congo, 11th Sept, 1967.

Record of a meeting at the Foreign Office 23-09.64

Reed A., "Southern Sudan: Report to Church World Service", 1971

Scherf T., The Sudan Conflict: Is History and Development, a Mimeographed Paper 1971

South Sudan Liberation Movement (SSLM), "Constitutional Recommendations to Addis-Ababa Conference 1972."

Soviet New Agency TASS, July 27, 1971, Moscow.

WCC Central Committee, "Unity and Human Rights in Africa Today", (unpublished)

(iii) Sudan Council of Churches (SCC) Khartoum Sudan

Ador N., "Islam", Sudan Council of Churches, Khartoum, (unpublished paper), 11/6/2000 Parker M., Guardians of the Ark: A Sudanese Pilgrimage of Faith, Presented to the Church in Sudan, February 1997.

(iv) New Sudan Council of churches (NSCC Nairobi, Kenya

"Draft framework for resolution of outstanding issues Arising our of the Elaboration of the Machakos Protocol," July 2003

Duany W., Report used in briefing the African Bureau of the Department of State, National Security, Congressional Committees on Africa, and the Non-Government Organisation Community, Washington, D.C., November 1994 Justice Africa, 'Prospect for Peace in Sudan", Briefing July-August 2003 (Unpublished report).

Marona J. and Lukudu P., "Let M People Choose": The Statement of the Sudanese Churches on the Right of Self-Determination for Southern Sudan and other Marginalized Areas, London, 6th March 2002.

"Dinka – Nuer Peace Conference" Wunlit, South Sudan 1999

(v) South Sudan Democratic Forum, London Offices, UK

Lomuro M., South Sudan Democratic Forum: "Contribution to the Civil Society Forum on Reconciliation and Good Governance in the Sudan during the interim period"' Entebbe, Uganda, October 2002, (unpublished)

The Civic Forum, "Time for Independence: Self-determination for South Sudan" May 1997. Wanji B., "The National and Nationality

Question and the Rise of the African States in South Sudan: A model, A paradigm for dialogue to be presented to the Steering Committee of South Sudan Civic Forum Scheduled for the 12th to the 17th of November 2001, Abuja – Nigeria".

(B) ARTICLES/CHAPTERS IN BOOKS

Al-Teraifi A. A., "Regionalism in Sudan: Characteristics, Problems and Prospects", in Peter Woodward (ed.), Sudan after Numeiri, London and New York, 1991, p. 104.

An-Na'im A.m, "Peaceful coexistence at Risk", in Kail C. Ellis (ed.), The Vatican, Islam and the Middle East, Syracuse University Press, New York 1987, p. 270

An-Na'im A., "Application of Shari'a (Islamic Law) and Human Rights Violation in the Sudan" In Religion and Human Rights: The case of Sudan, Proceedings of the Conference Convened by the Sudan Human rights Organisation, May 1992, pp. 87-101

Cardeiro C., "The Christian Minority in an Islamic State; The Case of Pakistan", in Kail

C.Ellis (ed.), The Vatican, Islam, and the Middle East, Syracuse University Press, New York, 1987,p. 285

Dafaalla G., Prime Minister of Siudan "Open Letter" to John Garang, 10th November 1985, in John Garang, The call for Democracy in Sudan, (ed.), Masour

Khalid, Kegan Paul Inernational, New York, pp 94-100

Harris C., "Christian and Muslim Women in Dialogue", in Stuart E. Brown, (ed.) Seeking an Open Society: Inter-faith relations and Dialogue in Sudan Today, Paulines Publications Africa Nairobi Kenya, 1997, pp.89-98

Johnson D.H., "North –South issues", in Peter Woodward, (ed.), Sudan after Numeiri, Routledge, London & New York, 1991, p. 134

Malwal B., "The Sudan: Between Unity in Diversity and Division", in the Bleuchot Herve, Delmet Christian, Hopwood Derek, Sudan, History, Identities Ideologies, Ithace Press,

Reading, Biblical Perspective for Peace, Development, Peace and Reconstruction: its Socio- Religious Implications for the Churches in Africa", in Isabel Phiri, Kenneth Ross and James

Cox N., (eds.), <u>The Role of Christianity in Development, Peace and Reconstruction,</u> Kolbe Press, Limuru, Kenha, 196, p. 36

SALIH K. O., "The Sudan, 1985-9: The Fading Democracy'" in Peter Woodward (ed.), Sudan After Numeiri, Rotuledge, London & New York, 1991, p. 62.

Wheeler Andrew C., "The Ministry of the Church Missionary Society in Northern Sudan", in Samuel E Kayana and Andrew C. Wheeler, (eds.) " <u>But God is Not defeated!", Celebrating the Centenary of the Episcopal Church of the Sudan:</u> 1898 – 1999, Paulines Publications Africa, Nairobi-Kenya, 1999, pp. 53-60.

(C) OTHER ARTICLES

Al-Surraj J. M., "Equality and Justice in Islam", Sudan Vision, Vol. 2 Issue No. 267, 19/6/04,p.6

Bowring P.Anya-Nya now holds the key, "Financial Times" 26-11-1971

Chadwick J., Moscow protested about the execution of communists in Sudan, "Day lead July" 21 197, Khartoum (Cxd/W WCC Archive

CMS, "The CMS Gleaner", 1 March 1918, pp. 1-4

DUP, SPLM and Umma Parties, Meeting in Cairo, Al Ayam Newspaper 29ᵗʰ May 2003.

Emeka Onwurah, "The Ethico-Moral Perspective in Nation Building", in African Journal of Biblical Studies, the Nigerian Association for Biblical Studies, Vol. VII No 2, 1962, pp. 45-52

Kerr D. "Islamic *Da`wa* and Christian Mission: "Towards A Compar000, pp. 151 –161ative Analysis", in International Review of Mission, Vol. LXXIX No 353, April 2000, pp. 151 -161

Sharkey Heather J., "Christians Among Muslims: The Church Missionary Society in Northern Sudan" Journal of African History, No. 43, 2002, Cambridge University Press, pp. 51-57.

(D) BOOKS

Abdel-Rahim M., The Development of British Policy in Southern Sudan, 1899-1947 Khartoum University Press, 1968

Sikainga A. A. and Daly M.W (eds), Civil war in Sudan, British Academic Press, London New York, 1930.

Ahmed H. M. M., Sudan: The Christian Design, A Study of the Missionary Factor in Sudan's Cultural and Political Integration: 1843-1986, The Islamic Foundation, The Markfield Conference Centre, Leicester, UK, 1989

Albino O., The Sudan: A Southern Viewpoint, Oxford University Press, 1970.

Alexander T Desmond. And Rosner Brian S., New Dictionary of Biblical Theology, Inter Varsity Press, Leicester, England, 2000.

Ali C. A., Developing Christian theology in the Context of Islam, Christian Study Centre, Rawalpindi, Pakistan, 1996.

Ali A., The Holy Qur'an Text Translation and Commentary, Published by Amana Corp. Brentwood Maryland, USA, 1983.

Alier A., Southern Sudan: Too Many Agreements Dishonored, 2nd edition, Ithaca Press, Reading, 1992.

An-Na`im A., (ed.) Proselytization and Communal Self-Determination Africa, Orbis Books, Maryknoll, New York, 1999.

Arou K. N., Post Independence Sudan, Center of African Studies University of Edinburgh, 1980

Awet A. M., The Ideology of an Islamic State and their Rights of Non-Muslims: With Reference to Sudan's Complex Social Structures, Cultural Diversities, and Political Rivalries, A thesis submitted to the school of Historical Studies, Department of Theology, University of Birmingham for the Degree f Doctor of Philosophy, 2001.

Ayubi N., Political Islam: Religion and Politics in the Arab World, Routledge, 1991.

Belts T., "The Southern Sudan: The Cease-Fire and After", Report Prepared for the Africa Publications Trust, London, 1974

Boff L., <u>Listen To The Poor,</u> Harper and Row Publishers, San Francisco, 1970.

Cox J., Ross K., and Phiri I., <u>The Role of Christianity in development, Peace and Reconstruction,</u> (eds.), All Africa Conference of Churches, Nairobi, 1996.

PM Holt and MW Daly, <u>A History of the Sudan: From the coming of Islam to Present Day,</u> Longmans 1999.

PM Holt and MW Daly, <u>A History of the Sudan: From the coming of Islam to the Present Day,</u> Pearson Education limited, Marlow, Essex, 2000.

Deng W. and Joseph O., <u>The Problem of the Southern Sudan,</u> Oxford University Press, London Karachi, Nairobi, 1963

Duany W., <u>Neither Palaces Nor Prisons</u>: <u>The Constitution of Order Among the Nuer,</u> Workshop in Political Theory and Policy Analysis, Indiana Universtity, PhD Thesis, 1992.

Duncan J. R. S <u>The Sudan: A Record of Achievements,</u> William Blackwood Edinburgh and London, 1952.

Ellis K. C., (ed.), <u>The Vatican, Islam, and the Middle East,</u> Syracuse University Press, New York 1987.

Fabunmi L.A., <u>The Sudan Anglo-Egyptian Relations</u>: Case of Studies in Power Politics (1800- 1956) Longman Green London 1960.

Fanon F., Black Skin, White Masks, First translation 1967 and Published in United Kingdom by Pluto Press, Archway, London 1986.

Fearon J. A. I., <u>Reconciliation A Religiously – Divided Community through Inter-Faith Dialogue: An Experiment in Wusasa - Zaria of Nigeria,</u> Hartford Seminary, 2001

Friedrich and Kittel G., (eds.) Theological Dictionary of the New Testament: A Bridged in One Volume, William B, Eerdmans Publishing Co., the Paternoster Press 1985.

Garang J., <u>The Call for Democracy in the Sudan,</u> Masour Khalid (ed.), Kegan Paul International, London and New York, 1987

Gehman R., <u>African Traditional Religion: Biblical Perspective,</u> Kijabe Printing Press, Kenya, 1993.

Gopin M., Walking the Tightrope of reconciliation: "Reconciliation, Coexistence, and Justice in Interethnic Conflicts: Theory and Practice", in Mohammed Abu-Nimer, (ed.), Lexington Books, 2001.

Government of Sudan, "The Sudan Charter", Published in January 1987, and enshrined in Article 24 of the 1998 Constitution of the Republic of the Sudan.

Government of Sudan, "Constitution decree No 7", October 16, 1993 Article 1.

Government of Sudan and South Sudan Liberation Movement Addis Ababa Agreement 1972, (Appendix III).

Hamdi E. The Making of An Islamic Political Leader: Conversations with Hassan Al-Turabi, Westview Press, Boulder, Colorado 1996.

Harris C., In Joy and in Sorrow: Travels among Sudanese Christians, Paulines Publications Africa, Nairobi 1999

Hot P. M The Mahdist State in the Sudan, 1881-1898: A Study of its Origins Development And Overthrow, Clarendon Press, Oxford 1958.

Holy Bible, New International Version, Holder and Stoughton, London Sydney Auckland

Herver B., Delmet C. and Hopwood. D, Sudan History, Identities, Ideologies, Ithaca Press, Reading, 1991

Howell P. P., A manual of Nuer Law: Being An Account of Customary Law, its Evolution and Development in the Courts established by the Sudan Government, Oxford University Press, London 1954.

Human Rights Watch in Africa, Behind the Red Line: Political Repression in Sudan, Human Right Warch, New York, 1996.

International Bible Society, The Devotional Study Bible, The Bible League, Zondervan Corporation, 1987

International Crises Group, Group, "Prospect of Peace in Sudan" interview, with al-Ayam Arabic Newspaper, 29th, 30th May, and, 18th June 2003.

Jakobielski S., "Christian Nubia at the Height of its Civilization", in Mel-Fasi, (ed.), General

History of Africa: III-Africa from the 7thto the 11ᵗʰ Century, London, Heinemann, 1988.

Johnson D.H., The Root Causes of the Sudan Civil Wars, James Currey, Oxford, 2003.

Johnson D.H., The Nuer Prophets: A History of Prophecy from the Upper Nile in the Nineteenth and Twentieth Centuries, Clarendon Press, Oxford 1994.

Jombi K. Caesar, Juridic Structure of the Christian Church in the Sudan: From the Origin of Christianity in Nubia before and after the diffusion of Islam, Tipografica Leberit,Tome, 1987.

Katerra D Badru and Shenk David W., Islam and Christianity: A Muslim and A Christian in Dialogue, Uzima Press, Nairobi-Kenya, 1997.

Keen A., An Account of the Constitution of Sudan, London, McCorquodale & Co (S) (1965).

Khalid M., Numeiri and the Revolution of Dismay, KPI Limited, London, 1985.

Khalid M., The Government They Deserve: the Role of the Elite in Sudan's Political Evolution, Kegan Paul International, London and New York 1990.

Knitter Paul F., One Earth Many Religions: Multifaith Dialogue and Global Responsibility, Orbis Books, Maryknoll, New York, 1995.

Knitter Paul F. No other Name? A critical Survey of Christian Attitudes Toward the World Religions, Orbis Books MaryKnoll New York, 2004.

Lado L., Mahgoub K., and Cottran T. S., Report of the Commission of Inquiry into the Disturbances in the Southern Sudan August, 1955, McCorqucdale and Co. (Sudan), Ltd Khartoum

Lessch A.M., The Sudan: Contested National Identities, Indiana University Press, Boomington and Indianapolis, James Currey, Oxford, 1998.

MacMichael H., The Anglo-Egyptian Sudan, Faber and Faber Limited, London, 1934.

Mohammed A., Imperialism and Nationalism in the Sudan, Khartoum University Press, 1986.

Mubarak K., Turabi's "Islamist" Venture: Failure and Implications, 2001.

Nikkel M.R., The Origin and Development of Christianity among the Dinka of Sudan, PhD Thesis, University of Edinburgh, 1993.

Niblock T., Class and Power in Sudan: The Dynamic of Sudanese Politics 1898-1985, Macmillan Press 1987.

Olaniyan R., (ed.), Africa History and culture, Longman Nigeria Limited, Lagos 1982.

Painter J., Theology as Hermeneutics, Rudolf Bultmann's Interpretation of the History of Jesus, Sheffield Academic Press, 1987.

Peter K., Africa Handbook, 3rd Edition, Colin Legum, Anthony Blond, London 1969.

Prichard-Evans E. E., Nuer Religion, Oxford University Press, 1956.

Robertson J., The Minutes of Juba Conference 1947, convened by the Civil Secretary of the Sudan (Sir James Robertson) on June 12th, 1947, published by British Administration.

Saderson N. and, Sanderson L. P., Education, Religion and Politics in Southern Sudan 1898-1964, Ithaca Press, London, Khartoum University Press 1981.

Schacht J. Elvevi-Provencal E. and Kramers H., Encyclopedia of Islam, New Edition Volume I, London, Luzac and Co., 1960.

Shenk W., and Katerregga D., Islam and Christianity, Uzima Press, St. John's Gate off Parliament Road Nairobi, 1997.

Sikainga A., and Daly M.W., (eds.), Civil War in the Sudan, British Academic Press, New York, 1993.

Spaulding J. L and R.S.O' Fahey, Kingdoms of the Sudan,: Studies in African History series, London, Methuen 1974.

Sudanese Minister of Education, "The Educational Policy of The Republic of Sudan" Full text of speech delivered on, 31st October 1959, Khartoum University Press (1959).

Taha M., The Second Message of Islam, Omdurman, Sudan 1967, First Published in English by Syracuse University Press, 1987.

The National Assembly, The Republic of the Sudan, Constitution Bill, being: 28 March 1998,

The Sudan Human Rights Organisation, <u>Religion and Human Rights</u>: <u>The Case of Sudan</u>, 1992.

The Sudan: A record of Progress 1898-1947, Published by Sudan Government (1947)

Twaddle M. and Hansen B., <u>Religious and Politics in East Africa</u>, James Currey Oxford, 1995.

White J. and Van Der Vyver.J.D., (eds.), Religious Human Rights in Global Perspective; Religious in Global Perspective Religious Perspective; Martinus Nijhoff Publishers The Hague/Boston, London, 1996.

Vincent O., Hobbes, Covenant, and Constitution, Workshop in Political Theory and Policy Analysis, Indiana University, 1980.

Warburg G., Islam, Nationalism and Communism in a Traditional Society: The Case of Sudan Frank Cass London, 1978.

Waterhouse E.S., "Secularism", in J Hastings, (eds.), Encyclopedia of Religion and Ethics, Vol. XI, Edinburgh, NY. 1936.

Wheeler A., Anderson W. and Werner R., Day of Devastation: Day of Contentment: The History of the Sudanese Church Across 2000Years, Pauline Publications Africa, Nairobi 2000

Woodward P. (ed.), Sudan After Numeiri, Rout ledge, London & New York, 1991.

Yoh J. Gai, <u>Christianity in the Sudan: Overview and Bibliography</u>, Royal Institute of Interfaith Studies, Amman, Jordan, 1996.

(E) SOURCES FROM THE INTERNET

"Christians and Muslims Together- A Charter for Dialogue of Life and Common Action, adopted by Arab Christian-Muslims Working Group "press release, PR-01-47, of 13
December 2001.
From the Worldwide Faith News Archives, www.wfn.org Sj.
Jacques Dupuis, "Religious Plurality and Christological Debate" A Paper Presented in Baar Switzerland, (9-15 January 1990) at a symposium sponsored by the "Dialogue with Living

Faiths" section of the WCC the author discusses, in the light of different paradigms of salvation, the Christological problem that is at the heart of a theology of religions: "Is Jesus Christ the One and Universal Saviour"? http:/sedos.organ/English/dupuis.htm.

Deng K Charles; The Role of Arab-Islamic Elite in the matters of war and peace: The North South relationship p., 26.

Polito Nicholas lo, Christian –Muslim Relations in Sudan: An Update, (1/10/2003), Solihull, West Mudlands, Network for Inter-Faith Concerns.

htt://www.anglicanifcon.org/sudanPF.htm Mathew Ed, "Applied Missiology" Volume 1, Number 1, April 1990, pp. 1-4, htt://bible .au. edu/missions/page.asp?/D=279.

ABOUT THE AUTHOR

Professional credentials:

Rev. Gabriel Gai Riam (PhD), Date and place of Birth: **01/01/1950**, Dirrror Payam, Akobo County Jonglei State - South Sudan. He is a holder of: Doctor of Philosophy in Religious Studies, from the Catholic University of Eastern Africa, Nairobi - Kenya; Master of Theology; Culture and Development (MTCD), The University of Edinburgh; Masters of Philosophy (MPhil) – The University of Edinburgh; Master's in Public Administration (M.PA), from the University of Liverpool – UK; Postgraduate Diploma in Public Administration - Sudan Academy for Administrative Sciences, the University of Khartoum – Sudan; Diploma in Public Finance and Management from the University of Juba- South Sudan; Postgraduate Diploma in Development Finance from the University of Birmingham UK; and Postgraduate Diploma - in Theology and Biblical studies - Hampstead Bible School London - UK.

Experiences:

He is a self-motivated person with a sense of individual ability, team work and with skills in conducting innovative research in social studies with emphasis on Christian, Islamic, social and economic developmental themes. His experiences have involved executive and administrative roles and duties; both in public and private sectors.

Publications:

1. Christian-Muslim Relations In Sudan: A Study Of The Relationship Between Church And State 1898 – 2005 (1st and 2nd editions)
2. Involvement of Religious Leaders in Conflict Resolution Initiatives in Jonglei State South Sudan, 2005-2016 (PhD Dissertation)
3. Nuer Culture: It's, Development, Social Change and Effects on Nuer Traditional Values (**Manuscript**)

APPENDIXES

APPENDIX I: THE DIVERSE SUDANESE PEOPLE SOUTHERN PEOPLES (34%):

A. Nilotic Linguistic Groups: Dinka (10%), Muer (5%), Shilluk 1%) Anuak, Acholi, Bor, Belanda, Jur, Shilluk Lwo, Pari.

B. Nilo-Hamitic Linguistic Groups: Bari speaking (Bari, Kuku, Latuko, Pojulu, Kakwa, Nyangwara, Mundari (2%); Nyepo, Lokoya, Lulubo, Latuko, Logit, Lango,, Toposa, Domijiro, Jiye, Mourle Group.

C. Sudanic Linguistic Groups: Azanbde (2%), Muru (1%), Ndogo, Sere, Mundo, Biri, (Balanda/Fertit), Madi, Bongo (Fertit), Baka, Feroge

Arabized Peoples of Northern Sudan

A. Ja'aliya Arab: Danagala Arabs, Hassaniya, Kawahla, Gima, Husainat

B. Juhayna Arabs: Jamala (kababish, Shukriya), Baqqara (Silaim, Hawazma, Misirya, Humr, Rizaiqat, Ti'aisha, Bani Rashid, Rashaida, Habaniya)

C. Gerzira Arabs: Mesellimya, Halawin,, Rufa's

D. Sibaidiaya Arab

E. Hawawir Arab (Berbernstock): hawawir, Jellaba, Hawara, Korobat

F. Mixed Arab-Nubian: Shaigiya, Manasir, 'rubata, Mirifab

G. Christian Arab: Copt, Syrian Orthodox

Non-Arabized Peoples of Northern

A. Beja (6%): Beni Amer, Amarar, Bisharin, Hadendowa

B. Dar-fur (2%): Daju, Beigo, Zaghawa, Berti, Masalit, Gimr, Tama

C. Nuba (5%): Over 50 groups including Nyimang, Temein, Katla, Tima, Tegali, Koalib-Moro (Heiban, Shwai, Otoro, Tira, Moro), Daju, Tulishi, Keiga, Miri, Kadugli, Korongo, Talodi-Meskakin, Lafofa, and "Hills Nubians"

D. Nubian (3%)

E. West African (Fallatata) (6%): Fulani, Hausa, Kanuri, Songhai (Zabrma)[259]

APPENDIX II

Policy Statement on the Southern Question: by President Nimeiri, 9 June 1969

'Dear Countrymen! Warm Congratulations and greetings to you on this historic occasion of your revolution.

No doubt you have heard of the broad aims of the revolution outlined in my speech and in that of the Prime Minister, which was broadcast on 25, May. Our revolution is the continuation of the October 21 popular revolution. It works for the regeneration of life in our country, for social progress and the raising of the standard of living of the masses of our people throughout the country. It stands against imperialism, colonialism and whole-heartedly supports the liberation movements' of the African and Arab peoples as well as other peoples throughout the world'

---

[259] Source: Adopted from Ann Mosely Lesch op.cit., p.17
However, the above figures may not be accurate

Historical Background

"Dear Countrymen, the Revolutionary government is fully aware of the magnitude of Southern problem and is determined to arrive at a lasting solution.

This problem has deep-going historical roots dating back to the last century. It is the result of the policies of British Colonialism, which left the legacy of uneven development between the Northern and the Southern parts of the country, with the result that on the advent of independence Southerners found themselves in an unequal position with their Northern brethren in every field. The traditional circles and parties that have held the reins of power in our country since independence have utterly failed to solve the Southern question. They have exploited state power for self-enrichment and for serving narrow partisan interests without caring about the interests of the masses of our people whether in the North or in the South.

It is important to realize also that most of southern leaders contributed a greater deal the present deterioration of the state of affairs in that part of our beloved country. Over the years, since 1950 to the present da they have sought alliances with the Northern reactionary circles and with imperialism whether from inside or outside the borders. Personal gain was the mainspring of their actions.

Dear Countrymen, the enemies of the North are also the enemies of the South. The common enemy is imperialism and neo-colonialism, which is oppressing and exploiting the African and Arab peoples, and standing in the way of their advance. Internally, our common enemies are the reactionary forces of counter-revolution. The 25 May Revolution is not the same as the coup *d'etat* of November 1958. That was reactionary move staged by the imperialists in alliance with local reacting in and outside the army. It was made to silence the demands of the masses of our people both in the North and the South for social change and genuine democracy.

The revolution of May 25 is the very opposite of the coup *d'etat* of 1958. Our revolution is, we repeat, direct against imperialism, the reactionary circles and corrupt parties that destroyed the October

Revolution and were aiming at finally liquidating any progressive movement and installing a reactionary dictatorship

Dear Countrymen, the revolutionary Government is confident and competent enough to face existing realities. It recognizes the historical and cultural differences between the North and the South and firmly believes that the unity of our country must be built upon these objective realities. The Southern people have the right to develop their respective cultures and traditions within a united Socialist Sudan'. Regional Autonomy Programmes

'You will realize that the building of broad socialist-oriented democratic movement in the South, forming part of the revolutionary structure in the North and capable of assuming the reins of power in that region and rebuffing imperialist penetration and infiltration form the rear, is an essential pre-requisite for the practical and healthy application of regional Autonomy.

Within this framework and in order to prepare for that day when this right can be exercised, the revolutionary Government is drawing up the following programmes

1. The continuation and further extension of the Amnesty Law,
2. Economic, social and cultural development of the South,
3. The appointment of a Minister For Southern Affairs and
4. The training of personnel

The government will create a special economic planning board for the South and will prepare a special budget for the South, which aims at the development of the Southern provinces at the shortest possible time.

Dear Southern countrymen, in order that we may be able to carry out this programme it is of utmost importance that peace and security should prevails in the South and that life to normal. It is primarily the responsibility of you all whether you be in the bush or at home to maintain peace and stability. The way is open for those abroad to return home and co-operate with us in building a prosperous Sudan, united and democratic'.

APPENDIX III

THE ADDIS-ABABA AGREEMENT ON THE PROBLEM OF SOUTH SUDAN

Draft Organic Law to organize Regional Self-Government in the Southern Provinces of the Democratic Republic of the Sudan In accordance with the provisions of the Constitution of the Democratic Republic of the Sudan and in realization often memorable May Revolution Declaration of June 9, 1969, granting the Southern Provinces of the Sudan Regional Self-Government with a united socialist Sudan, and in accordance with the principle of the May Revolution that the Sudanese people participate actively in and supervise the decentralized system of the government of their country. It is hereunder enacted:

Article 1:

> This law shall be called the for Regional Self-Government in the law for Regional Self-Government in the Southern Provinces: It will come in force in on a date within a period not exceeding thirty days from the date of the Addis-Ababa Agreement.

Article 2:

> This law shall be issued as organic law, which cannot be amended except by a three- quarters majority of the people's National Assembly and confirmed by two-thirds majority in a Referendum held in the three Southern Provinces of the Sudan.

CHAPTER II: DEFINITIONS

Article 3:

> (i)   Constitution', refers to the Republic Order No. 5 or any other basic law replacing or amending it.

(ii)   'President', means the President of the Democratic Republic of the Sudan.

(iii)   'Southern Provinces of the Sudan', means the Provinces of Bahr El Ghazal, Equatoria and Upper Nile in accordance with their boundaries as they stood on January 1, 1956, and any areas that were culturally and geographically part of The Southern Complex as may be decided by a referendum.

(iv)   'People's Regional Assembly', refers to the legislative body for Southern Region of Sudan.

(v)   'High Executive Council', refers to the Executive Council appointed by the President on the recommendation of the High Executive Council and such body Shall supervise the administration and direct public affairs in the Southern Region of the Sudan.

(vi)   'President of High Executive Council', refers to the person appointed by the President on the recommendation of the People's Regional Assembly to lead and supervise the executive organs responsible for the administration

(vii)   "People's Regional Assembly', refers to the National Legislative Assembly representing the people of the Sudan in accordance to the constitution.

(viii)   'Sudanese', refers to any Sudanese citizens as defined by the Sudanese National Act 1957 and any amendments thereof.

CHAPTER III

Article 4:

The Province of Bahr El Ghazal, Equatoria and Upper Nile as defined in Article 3
(iii) shall constitute as Self-Government Region within the Democratic Republic of the Sudan and shall be known as Southern region.

Article 5:

The Southern Region shall have legislative and executive organs, the functions and powers of which are defined by this law.

Article 6:

Arabic shall be the official language for the Sudan and English the Principle language for Southern Region without prejudice to the use of any other language or languages, which may serve a practical necessity for the Efficient and expeditious discharge of executive and administrative Functions of the region.

CHAPTER IV

Article 7:

Neither the People's Regional Assembly nor the High Executive Council shall Legislate or exercise any powers on matters of national nature,
Which are:
(i)   National Defence
(ii)   External Affairs
(iii)   Currency and Coinage
(iv)   Air and Inter-Regional River Transport
(v)   Communications and Telecommunications
(vi)   Customs and foreign trade, except for Border Trades and certain Commodities which the Regional Government may specify with the Approval of Central
(vii)   National and Immigration (Emigration)
(viii) Planning for Economic and Social Developments
(ix)   Educational Planning
(x)   Public- Audit

CHAPTER V: LEGISLATURE

Article 8:

> People's Regional Assembly elected exercises regional Legislature in Southern Region by the Sudanese citizens resident in the Southern Region. The constitution and conditions of membership of the Assembly shall be determined by Law.

Article 9:

> Members of People's Regional Assembly shall be elected by direct secret ballots

Article 10:

(i) For the first Assembly, the President may appoint additional members to the members to the People's Regional Assembly where the conditions for elections are not conducive to such elections as stipulated in Article 9, provided that such appointed members shall not exceed on quarter of the Assembly.

(ii) The People's Regional Assembly shall regulate the conduct of its business in accordance with rules of procedures to be laid down by the said Assembly during its first setting.

(iii) The People's Regional Assembly shall elect one of its members as a Speaker, provided that the first sitting shall be presided over by the Interim President of the High Executive Council.

Article 11:

> The People's Regional Assembly shall legislate for the preservation of public order, internal security, efficient administration and the development of the Southern Region

in culture' economic and social fields and in particular in the following:-

(i)   Promotion and utilization of regional financial resources for the development and administration of the Southern region.

(ii)   Organization of the machinery for regional and local administration.

(iii)   Legislation on traditional law and Custom within the framework of National law.

(iv)   Establishment, Maintenance and administration of prisons and Reformatory institutions

(v)   Establishment, maintenance and administration of Public Schools at all levels in accordance National plans for education, economic and social development

(vi)   Promotion of local languages

(vii)   Town and villages planning and the construction of roads in accordance with National Plans and Programs.

(viii) Promotion of trade; establishment of local industries and markets; issue of traders' licenses and formation of co-operative societies.

(ix)   Establishment, maintenance and administration of public hospitals

(x)   Administration of environmental health services;; maternity care; Child welfare, supervision of markets; Combat of epidemic diseases; training of medical assistants and rural wives, establishment of health centers, dispensaries and dressing stations.

(xi)   Promotion of animal health control of epidemic sand improvement of animal productions and trade

(xii)   Promotion of tourism

(xiii) Establishment of zoological gardens, Museums, organization of trade and cultural exhibitions.

(xiv) Mining and quarrying without prejudice to the right of the Central government in the event the discovery of natural gas and minerals.

(xv) Recruiting for organization and administration of police and prison services in accordance with the national policy and standards

(xvi) Land use in accordance with National laws and plans

(xvii) Control and prevention of pests and plant diseases.

(xviii) Development, utilization and protection of forest crops and pastures in accordance with national laws.

(xix) Promotion and encouragement of self-help programmes

(xx) All other matters delegated by the President or the People's National Assembly for legislation

Article 12:

The People's National Assembly may call for facts and information concerning the conduct of the administration of Southern Region.

Article 13:

(i) The People's Regional Assembly may, by a three-quarters majority and for special reasons relating to public interest, request the National President, to relieve the President or any other member of High Executive Council from office. The President shall accede to such request

(ii) In case of vacancy, relief of resignation of the President of the High Executive Council the entire body shall be considered as having automatically resigned.

Article 14:

The People's Regional Assembly may by a two-third majority request the president to postpone the coming into force of any law, which in their view of the members, adversely affects the welfare and the interests of the citizens of the Southern Region. The President may, if he thinks fit, accede to such request

Article 15

(i)   The People's Regional Assembly may, by a majority of its members, request the President to withdraw any bll presented to the People's National Assembly, which in their view affects adversely the welfare, rights or interests of the citizens of the Southern Region, pending the communication of the view of the Regional Assembly.

(ii) If the President accede to such request, the People's Regional assembly shall present its view within 15 days from the date of accession to be request.

(iii) The President shall communicate any such views to the People's National Assembly together with own observation if deems necessary.

Article 16:

The People's National Assembly shall communicate all Bills and Act to the People's Regional Assembly shall act similarly

CHAPTER VI: THE EXECUTIVE

Article 17:

The regional executive authority is vested in a High Executive Council.
Which acts on behalf of the President.

Article 18:

The High Executive Council shall specify the duties of the various departments in the Southern Region, provided that on matters relating to central government agencies, it shall act with the approval of President.

Article 19:

The President of the High Executive Council shall be appointed and relieved of the office by the President on the recommendation of the People's Regional Assembly.

Article 20:

The High Executive Council shall be composed of members appointed and relieved of the office by the President on the recommendation of the President of the High Executive Council.

Article 21:

The President of High Executive Council and its members are responsible to the president and to the People's Regional Assembly for efficient administration in the Southern Region. They shall take an oath of office in before the President.

Article 22:

The President of the High executive Council may attend and participate in the deliberations without the right to vote, unless they are also members of the People's regional Assembly.

CHAPTER VII

Article 23:

The President shall from time to time regulate the relationship between the High Executive Council and the central ministries

Article 24:

The High Executive Council may initiate laws for creation of a regional public service. These laws shall specify the terms and conditions of service for the regional Public Service.

CHAPTER VIII

Article 25:

The People's Regional Assembly may levy Regional duties and taxes in addition to National and local duties and taxes. It may issue legislation and orders to he collection of all public monies at different levels

Article 26:

(a)   The sources of revenue of Southern Region shall consist of the following:-
- (i)   Direct and Indirect Regional Taxation
- (ii)   Contributions from People's Local Government Councils.
- (iii)   Revenue from commercial, industrial and agricultural projects in Accordance with the National Plan
- (iv)   Funds from the National Treasury for established services.
- (v)   Funds voted by the People's National assembly I accordance with the requirements of the region.
- (vi)   The special Development Budget for the south as presented by the People's Regional Assembly for the acceleration of economic and social advancement of the Southern region as envisaged in the declaration of June 9, 1969.
- (vii)   Any other resources.
- (viii)   The Regional Executive Council shall prepare a budget to meet the expenditure of regional services, security,

administration, and development in accordance with national plans and programmes and shall submit it to the People's Regional Assembly for approval.

CHAPTER IX: OTHER PROVISIONS

Article 27:

(i)   Citizens of Southern Region shall constitute a sizeable proportion of the People's Armed Forces in such reasonable numbers as will correspond to the population of the region.

(ii) The use of the Peoples Armed Forces within the region and outside the framework of national defence shall be controlled by the President on the advice of the President of High Executive Council.

(iii) Temporary arrangements for the composition of units of the People's Armed Forces in the Southern Region are provided for in the Protocol on Interim Arrangements.

Article 28:

The President may veto any Bill which he deems contrary to the provisions of the National Constitution provided the People's Regional Assembly, after receiving the President's views may reintroduce.

Article 29:

The President and members of High Executive Council may initiate laws in the People's Regional Assembly.

Article 30:

Any member of the People's Regional Assembly may initiate any law provided that Financial bills shall not be presented without sufficient notice to the President of High Executive Council.

Article 31:

The People's Regional Assembly shall strive to consolidate the Unity of the Sudan and respect the spirit of the National constitution.

Article 32:

All citizens are guaranteed freedom of movement in and out the Southern Region provided restrictions or prohibition of movement may be imposed on named citizens solely on grounds of public health and order.

Article 33:

(i)   All citizens resident in the Southern Region are guaranteed equal opportunities of education, employment, commerce and the practice of any profession.

(ii) No law may adversely affect the rights of citizens enumerated in The previous items on the basis of race, trial origin, religion, place Of birth, or sex.

Article 34:

Juba shall be the capital of the Southern Region and the seat of the Regional Executive and Legislature.

FUNDAMETAL RIGHTS AND FREEDOMS

The following should be guaranteed by the Constitution of the Democratic Republic of the Sudan:

1.   A citizen should not be deprived of his citizenship.

2. Equality of Citizens
   (i)   All citizens without distinction based on race, national origin, birth, Language, sex, economic or social status, should have equal rights and duties before the law Have rights to institute
   (ii)   All persons should be equal before the courts of law and should have Rights to institute legal proceedings in order to remove any Injustice of declare any rights in an open court without delay Prejudicing their interests.
   (iii) Retrospective penal legislation and punishment should be prohibited.
   (iv)   The right of the accused to defend himself personally or through an agent should be guaranteed.
   (v)   No person should be arrested, detained or imprisoned except in Accordance with the due process of law, and no person should remain in custody or detention for more than twenty-four hours without judicial order.
   (vi)   No Accused persons should be subjected to inducement, intimidation or torture in order to extract evidence form him whether in his favour or against him or against any other person,

3. Freedom of Religion and conscience
   (i)   Every person should enjoy freedom of religious opinion and conscience and the rights to profess them publicly and privately and establish religious institutions subject to reasonable limitations in favour of morality, health or public order as prescribed by law.

4. Protocol of Labour.
   (i)   Forced or compulsory labour of any kind should be prohibited except when ordered for military or civil necessities or pursuant to penal punishment prescribed by law.
   (ii)   The rights to equal pay for equal work should be guaranteed.

5. Freedom of minority to use their languages and to develop their Culture should be guaranteed

DRAFT ORDINANCE ON ITEMS OF REVENUE AND GRANTS-IN–AID FOR THE SOUTHERN REGION

(i) Profit accruing to the Central Government as a result of exporting products of the Southern Region.

(ii) Business profit tax of the Southern Region that is at present in the central list of the ministry of treasury.

(iii) Excise duties on alcoholic beverages and spirits consumed in the Southern Region.

(iv) Profit on sugar consume in Southern Region.

(v) Royalties of forest products in the Southern Region.

(vi) Royalties of leaf tobacco and Cigarettes.

(vii) Taxation on property other than the provided in the rate ordinance

(viii) Taxes and rates on Central and Local Government projects (5% of net profits of factories, cooperative societies, agricultural enterprises and cinemas

(ix) Revenue accruing from Central government activities in the Southern Region, sales, sales of forms and documents, stamp duties and any other items to be specified from time to time provided the region can bear the maintenance expenses, e.g Post Office revenue, Land.

(x) Licences other than those provided in the People's Local Government Act. 197.

(xi) Special development tax to be paid by residents in the Southern Region, rate of which should be decided by the People's regional Assembly.

(xii) Income tax collected from officials and employees working in the Southern Region both in the local and national civil series as well as in the Army, police and Prisons Judiciary, and Political establishment.

(xiii) Corporation tax on any factory and / or agricultural Projects established in the region but not run by the regional government (5% of initial cost).

(xiv) Contributions from the Central Government of encouragement of Constructions and development for every agricultural project, industrial projects and trading enterprise (20% of the initial cost as assessed by the Central Government.

(xv) New Social Service Projects to be established by the region or any of its Local Government units, and for which funds are allocated, shall receive funds form the national treasury in the following manner:

- Education Institutions, 20%b of expenses
- Trunk, and through roads and bridges, 25% of the expenses
- Relief and Social amenities, 15% of expenses.
- Tourists attraction projects, 25% of expenses
- Security 15% of expenses
- Grants for Post Secondary and University Education within the Sudan, 20% of the grants; Outside the Sudan, 30% of grants
- Contribution for Research, Scientific Advancement, and Cultural
- Activities, 25% of expenses.

AGREEMENT IN THE CEASE-FIRE IN THE SOUTHERN REGION

Article 1:

This Agreement shall come into force on the date and time specified for the ratification of the Addis Ababa Agreement.

Article 2:

There will be an end to all military operations and to all armed actions in the Southern Region from the time of cease-fire.

Article 3:

All combat forces shall remain in the area under their control at the time of the cease-fire,

Article 4:

Both parties agree to forbid any individual or collective acts of violence any underground activities contrary to public order shall cease

Article 5:

Movements of individual members of both combat forces outside the areas under their control shall be allowed only if these individuals are unarmed and authorized by their respective authorities. The plans for stationing troops form the national army shall be such as to avoid contact between them and Southern Sudan Liberation Movement combat forces.

Article 6:

A Joint Commission is hereby created for the implementation of all questions related to the cease-fire including the repatriation of the refugees. The Joint Commission shall include members from all members bordering the Southern Region as well as representatives of International Committee of the Red Cross, World Council of Churches, All Africa conference of Churches and the United National High Commissioner for

Article 7:

The Joint Commission shall propose all measures to be undertaken by both parties in dealing with all incidences after a full inquiry on the spot.

Article 8:

Each party shall be represented in the Joint Commission by one senior military officer a maximum of five members.

Article 9:

The Headquarters of the Joint shall appoint local commission in various centers of the southern Region composed of two members from each party

Article: 10

The Joint Commission shall appoint local commission in various centers of the Southern Region composed of two member from each party.

PROTOCOLS ON INTERIM ARRANGEMENT
CHAPTER 1: INTERIM ADMINISTRATIVE ARRANGEMENTS
(Political, Local Government and Civil Services)

Article 1:

The President of the Republic of the Sudan shall, in consultation with the Southern Sudan Liberation Movement (SSLM) and branches of the Sudanese Socialist Union in the Southern region, appoint the President and members of interim High Executive Council.

Article 2:

The Interim High Executive Council shall consist of the President and other Members with portfolios in:

a. Finance and economic Planning
b. Education
c. Information, Culture and Tourism
d. Communication and Transport
e. Agriculture, Animal Production and fisheries
f. Public Health
g. Regional Administration (Local Government Legal Affairs, Police and Prison)
h. Housing, Public Work and Utilities
i. Natural Resources and Rural Development (Land use, Rural Water Supply, Forestry and Cooperatives)
j. Public Service and Labour
k. Minerals and Industries, Trade and Supply

Article 3:

The Interim High Executive Council shall, in accordance with National laws, establish a Regional civil service subject to the Ratification by the People's Regional Assembly.

Article 4:

The President shall, in consultation with the Interim High executive Council, determine the date for the election to the People's, Regional Assembly and the Interim High executive Council shall make arrangements for the setting up of the Assembly.

Article 5:

In order to facilitate the placement in and appointment of both Central and regional institutions, the southern Sudan Liberation Movement shall compile and communicate lists of citizens of the Southern Region outside the Sudan in accordance with details to be supplied by the Ministry of Pubic service and administrative reform

Article 6:

The Interim High Executive Council and the Ministry of Public Service and Administrative Reform shall undertake to provide necessary financial allocation with effect from the 1972- 1973 budget for such placement and appointments.

Article 7:

The mandate of the Interim High Executive Council shall not exceed a period of 18 months.

CHAPTER II: TEMPORATY ARRANGEMENT FOR THE COMPOSTION OF UNITS OF THE PEOPLE'S ARMED FORCES IN THE SOUTHERN REGION

Article 1:

The arrangement shall remain in force for a period of five year Subject to revision by the President on the request of the President of High Executive Council acting with consent of the People's Regional Assembly.

Article 2:

The People's Armed Forces in the Southern Region shall consist of A national force called the Southern Command composed of 12,000Officers and men of whom 6,000 shall be citizens from the Southern Region and the other 6,000 from outside the Southern Region.

Article 3:

The recruitment and integration of citizens from the Southern Region within the aforementioned Forces shall be determined by a Joint Military Commission taking into account the need for initial Separate deployment of troops with a view to achieve smooth integration in the national force. The commission shall ensure that this deployment shall be such that an atmosphere of peace and confidence shall prevail in the Southern Region.

Article 4:

The Joint Military Commission shall be composed of three Senior Military Officers from each side. Decisions of the Joint Military Commission shall be taken unanimously. In case of disagreement, such matters shall be referred to the respective authorities.

CHAPTER III: AMNESTY AND JUDICIAL ARRANGEMENTS

Article 1:

No action or other legal proceedings whatsoever, civil or criminal,. Shall be instituted against any person in any court of law for or on account of any act or matter done inside or outside the Sudan as from the 18th day of August 1955. If such act or matter was done in connection.

Article 2:

If a civil suit in relation to any acts or matters referred to in Article 1 is instituted before or after the date of ratification of the Addis Ababa agreement, such a suit shall be discharged and made null and void.

Article 3:

All persons serving terms of imprisonment or held in detention in respect of offences herein before specified in Article 1 shall be discharged or released within 15 days from the date of ratification of the Addis Ababa Agreement.

Article 4:

The Joint Cease-fire Commission shall keep a register of all civilian returnees which if registered, shall serve to certify the persons therein named are considered indemnified within the meaning of this agreement provided that the commission may delegate such power to the diplomatic missions of the Democratic Republic of the Sudan in case of the citizens from the Southern Region living abroad and to whom the provisions of this agreement apply.

Article 5:

In the case of armed returnees or those belonging to a combat force the Joint Military Commission shall keep a similar register of those person who shall be treated in the same manner as provided for in Article 4.

Article 6:

Notwithstanding the provision of Articles 4 and 5, a special tribunal with ad hoc judicial powers shall be established to examine and decide on those cases which in the estimate of the authorities does not meet the conditions for amnesty specified in Article 1 of this agreement. The special tribunal shall be composed of a President appointed by the President of the Republic and not more than four members named by the cease-fire commission.

Article 7:

Cases referred to in Article 6 shall be brought to the attention of the special tribunal by request of the Minister of Justice.

Article 8:

The Amnesty provision contained in this agreement as well as the powers of the Special Tribunal shall remain in force until such time as the president after consultation with the commissions referred to in this agreement; decide that they have fulfilled their functions.

CHAPTER IV: REPARTIATION ABND RESETTLEMENT COMMISSION

I. Repatriation

Article 1:

There shall be an established special commission inside and where required outside the Southern Region charged with the responsibility of taking all administrative and other measures as may be necessary in order to repatriate all citizens from the Southern Sudan who today are staying in other countries and especially in the neighbouring countries. The Headquarters of the Commission shall be in Juba.

Article 2:

> The commission shall be composed of at least three members including one representative of the Central government, and one representative of the Central government, one representative form the Southern Region, and one representative of UN High Commissioner for Refugees. For those commissions operating outside the Sudan, representatives of the host government

Article 2:

> The commission shall be composed of at least three members including one representative of the Central government, one representative from the Southern Region, and one representative of UN High Commissioner for Refugees. For those commissions operating outside the Sudan, representatives of the host government shall be included, plus the Central government representative who shall be the Ambassador of the Sudan or his representative.

Article 3:

> The control of repatriation at the borders shall be assumed by competent border 90authorities in co-operation with the representatives of Repartition Commission.

Article 4:

> The Repatriation Commission shall work closely with the Commission for Relief and Resettlement to ensure that the operation and timing of the returning of refugees from across the borders is adequately coordinated

II RESETTLEMENT

Article 1:

There shall be established a Special Commission for Relief
and Resettlement under the President of the Interim High
Executive Council with headquarter in Juba and provisional
branches in Juba, Malakal, and Wau. The commission,
it branches and whatever units it may deem fit to create
in other localities in order to facilitate its functions, shall
be responsible for co-ordination and implementation of
all relief services and planning related to resettlement and
rehabilitation of all returnees, that is:

a. Refugees from Neighbouring countries
b. Displaced persons resident in the main centers of the
    Southern Region and other parts of the Sudan.
c. Displaced persons including residual Anya Nya personnel
    and supporters in the bush
d. Handicapped and orphans

Article 2:

Although resettlement and rehabilitation of refugees and
displaced persons is administratively the responsibility of the
Regional Government, the present condition in the Southern
Region dictate that efforts of the whole nation of the Sudan
and International Organization should be pooled to help and
rehabilitate persons affected by the conflict. The relief and
Resettlement Commission shall co-ordinate activities and
resources of the Organization within the Country.

Article 3:

The first propriety shall be the resettlement of displaced
persons within the Sudan in the following order:

a. Persons presently residing in overcrowded centers in Southern Region, and persons desirous to return to their original areas or homes..
b. Persons returning from bush including Anya Nya supporters
c. Handicapped persons and orphans

Article 4:

The second priority shall be given to returnees form the neighbouring and other countries according to an agreed plan. This plan shall provide for:
a. Adequate reception centers with facilities for shelters, food supplies, medicines and
b. Medicaments
c. Transportation to permanent resettlement villages or places of origin
d. Materials and equipment

Article 5:

The Relief and Resettlement Commission shall:
a. Appeal to International organization and voluntary agencies to continue assistance for students already under their support particularly for students in Secondary Schools and Higher Institutions until appropriate arrangements are made for their repatriation.
b. Compile adequate information on students and persons in need of financial support from the Sudan Government.

Article 6:

The relief and Resettlement Commission shall arrange for the education of all returnees who were attending primary schools.

The Agreement is hereby concluded on this twenty-seventh day of the month of February in the year one thousand nine hundred and seventy two, AD, in this City, Addis Ababa, Ethiopia, between the Government of the Democratic Republic of the Sudan on one hand and the Southern Liberation Movement on the other hand. It shall come into force on the date and hour that has been fixed for its ratification by the President of the Liberation Movement. It shall be ratified by the said two leaders in persons or through their representative authorized representative in this city, Addis Ababa, Ethiopia, at the twelfth hour at noon, on the twelfth day of the month of March, in the year one thousand nine hundred and seventy two, AD.

In witness whereof, We the Representatives of the Government of the Democratic republic of Sudan and the Representatives of the Southern Liberation Movement hereby append our signatures in the presence of the Representatives of His Imperial Majesty the Emperor of Ethiopia and The Representatives of His Imperial Majesty the Emperor of Ethiopia and The Representatives of the World Council of churches, the All Africa Conference of Churches, and the Sudan Council of Churches. For the Government of the Democratic Republic of the Sudan

1. Abel Alier – Wal Kuai, Vice-Present and Minister of State Southern Affairs
2. Dr Mansour Khalid, Minister for Foreign Affair
3. Dr Gaafar Mohamed Ali Bakheit, Minister for Local Government
4. Major GENERAL Mohamed Ali Baghir Ahmed, Minister of Interior
5. Abdel Rahman Abdalla, Minister of Public Service and Administrative reform
6. Brigadir Mirghani Suleiman
7. Colonel Kamal Abashar

For the Southern Sudan Liberation Movement

1. Ezboni Mondiri Gwonza, leader of the Delegation
2. Dt Lwarence Wo Wol, Secretary of the Delegation
3. Mading de Garang, Spokesman of the Delegation

4. Colonel Fredrick Brian Maggot, Special Military Representative
5. Oliver Batali Albino, member
6. Rev. Paul Pot, member
7. Job Adier De Jok, member

Witness

1. Nabieyelul Kifle, representative of his Imperial Majesty, the Emperor of Ethiopia
2. Leopoldo J. Niilus, Representative of the World Council of Churches
3. Kodwo E. Ankrah, Representative of the World Council of Churches
4. Burgess Carr, General Secretary all Africa Conference of Churches
5. Samuel Athi Bwogo, Representative of Sudan Council of Churches

Attestation

I attest that these signature are genuine and true,
Burges Carr, Moderator.

APPENDIX IV:

"Let My People Choose ": The Statement of the Sudanese Churches on the Right of Self-Determination for Southern Sudan and other Marginalized Areas

Introduction:

The right of the people of Southern Sudan to self-determination has been and still is widely accepted by all the Sudanese political forces. Indeed, in a country famous for absence of a national consensus on the fundamentals of nation and state building, the Sudanese political forces have achieved a consensus on the Right for Self-Determination (herein after abbreviated as RSD). It is not only a regionally and internationally recognized human rights. It is the Right of all people to freely determine their political status and pursue their economic, social and cultural development. It is also an effective facility for conflict resolution, particularly in those countries, which nave experience prolonged conflict, and suffering, and no any other prospect of military victory for any of the parties. In such a situation, once parties to the conflict accept and apply it and abide by its outcome, war usually comes to an end.

Under traditional international law, the RSD was generally seen as a desalinization facility. It was also seen as applicable to what could be describes as "internal colonialism" in formally independent state. It has been argued that conditions for internal colonization arise when one race or culture group dominates other groups using its control of power and resources of the formally independent state.

In the sixties and the late seventies the UN Extended the RSD to non-colonial situations. Accordingly common article 2 of the covenant for Civil and Political Rights and the Covenant for Economic, Social and Cultural Rights 1966, affirmed the RSD for people in general without confining it to decolonization context. In Africa, the principle of *Uti possidetis* (the retention of pre-independence borders drawn by the colonialist) was effectively used to oppose claims of the RSD by oppressed groups struggling for independence form independent states. But the Eritrea example suggest that under certain conditions that principle could be ignored. Importantly, experiences of successor States to the former Soviet Union, former Yugoslavia and consensual separation of Slovakia Czech Republic suggest that there are conditions under which independent State hood could be attained without sanctions form international law.

In the case of the Sudan, we may refer to constitutional Self-Determination. This is a process of Self-Determination based on the consensus of the people, the political forces and the government of the day. It is argued here that such consensus exists and it is evidenced by a number of documents and Covenant signed by the parties to the conflict and by public declarations of the representatives of the political forces. Where such consensus exits, the important question is to ensure the implementation of this consensus. In case of any demonstrable delay in the implementation, the task is to ascertain the reasons for such a delay and encourage the parties to scrupulously abide by their undertakings.

Argument as to "who is self" in the Sudan and "that the exercise of RSD will lead to separation" need not detain us here. They have been raised before. They also have been answered,. What needs to be confronted now is: given the consensus by the Sudanese political forces on RSD, what should be done to implement it? Does the delay in implementation of this consensus suggest lack of seriousness on the part of the signatories? If so, what should be done by the ecumenical family and international community to convince all signatories that a scrupulous implementation of RSD for the people of the Southern Sudan and other marginalized people is the only recipe for justice and peace in the Sudan?.

Background to RSD

The Sudanese as a people were supposed to exercise the RSD in a plebiscite under the Cairo Anglo-Egyptian Agreement 1953. It was not to be. Instead of a countrywide plebiscite, the parliament in Khartoum voted in December 1955 to request the Condominium powers (Britain and Egypt) to recognize the Sudan as an independent state effective from January 1st 1956. The Southern Sudanese representative voted for the independence motion on the understanding that the South will have a federal status in the post-independent Sudan. The understanding was based on a special motion in the parliament, which according to Mohammed Ahmed Mahjoub, two time Prime Minister of the Sudan, was passed to "please the Southerners". The motion prepared by prominent northern Sudanese members of parliament including Mahjoub himself. Promise to consider federal status for the South. It was admittedly not meant to be honoured. Self-Determination vote of

1955 was obtained by fraud and therefore not binding on the Southern Sudanese.

During the first armed resistance (1955-1972), south its claim to exercise the RSD in the Round Table Conference (RTC). The northern political parties rejected that claim. The Southern Sudanese parties then presented confederal scheme as a minimum acceptable position. The northern Sudanese parties ending up conceding a restricted local autonomy for the South in which the central government would still retain considerable powers over the police, security, finance, appointments of the chief executive and judiciary in the South. Importantly, the South was to be governed as three separate regions.

The Southern Sudanese parties predictably rejected the northern Sudanese scheme. However, when the May Regime under Numeiri in subsequent negotiations conceded those points raised by the south, the southern Sudan Liberation Movement (SSLM) accepted the Addis Ababa Agreement of 1972. Under this agreement, the South won significant powers of Self-government. However northern Sudanese traditional forces combined with Numeiri opportunism dismantled the regional self-rule for the South in June 1983.

The SPLM/A, which launched its struggle in mid-1983, stated its objectives then as a "the destruction of the old Sudan, and the creation of a New, just democratic united Sudan". This mission statement did not mean that the Southerners had renounced their right to self-determination. This must be emphasized since the SPLM/A did not see itself as merely a southern Sudanese movement, but a movement for the whole Sudan. It was therefore left for Southern Sudan to articulate claims that were specifically southern. Accordingly when the national Islamic Front (NIF) seized power in June 1989, and adapted Islamic fundamentalist programme, which threatened to negate most of what the South stood for, the stage was set programme, which threatened to negate most of what the South stood for, the state was set for decisive choice for the south. Little wonder that the RSD for the Southerners was re-asserted by southerners in the government convened National dialogue conference of September-October 1989 in Khartoum. With the intensification of oppressing, and with the launching of Jihad against the southerners, the Nuba and the people of southern Blue Nile, the demand for self-determination gathered popularity. It was therefore after the southern Sudanese in the government controlled areas who led demand for self-determination.

Mounting consensus over RSD

Claiming the RSD is one thing, and an important thing at that. However, working for RSD in a systematic, programmatic and consistent manner is quite another. The south is today called upon to pursue the latter course i.e working for the RSD in a systematic, programmatic and consistent manner. A strategy for self-determination in form of a Vision, Mission and Programme is therefore called for. The strategy would consist of the following:

1. Public Awareness. Deepening of public awareness among southerners in the Sudan and in Diasporas about self-determination. This means the development of civic education programe about this theme and related themes such as human rights. Rule of law, humanitarian principles, good governance, democracy, etc. This public awareness would include matters such as the distinction between RSD and separation, federation, free, fair and internationally supervised referendum.
2. Such educational programme may be carry out by the civil society organizations in which the Churches, youth, women groups and professional organizations play their roles.
3. Lobby for an early enactment of a referendum law that would ensure the following:
    a. Fair, free and internationally supervised referendum
    b. Clearly defined options, which would include independent statehood. Needless to add that the referendum law must be a part of the interim arrangements which shall be put in place.

4. Dialogue with all political forces and personalities in support for holding of a free, fair internationally supervised referendum before the expiration of fixed interim period.

5. Churches to develop a comprehensive programme for securing regional and International support

6. Call on WCC to lobby at the UN and members of the Security Council, African Union (AU) and other regional bodies such as the Arab-League, European Union, Organization of Islamic States, e.tc for their support for RSD

7. Promotion of peace making and conflict prevention, mitigation and resolution capacities of civil society or organization and civil authority to ensure that the Southerners are capable of maintaining peace and stability by themselves.

8. The church would work with the civil society and civil authority to promote good governance in which justice and human rights are respected.

All the above are designed to bring about a state of affairs that convinces the people, partners and observers that the southerners are capable of running their affairs by themselves. Basis for peace making through self-determination process:

While the Sudanese churches support the IGAD sponsored mediation, based on the Declaration of Principles (DoPs), it is hereby stressed that the mediators hold the parties to bilateral or multi-lateral covenants they have sealed. To date, the Sudanese political forces have signed a number of agreements or declarations affirming their commitment to the RSD for the people. These are:

1. Frankfurt Agreement between the Nasir Faction at that time and GoS (Government of Sudan) agreeing of Self-Determination for the southern Sudanese (1992)

2. Nairobi Declaration of March 1993, between NDA parties agreeing that the basic human rights norms, including the RSD, be the basis of the future constitution of the Sudan.

3. Washington Declaration, October 1993, between SPLM/A (Dr. John Garang) and SPLM/A United (Dr. Riek Machar) agreeing on the RSD for the southern.

4. IGAD Declaration of Principles (DoP) of 1994, affirming the RSD for rthe south and conditional RSD for all the people of the Sudan:

5. Chukudum Agreement (December 1994) between APLM/A and the UMMA Party agreeing on the RSD for the people of Southern Sudan including Abbey;

6. Asmara Agreement of December 1994 between NDA parries affirming the RSD for the people of South;

7. Asmara Agreement by NDA June 1995, affirming the RSD choosing between federation-confederation on one hand and independence of the Southern Sudan on the other. Furthermore internal accommodation for the people of Nuba mountains and southern Blue Nile was to be under taken and if failed these people would be entitled to the RSD.

8. The Khartoum Peace Agreement April 1997 between United Democratic Salvation from (UDSF) led by Dr. Rick Machar on one hand and the GoS on the other, agreeing the RSD through a referendum to be held in the year 2002:

9. The Fashoda Peace Agreement of the SPLM/A-United (Dr. Lam Akol) and the GoS September 1997 agreeing the RSD for the South;

10. Djibouti National call of 1999 between the UMMA party and the Gos recognizing the RSD for the people of Southern Sudan. The call was the first agreement among northern Sudanese leaders in which they recognized the RSD for the people for the South.

11. Article 113 of the Sudan Constitution of 1998 adopts the RSD for the South with two options: of unity or secession of Southern Sudan.

12. Geneva Agreement of 2001 between the People's National Congress (Dr. Hassan El Turabi) and the SPLM/A (Dr. John Garang) recognizing the RSD for the people of the

Southern Sudan and criticizing the GoS for back tracking form commitment to RSD;

13. Nairobi Declaration of January 2002 between Dr. John Garang 9SPLM/A) and Dr. Riek Machar (SPDF) affirming the RSD for the people of southern Sudan, Nuba Mountains and Southern Blue Nile;

From the above listed agreements the following become very clear:

1. RDS has generally been accepted as one of the ways of resolving the Sudanese conflict.
2. RSD for the people of the Southern Sudan has been generally accepted
3. The options open to the Southerners are unity and independent statehood.

The Asmara Declaration by the NDA June 1995, (#7 above), the Khartoum Peace Agreement 1997, (#8 above) and article 113 of the Sudan Constitution 1998, (#11 above) are categorical about the options of unity on one hand and independence for the South Sudan o the other. In none of the above listed agreements has the options been left ambiguous. At no time have term RSD been used to mean internal self-determination, i.e option within the untied the Sudan only. However, in some of the agreements the RSD was to be exercised by the people of Southern Blue Nile and Nuba Mountains.

CONCLUSION

The Sudanese Churches firmly believe that the conflict in the Sudan is principally about justice. The struggle is against injustice and it is about providing justice for all irrespective of creed, colour, belief and race. It is therefore not about the unity of the country. Because in a country where justice prevails, there will be no incentive or reason for separation of fragmentation. It is injustice that breaks up families, tribes and countries. It is the course of maintaining the unity of the Sudan and the struggle for justice, the oppressed people have paid dearly. To date, over 2.9 million displaced; thousands of people maimed and wounded; millions widowed and orphaned; besides the opportunity cost of the war in terms of education, services and development in beyond qualification enough is enough.

It is time that the international opinion and the people of good will and above all the ecumenical family, should see to it that suffering comes to an end. It must end in peace with justice, or our suffering people should therefore be allowed to freely determine their political status and pursue their economic social and cultural development. We believe that nobody is wise or knowledgeable enough to make choices for them. The elite on the previous occasions had concluded Agreements on their behalf. Systems have been imposed on them but they have lasted. Attempts are being made to prescribe certain choices for them and we believe that such prescriptions are not the correct recipes for a just and lasting peace. It is therefore time that the IGAD committee on the Sudan and the IGAD Partners From press for the oppressed people to freely choose their destiny and for the political forces in the Sudan and the international community to abide by the outcome of such a choice whatever it might be.

Signed:

His Grace   His Grace
Archbishop Paulino Lukudu   Archbishop Joseph Marona
President   Primate
Sudan Catholic Bishops' Conference   Episcopal Church of the
                                            Sudan

Rev Peter Makuac Nyak
Associate Moderator
Presbyterian Church of the Sudan

Rev Taban Eloni Andarago   Fr. Mark Kumbonyakia
Chairman SCC   Chairman NSCC

Venue
London, 6th March 2002

INDEX

Abboud: 4, 49, 50, 51, 56, 67, 69, 113, 122

Abel Alier: 59, 75, 78, 99, 223

Addis Ababa Agreement: 4, 6, 75, 79, 80, 81, 94, 136, 138, 187, 199, 212, 218, 227

Addis Ababa Peace Conference: 68, 79

Aggrey: 55, 64

al-Gizouli Dafa'alla: 101

Ali Baldo: 50

Ali Mirghani: 38

Al-khalifa: 56

All Africa of Council of Churches: 4

Allen Reed: 60, 61, 62

Al-Mahdi: 3, 31, 57, 58, 59, 87, 90, 91, 97, 101, 102, 103, 104, 105, 106, 107, 108, 109, 110

Al-Turabi: 32, 89, 90, 91, 93, 94, 96, 98, 105, 110, 111, 187

Anglo-Egyptian Condominium: 1, 3, 13, 14, 17, 19, 21, 23, 31, 34, 35, 43, 51, 53, 136, 138, 140, 141, 177

Angus Cameron: 20

Ansâr: 12, 13, 31, 32, 88

Anya Nya Movement: 55, 61, 63, 64, 66, 73

Anya-nya: 55, 61, 62, 63, 64, 66, 68, 184

Augustino Baroni: 65

Babiker el-Nur: 63

Bari Wanji: 64

British: 1, 3, 4, 11, 13, 18, 19, 23, 24, 28, 31, 35, 37, 38, 39, 40, 41, 43, 44, 46, 51, 52, 54, 66, 123, 177

Change of British Policy: 35

Christian Missionaries: 19, 34, 49, 50, 51, 122, 140, 141, 177

Christian - Muslim Relations: 1, 2, 3, 5, 6, 67, 107, 123, 138, 139, 172, 178

Church Missionary Society: 6, 19, 20, 52, 65

Church-state relations: 1, 2, 3, 4, 5, 6, 47, 51, 66, 90, 100, 120, 124, 138, 177

Contextual Theology: 138, 139, 140, 141, 142, 148

Covenant: 84, 142, 143, 144, 145, 147, 148, 149, 150, 151, 152, 153, 154, 156, 157, 158, 163, 165, 172, 174, 178

Daly and Sikainga: 95

Discovery of Oil: 93, 94

Education Development: 22, 27
Education Policy: 48, 53, 54
Eliana Ngalamu: 65
Eric Sabiti: 65
Father Hillary Boma: 124
Fatma Ahmad: 99
Gaafar Mohammed: 75
General Neguib: 39
George Appleton: 65
Goodwill Visit: 57, 65, 73
Gordon Mortat: 64
Government of Sudan: 3, 4, 18,
    23, 24, 28, 30, 65, 125, 126,
    132, 174
Harold MacMichael: 22
Hashim al-Atta: 63
High Executive Council: 81, 93,
    99, 200, 201, 202, 204, 205,
    206, 207, 208, 209, 215,
    216, 221
Ibrahim Nagud: 99
Islamic State: 3, 5, 9, 32, 85, 87, 89,
    93, 99, 108, 109, 110, 111,
    115, 116, 118, 124, , 173
Islamization: 1, 4, 24, 59, 67, 85,
    86, 87, 90, 93, 95, 96, 100,
    103, 109, 111, 112, 113, 116,
    120, 124, 125, 136, 138,
    140, 141
Isma'il al-Azhari: 4, 41
Johnson: 28, 32, 76, 83, 87, 93,
    95, 103, 107, 129, 131, 144,
    145, 146
Joseph Garang: 63
Joseph Lagu: 64, 79, 80, 99
Josiah Atkins Idowu-Fearon: 167
Juba Conference: 35, 37, 38, 44,
    48, 128
Kandolo Modi: 62

Karam Allah: 13
Kodwo Ankrah: 65, 71, 75
Legislative Assembly: 35, 38,
    41, 200
Lesch: 44, 87, 90, 91, 92, 93, 95, 97,
    98, 99, 110, 112, 127, 196
Machakos Protocol: 5, 85, 132, 137,
    172, 174, 175
Mahdî: 3, 11, 12, 13, 17, 19, 24, 31,
    32, 57, 58 59, 87, 88, 90, 91,
    97, 101, 102, 103, 104, 105,
    106, 107, 108, 109, 110, 121,
    140, 177
Mahmud Taha: 32, 88, 150, 151,
    160, 162
Masour Khalid: 12, 49
Max Warren: 65
Missionary Societies Act: 50, 51,
    66, 67
Missionary Spheres: 26, 27
Mohammad Ahmad Majob: 57
Mohammed Saleh Shinghti: 38
Naivasha Peace Agreement: 132,
    136, 138, 163
National constitution: 4, 5, 39,
    58, 74, 88, 96, 103, 142,
    208, 209
National Islamic Front: 5, 89, 104,
    107, 109, 128, 227
National Reconciliation: 60, 90, 91,
    92, 99, 178
Ngundɛng: 145, 146, 148
Niblock: 64, 73, 95, 96, 103, 104
Numeiri: 4, 5, 59, 60, 62, 63, 67,
    69, 74, 84, 85, 87 89, 90, 91,
    92, 93, 94, 95, 96, 97, 98,
    99, 100, 101, 102, 103, 107,
    111, 119, 127, 128, 136, 150,
    151, 163, 173

Oboyo Saturlino: 46
Omar Bashir: 6
Philip Ghabbush: 90, 99
Policy Statement: 60, 196
Pope John Paul II: 122
Qur'an: 8, 13, 22, 27, 44, 54, 76,
     88, 98, 110, 113, 117, 118,
     148, 149, 150, 157, 160, 161,
     162, 167, 168
Right to self-determination: 130,
     132, 133
S. H. Amissah: 57
Samuel Amissah: 65
Samuel Athi Bwogo: 65
Sayed Ali Abdel Rahman: 48
Shari`a Law: 96, 97, 102, 105, 107,
     112, 118, 120, 173
Sir Francis Akau Ibiam: 57
South Sudan Liberation Movement:
     4, 58, 182
Southern Policy: 19, 23, 24, 25, 30,
     34, 36, 37, 43, 45, 46

Storrs McCall: 64
Sudan Communist Party's: 59
Sudan Council of Churches and
     the New Sudan council of
     churches: 1, 6, 139
Sudan's Permanent Constitution: 86
Swailem Sidhom: 57
Swar al-Dahab: 101, 102
The 1998 Constitution: 109, 115,
     116, 117, 118, 120, 124, 163
The Anglo-Egyptian Agreement:
     18, 35, 39, 40
Turco-Egyptian: 9, 10, 11, 12,
     31, 140
Umma: 11, 12, 31, 32, 57, 87,
     88, 90, 91, 97, 105, 106,
     172, 184
World Council of Churches: 4, 6,
     47, 65, 67, 154
Yeremia Dotiro: 65
Zakat: 98, 117, 118